Building Safety Act 2022

Other titles available from Law Society Publishing:

Client Care in Conveyancing
Priscilla Sinder

Conveyancing Checklists, 4th edition
Frances Silverman and Russell Hewitson

Conveyancing Handbook, 30th edition
General Editor: Frances Silverman

Conveyancing Quality Scheme Toolkit, 4th edition
The Law Society

Forfeiture of Leases
Peter Petts and Jamal Demachkie

Housing Law Handbook, 2nd edition
General Editor: Stephen Cottle

Post-completion: A Conveyancer's Guide to Process, Risk and Compliance
(forthcoming, 2024)
Fiona du Feu and Priscilla Sinder

Property Development, 4th edition
Gavin Le Chat

Property Practitioner's Guide to the First-tier Tribunal
Andrea Nicholls and Julia Petrenko

Renewal of Business Tenancies, 3rd edition
Michael Haley

Residential Conveyancing Practice, 2nd edition
Russell Hewitson

Stamp Duty Land Tax Handbook, 2nd edition
Sean Randall

Titles from Law Society Publishing can be ordered from all good bookshops or direct (visit our online shop at **www.lawsociety.org.uk/bookshop**).

BUILDING SAFETY ACT 2022

A Guide for Property Lawyers

General Editors: Andrew Butler KC and Ian Quayle

The Law Society

ISBN-13: 978-1-78446-242-0

Published in 2024 by the Law Society
113 Chancery Lane, London WC2A 1PL

Typeset by Data Standards Ltd, Frome, Somerset
Printed by Hobbs the Printers Ltd, Totton, Hants

FSC www.fsc.org MIX Paper from responsible sources FSC® C020438

The paper used for the text pages of this book is FSC® certified. FSC (the Forest Stewardship Council®) is an international network to promote responsible management of the world's forests.

Contents

Foreword

The barrage of criticism directed towards the Building Safety Act (BSA) 2022 since the first of its provisions came into force has been voluble. Some of it has been fair, some less so, and some of it is based on misunderstandings of the Act and the secondary legislation made under it. However, there is no doubt the Act imposes onerous and far-reaching obligations on many who are involved in the ownership and development of real estate in England and Wales.

This book, as far as we are aware, is the first to be published on this difficult and important topic. It focuses on the Act's real estate aspects, in line with the specialism of the barristers at Tanfield Chambers who have written all but two of the chapters. Chapter 3 provides an overview of the Act's impact on the construction industry, but this is not covered in detail. As befits a book published by the Law Society, it is written with the legal practitioner in mind, and attempts to provide practical solutions to the formidable difficulties which, we understand, are frequently being encountered in practice.

Ian's chapters provide his valuable and contrasting perspective, as a respected conveyancer and trainer of many years' standing.

On the one hand, there is a certain freedom in writing a book on an Act which is not yet the subject of much authority. On the other hand, to do so is a challenge, and a daunting one at that. It does not help that both the primary and secondary legislation is – not to pull punches – riddled with drafting errors, including defective syntax, cross-references to non-existent provisions, and what seems to have been a general lack of coordination between the respective drafters. The authors have done the best they can with these challenges, but where views are expressed about the meaning and effect of the Act's provisions, they are obviously hostages to fortune. No responsibility can be accepted for errors, and the book should not be used as a substitute for formal legal advice. Views expressed in chapters about the state of the law are those of the author of the chapter in question.

I am grateful to the Law Society for entrusting this work to us, and to my colleagues who have contributed their time and expertise; also of course to Ian for his boundless enthusiasm and energy, without which this project would probably not have reached the starting line, let alone the finish.

The law is stated as at 1 February 2024.

Andrew Butler KC
February 2024

Following on from years of experience as a conveyancer, I have spent over 20 years training solicitors and conveyancers working for Central Law Training, local law societies and numerous professional bodies and organisations. I have delivered in excess of 2,000 webinars and training courses covering a variety of topics and have worked for national housebuilders and developers with a particular interest in residential leasehold issues.

The BSA 2022 became of real interest to me when practitioners began bombarding me with questions and problems concerning the Act and the practical issues arising particularly with Sched.8. At the start of my journey with the BSA 2022 I was fortunate to make the acquaintance of Andrew and his colleagues at Tanfield Chambers, many of whom have worked on this text. Their combined knowledge and ability to translate key sections of the Act and associated regulations has been a godsend in enabling me to share with the relevant professions the problems with the Act, together with where possible, I am delighted to say, solutions.

Ian Quayle
February 2024

About the editors

Andrew Butler KC is a member of Tanfield Chambers where his practice encompasses both the real estate work for which the set is best known, and a wide-ranging commercial caseload.

He specialises in development disputes and professional negligence matters, with company law issues also forming an increasing area of activity. Since the enactment of the Building Safety Act 2022, he has lectured and written extensively on its provisions, and advised a wide range of clients, including purchasers, developers and large estates.

Andrew is a qualified mediator and a member of both the Chartered Institute of Arbitrators and the London Court of International Arbitration. He was appointed Queen's Counsel in 2018 and shortlisted for *The Lawyer*'s Barrister of the Year award in 2020.

Ian Quayle qualified as a solicitor and worked in private practice for 12 years specialising in property law matters generally, including residential conveyancing, development work, commercial leasehold transactions and property joint ventures.

Since 1998 he has worked in-house as a consultant for national house builders and national and international property developers advising on all aspects of property, landlord and tenant, transactional and management issues.

For over 20 years Ian has provided training to the legal profession throughout England, working for some of the most prominent providers of legal training as well as providing training privately to firms and organisations. This has in the main been offered via in-house and public courses, as well as conferences and webinars. In 1999 he created IQ Legal Training Limited, which has quickly gained a reputation for providing quality legal training for property lawyers.

Table of cases

Table of statutes

Table of statutory instruments

Table of European legislation

Abbreviations

STATUTES

AA 1997	Architects Act 1997
BA 1984	Building Act 1984
BSA 2022/the Act	Building Safety Act 2022
DPA 1972	Defective Premises Act 1972
LTA 1954	Landlord and Tenant Act 1954
LTA 1985	Landlord and Tenant Act 1985
LTA 1987	Landlord and Tenant Act 1987

STATUTORY INSTRUMENTS

711 Regulations	Building Safety (Leaseholder Protections) (England) Regulations 2022, SI 2022/711
859 Regulations	Building Safety (Leaseholder Protections) (Information etc.) (England) Regulations 2022, SI 2022/859
275 Regulations	Higher-Risk Buildings (Descriptions and Supplementary Provisions) Regulations 2023, SI 2023/275
315 Regulations	Building Safety (Registration of Higher-Risk Buildings and Review of Decisions) (England) Regulations 2023, SI 2023/315
396 Regulations	Higher-Risk Buildings (Key Building Information etc.) (England) Regulations 2023, SI 2023/396
895 Regulations	Building Safety (Leaseholder Protections etc.) (England) (Amendment) Regulations 2023, SI 2023/895
906 Regulations	Building (Approved Inspectors etc. and Review of Decisions) (England) Regulations 2023, SI 2023/906
907 Regulations	Higher-Risk Buildings (Management of Safety Risks etc) (England) Regulations 2023, SI 2023/907
909 Regulations	Building (Higher-Risk Buildings Procedures) (England) Regulations 2023, SI 2023/909
911 Regulations	Building Regulations etc. (Amendment) (England) Regulations 2023, SI 2023/911

40 Regulations	Building Safety Act 2022 (Commencement No.6) Regulations 2024, SI 2024/40
41 Regulations	Higher-Risk Buildings (Keeping and Provision of Information etc.) (England) Regulations 2024, SI 2024/41

EU REGULATION

2011 Regulation	Regulation (EU) No 305/2011 of the European Parliament and of the Council of 9 March 2011 laying down harmonised conditions for the marketing of construction products and repealing Council Directive 89/106/EEC (2011) OJ L 88/5

TERMINOLOGY

AAP	appropriate accountable person
ACM	aluminium composite material
AP	accountable person
ARB	Architects' Registration Board
BLO	building liability order
BSF	Building Safety Fund
BSR	building safety risk
CCO	costs contribution order
CPR	Civil Procedure Rules
FLC	former landlord's certificate
FTT	First-tier Tribunal
HHSRS	Housing Health and Safety Rating System
HRB	higher-risk building
HRRB	higher-risk residential building
HSE	UK Health & Safety Executive
IO	information order
JCA	Joint Competent Authority
JIT	Joint Inspection Team
JRG	Joint Regulators' Group
LC	landlord's certificate
LDC	leaseholder deed of certificate
NRCP	National Regulator for Construction Products
OPSS	Office for Product Safety and Standards
PAP	principal accountable person
RCO	remediation contribution order
RMC	resident management company
RO	remediation order
RP	responsible person

RTM	Right to Manage
SMM	special measures manager
SMO	special measures order

CHAPTER 1

Introduction

Timothy Polli KC

1.1 THE GRENFELL TOWER TRAGEDY[1]

The Grenfell Tower was a 24-storey block of residential flats. It was constructed between 1972 and 1974 as the first phase of the Lancaster West development. Its last refurbishment was completed in 2016, as part of which, among other things, the external rainscreen cladding was renewed.

At 00:54 on 24 June 2016 an emergency call was made to the London Fire Brigade, reporting that a fire had broken out in the kitchen of Flat 16 on the 4th floor of the tower. Firefighters entered the kitchen at 01:14 to put out the blaze; but, by then, the fire had already passed from Flat 16 into the exterior cladding on the east face of the tower.

That exterior cladding comprised aluminium composite material (ACM) rainscreen panels with polyethylene cores. The polyethylene was combustible and the fire climbed the east façade of the tower rapidly. Behind the ACM panels were polyisocyanurate and phenolic foam insulation boards set 50mm behind the rear face of the ACM panels. Those insulation boards and the 50mm cavity, which acted like a flue, also contributed to the rate at which the fire spread vertically. By 01:27 the fire had reached the roof of the tower, from where it started spreading horizontally to the north face of the building and more generally around the crown. The melting polyethylene dripped down, igniting fires lower down the façade of the tower, which then climbed back up the façades. By 02:00 the fire was travelling across the north and east elevations of the tower; and by 03:30 the fire had spread across the south and west elevations of the tower.

Internally, many of the lobbies had started filling with smoke by around 01.20. By 02.00 a significant number of them were heavily smoke-logged. The stairs remained relatively smoke-free until about 01:50. From about then, however, the staircases started to fill with smoke; and by 02:20 the smoke on the stairs posed a risk to life, even though the stairs were not absolutely impassable by all.

[1] For a comprehensive account of the fire and the response of the emergency services, see Part 2 of the first report of the Public Enquiry into the Fire at Grenfell Tower, published in October 2019.

The first report of smoke entering a flat from a lobby was made at 01:25. As was and remains common with tall residential buildings, Grenfell's fire safety strategy was based on containing any fire to give the fire services an opportunity to extinguish it and avoid the need for a mass evacuation. Accordingly, any occupant of the building who contacted the London Fire Brigade was initially advised to 'stay put'. At 02:35 the London Fire Brigade control room revoked the 'stay put' advice, and told all occupants contacting them to try to escape the building. However, the staircases were, by then, hazardous and difficult to pass.

In total, more than 250 firefighters and 70 fire engines from stations across London fought to control the fire and rescue as many occupants as possible. The tower nevertheless burned for over 60 hours and 72 people died.

1.2 DAME JUDITH HACKITT'S REVIEW OF BUILDING REGULATIONS AND FIRE SAFETY

The Ministry of Housing, Communities & Local Government (now known as the Department for Levelling Up, Housing and Communities) established a building safety programme and appointed Dame Judith Hackitt, a former chair of the UK Health & Safety Executive (HSE), to conduct an independent review of the building regulations and fire safety. Her review published an interim report on December 2017, and its final report in May 2018 (the Hackitt Report). Dame Hackitt concluded that the regulatory system covering the safety of high-rise and complex buildings was not fit for purpose. Ignorance of the applicable regulations and/or indifference to those regulations and the potential consequences of their breach had created a 'race to the bottom' within the built environment industries, with insufficient regard being paid to the need to ensure that occupants of buildings were safe and felt safe. In particular, the review identified the following general failings:

- The building regulations and guidance were too complex and unclear, leading to confusion and misinterpretation in their application to high-rise and complex buildings.
- It was not sufficiently clear where responsibility for compliance lay. Even where there were requirements for key activities to take place in respect of the design, construction and/or maintenance of buildings, it was not always clear who had responsibility for making those things happen and, consequently, all too often no one ensured that those requirements were met.
- Although many in the built environment industry followed and demonstrated good practice, the means of assessing and ensuring the competency of key people throughout the system was considered to be inadequate. In particular, there was often no differentiation in competency requirements for those working on high-rise and complex buildings.

- The processes to ensure and enforce compliance and to sanction non-compliance when necessary were too weak. As a consequence, what was being designed was not what was being built and there was a lack of robust change control. Without the threat of meaningful sanctions for failures of compliance, too many people chose to behave incorrectly.
- There was no clear and effective way for residents to escalate their concerns about building safety. Within Grenfell itself, the residents had expressed concerns about the safety of the building but felt they were not being taken seriously.
- The system of product testing, marketing and quality assurance across the construction industry was not clear.

In her final report, Dame Hackitt made 54 specific recommendations. Those recommendations were not to be regarded as a menu, from which the Government could pick and choose. Rather, they constituted a collective whole and, together, were intended to effect deep systemic reform to the regulatory oversight of the construction and management of high-rise multi-occupancy buildings. They were intended to create a new and comprehensive regulatory framework specifically structured to drive real and meaningful culture change and the right behaviours across the entirety of a building's lifecycle.

Dame Hackitt considered it to be crucial to recognise that high-rise buildings were complex systems. A 'one size fits all' approach to building safety was therefore inappropriate. Rather, the different layers of protection that might be required to make a building safe had to be considered on a case-by-case basis by reference to the potential risk to those in or around the building. It followed that the regulatory framework had to focus on outcomes, rather than rigid prescriptive rules. It also had to recognise that complex systems designed for residential multi-occupancy had to be subject to a higher level of regulatory oversight that was proportionate to the number of people who were potentially put at risk. She therefore proposed that the most intensive regulatory framework was to be targeted at new and existing high-rise residential properties of 10 storeys or more. She labelled such buildings 'Higher Risk Residential Buildings' (HRRBs).

The new regulatory framework had to be simpler, clearer and more effective than what had gone before. Precisely because of the complexity of modern buildings, the actions of any one person could compromise the safety of the system as a whole. Accordingly, Dame Hackitt's report recommended that clear duties be imposed upon specific, identified dutyholders – including the client, the building designer(s), the building contractor(s) and the eventual building owner(s) – to ensure that, throughout the design, construction and ownership/management stages of a building's lifecycle, due and proper consideration would be given to building safety. Where duties were breached, she recommended that the sanctions applied to those dutyholders should be meaningful and sufficient to create an effective deterrent.

Most significantly the review noted that the existing regulatory framework covering the life cycle of high-rise residential buildings involved several different regulators working under several different legislative frameworks. Standards of design and construction were overseen by building control bodies (either local authority building control or private sector approved inspectors) although, at certain stages in the process, those building control bodies were obliged to consult with fire and rescue authorities in respect of the fire safety of the building. During the building's occupation those fire and rescue authorities had regulatory oversight of the fire safety of the common parts of the building. At all times, regulatory oversight for the safety of workers on or in the building lay with the HSE.

A key plank of the new regulatory regime proposed by Dame Hackitt was the formation of a new Joint Competent Authority (JCA), which would comprise the combined expertise and knowledge of local authority building standards and the fire and rescue authorities, but with the addition of the HSE.[2] She envisaged that the new JCA would have regulatory oversight of building safety within HRRBs across their entire life cycle. She did not propose that the existing regulatory bodies should merge into the new JCA. Rather, the JCA would provide a space, within which those bodies (which would remain independent) would work together to assess building safety more rigorously and to create a more unified and consistent intervention process.

By way of very brief summary, the JCA was to become involved during the design and construction of HRRBs at three 'gateway points'[3] at which the relevant dutyholders would be obliged to demonstrate to the JCA that their plans were detailed and robust, that their understanding and management of building safety was appropriate, and that they could properly account for the safety of the completed building. Only with the JCA's consent would the proposed HRRB be entitled to move onto the next stage of development and, in due course, occupation. Any major changes from the approved plans were to be reported to the JCA and could not be constructed before the JCA had approved the changes. A 'golden thread' of relevant information about HRRBs was to be compiled and maintained by dutyholders at all stages of a building's lifecycle, not just recording the building's initial design and construction, but also recording the details of all alterations to the building. The maintenance of such information and the provision of it to subsequent dutyholders would empower those future dutyholders to comply with their obligations more effectively.

Throughout the occupation and maintenance of HRRBs, specific dutyholders were to be responsible for making sure that the whole building was safe. They were to manage risks proactively, to work with residents to ensure that the building remains safe throughout its life cycle by carrying out regular safety reviews,

---

2 *Building a Safer Future: The Final Report of the Independent Review of Building Regulations and Fire Safety* Cm 9607 (May 2018), ch 1 ('*Building a Safer Future*').

3 When applying for planning permission, before commencing construction and before commencing occupation. See *Building a Safer Future*, ch 2, Part 2.

and to maintain the 'golden thread' of information. Those dutyholders would be expected to demonstrate to the JCA that they were complying with their obligations. In order to ensure that residents felt safe in their homes, Dame Hackitt proposed[4] that the dutyholder for an HRRB should have a statutory duty to provide residents with prescribed information to enable them to understand the layers of protection in place to keep their building safe and to engage with those residents. Such transparency and engagement was the means by which residents' trust in the regulatory regime would be rebuilt. For their part, residents too should have responsibilities to cooperate with the dutyholder(s) and not to compromise the fire safety of their flats and/or the building.

The Government accepted all Dame Hackitt's recommendations in their entirety. The Building Safety Act (BSA) 2022[5] is the primary legislation by which the Government sought to carry those recommendations into effect.

1.3 AN OVERVIEW OF THE BUILDING SAFETY ACT 2022

BSA 2022, Part 2 establishes the Building Safety Regulator and sets out its regulatory objectives and duties. It is the Regulator which, in general terms, will perform the functions that Dame Hackitt intended would be performed by the JCA. Part 2 is considered in more detail at **1.4**.

BSA 2022, Part 3 makes various amendments to the Building Act (BA) 1984 to facilitate the new regulatory regime introduced by the Act. Sections 31–41 introduce a new regime for the design and control of buildings. Of particular note are ss.34 and 35 which permit regulations to be made to impose duties on persons involved in the design and construction of new buildings, and the refurbishment and maintenance of existing buildings – all buildings, and not just higher-risk buildings (HRBs) – to sit alongside the duties imposed by the Construction (Design and Management) Regulations 2015, SI 2015/51 (usually referred to as the 'CDM Regulations'). All persons carrying out any design or building work must be competent to do so. Further, a duty is imposed upon those who appoint any such person to take reasonable steps to ensure that the person they appoint meets this requirement. Sections 42–53 establish the new regulatory regime for the building control industry, overseen by the Regulator. The Regulator must establish and maintain two registers: one of local authority building inspectors and another of building control approvers (to replace the existing approved inspectors). There are to be codes of conduct and codes of practice for both registered building inspectors and registered building control approvers, with sanctions for professional misconduct. The intention is to impose clear professional standards and to create personal responsibility on persons to meet those professional standards. Part 3 is considered in more detail in **Chapter 2**.

4 *Building a Safer Future*, ch 4.

5 Also referred to in this book as 'the Act'.

BSA 2022, Part 4 imposes obligations upon specific dutyholders: the 'accountable person(s)' (AP) and the 'principal accountable person' (PAP).[6] The PAP is obliged to register HRBs[7] with the Regulator and thereafter to deal with the Regulator as required. The APs are obliged to be proactive to promote the safety of those parts of HRBs for which they are responsible.[8] They are to assess building safety risks (BSRs)[9] as soon as reasonably practicable after a building is occupied or after they become responsible for the building, and regularly thereafter; and must take all reasonable steps to prevent a BSR from materialising and to reduce the severity of any incident resulting from such a risk occurring. APs are required to retain and update as necessary information and documents relating to HRBs (Dame Hackitt's 'golden thread' of information) and to report to the Regulator when required. The PAP is obliged to engage with residents of HRBs. Provision is made for criminal sanctions and/or enforcement by the Regulator when those duties are neglected.

In most cases the leasehold structure in multi-occupancy buildings would provide that leaseholders were liable in full through their service charge for the costs of remedying building safety defects. BSA 2022, Part 5 and the accompanying Sched.8 introduce varying levels of protection for *some* leaseholders in *some* buildings from *some or all* of the cost of remediating *some* building safety works. It should be noted that more buildings fall within the provisions in Part 5 ('relevant buildings'[10]) than fall within the provisions of Part 4 ('higher-risk buildings').[11] The financial protections introduced by the Act generally seek to protect ordinary residential tenants in relevant buildings, but not commercial landlords/investors, nor business tenants. Broadly speaking, the effect of these protections is (or is intended to be) to let the costs of remediating building safety defects lie where the obligations to carry out the work fall – which is usually with a landlord or management company – and not with the tenants protected by the statutory provisions.

Part 5 makes consequential amendments to the Landlord and Tenant Act (LTA) 1985 and the Landlord and Tenant Act (LTA) 1987 to imply landlords' and tenants' covenants into relevant leases, enabling landlords and tenants to enforce the others' respective obligations;[12] to compel landlords to take reasonable steps to try to find alternative sources of funding for remedial works;[13] but also to

6 The definitions of 'accountable person' and 'principal accountable person' are considered in **Chapter 5**.

7 The definition of 'higher-risk building' is considered in **Chapter 4**.

8 The duties on the accountable persons and the principal accountable person are considered in **Chapter 6**.

9 The definition of 'building safety risk' is considered in **Chapter 3**.

10 The definition of relevant buildings in Part 5 is considered in **Chapter 9**.

11 The definition of 'higher-risk building' is considered in **Chapter 4**.

12 These provisions are considered in **Chapter 12**.

13 These provisions are considered in **Chapter 13**.

enable landlords to recover through the service charge their reasonable costs of complying with their new obligations to manage the safety of their buildings.[14]

Part 5 also makes provision for new two new remedies: remediation orders, which compel landlords to remedy defects; and remediation contribution orders which compel landlords to pay for the costs of remediation works that might already have been carried out or are being arranged.[15] In those cases where the title involves several strata of leasehold interests, regs.3–5 of the Building Safety (Leaseholder Protections) (Information etc.) (England) Regulations 2022, SI 2022/859 (the 859 Regulations), provide for a mechanism for sharing the costs of qualifying remediation works among the various landlords.[16] Given that leaseholders' rights turn on facts concerning the building and/or their landlord and/or the other landlords in the building that might not be apparent or readily available to them, it was necessary to create a mechanism to provide leaseholders with the information that they need in order to establish their rights. That has been done by the Building Safety (Leaseholder Protections) (England) Regulations 2022, SI 2022/711 (the 711 Regulations), which introduced complicated provisions for the service of 'landlord's certificates' by which the necessary information can be called for and must be provided. The obligations initially placed on landlords by those regulations in their original form were so onerous that the regulations have already been amended to ease the burden (albeit only a little).[17] The effects of Part 5 and Sched.8 and the associated regulations are considered in detail in **Chapters 9–13**.

Finally, Part 5 also variously provides for: new building liability orders, which are to spread the 'relevant liability' of a corporate body to other corporate bodies with which the former has been 'associated'[18] in the 'relevant period' (ss.130–132);[19] the creation of a New Homes Ombudsman Scheme (ss.136–143);[20] the protection provided by new build home warranties to be enhanced (ss.144 and 145); new provisions enabling claims to be brought against the manufacturers of unsafe construction products (ss.146–155);[21] amendments to the regulation of architects (ss.157–159);[22] and the easing of restrictions on who can make a complaint to a housing ombudsman (s.160).

---

14 See **Chapter 12**.

15 Remediation orders and remediation contribution orders are considered in **Chapter 14**.

16 This mechanism for sharing costs is known as the 'waterfall' and is considered in more detail in **Chapter 9**.

17 Landlord's certificates and leaseholder deeds of certificate are considered in **Chapters 10** and **11**.

18 The definition of 'association' is considered in **Chapter 18**.

19 BSA 2022, ss.130–132 are considered in more detail in **Chapter 15**.

20 Note that at the time of writing BSA 2022, ss.136–143 are not yet in force.

21 BSA 2022, ss.146–155 are considered in detail in **Chapter 17**.

22 BSA 2022, ss.157–159 are considered in detail in **Chapter 16**.

1.4 PART 2 OF THE BUILDING SAFETY ACT 2022: THE BUILDING SAFETY REGULATOR

BSA 2022, s.2 establishes the HSE as the Building Safety Regulator (the Regulator). The Regulator is obliged by statute to exercise its functions 'with a view to: (a) securing the safety of people in or about buildings in relation to risks arising from buildings, and (b) improving the standard of buildings' (s.3(1)); and is to carry out its regulatory activities in a way which is 'transparent, accountable, proportionate and consistent', and 'targeted only at cases in which action is needed' (s.3(2)). Initial indications are that the Regulator is aware of the need for proportionality; by its statement of intent[23] the Regulator explained:

> In securing sustained safety outcomes, the Building Safety Regulator's response will be proportionate to the safety risks and to the seriousness of any breach of the law. Regulatory intervention will be targeted on activities where there is high actual or potential harm arising from any breach. In judging how far dutyholders have taken steps to reduce or mitigate safety risks, the Building Safety Regulator will balance the degree of risk against the money, time or trouble needed to avert that risk in the particular circumstances, as well as the impact of any action on businesses and residents.
>
> The Building Safety Regulator will expect that dutyholders, in turn, will adopt a sensible and proportionate approach to managing safety, focusing on significant risks.
>
> The Building Safety Regulator's approach to formal enforcement and sanctions will serve the public interest and will be undertaken in a fair, equitable and consistent manner, targeting and taking firm action against those who repeatedly offend, act irresponsibly, or whose actions could cause serious harm. It promotes the principle that those who create the risk are responsible for managing that risk and are held accountable when they fail to do so.

The Regulator has recognised that it is not always possible to retrofit current standards. It has said that alterations may be phased but interim measures may be required in the process. For existing buildings, the new regime may require improvements or alterations to be made, but only up to the point where people are safe from the spread of fire and structural failure.

The Regulator's specific statutory duties are set out in BSA 2022, ss.4–8. Section 4 obliges the Regulator to provide such assistance and encouragement to relevant persons as it considers appropriate with a view to facilitating their securing the safety of people – and, in particular, disabled people[24] – in or about HRBs in relation to BSRs as regards those buildings. The 'relevant persons' to whom such assistance is to be provided are: (a) residents of HSBs, as defined in Part 4;[25] (b) owners of residential units in such buildings; (c) persons who are APs[26]

[23] 'Building Safety Regulator approach to enforcement: Statement of intent', published on the . GOV website, and last updated on 25 July 2022.

[24] Somewhat stark though it may be, this is the language used in the statute.

[25] The definition of 'higher-risk building' is considered in **Chapter 4**.

[26] The definition of 'accountable persons' is considered in **Chapter 5**.

as defined in Part 4; and persons upon whom duties are imposed by virtue of BA 1984, Sched.1, para.5B (dutyholders).[27]

Section 5 requires the Regulator to keep under review '(a) the safety of people in or about buildings in relation to risks as regards buildings; and (b) the standard of buildings'. This obligation concerns not just the specific buildings on the Regulator's register of HSBs, but all buildings in general. In this way, the legislation provides for the Regulator to be responsible for improving the safety of people in and about the built environment generally.

The new regulatory scheme does not just require the Regulator to oversee compliance and enforce non-compliance. Section 6 requires the Regulator to be more involved, by providing such assistance and encouragement as it considers appropriate to (a) persons in the built environment industry, and (b) registered building inspectors,[28] with a view to 'facilitating their improving' (in the inelegant words of the Act) the competence of persons in that industry or members of that profession (as the case may be). The 'built environment industry' is defined broadly in BSA 2022, s.30(1): '(a) persons carrying on, for business purposes, activities connected with the design, construction, management or maintenance of buildings, and (b) employees of such persons; and references to a person "in" the industry are to any such person or employee'.

Section 7 gives the Regulator a key role in the making of regulations under BSA 2022, Parts 2 and 4 (save for regulations under ss.62, 65 or 69). The Regulator may suggest to the Secretary of State that regulations be made (s.7(1) and (2)), but must first consult with such persons as it considers appropriate (s.7(3)). Further, the Secretary of State cannot make regulations under Parts 2 or 4 (save for regulations under ss.62, 65 or 69) that the Regulator has not proposed without first consulting the Regulator (and such other persons as the Secretary of State considers appropriate) (s.7(4)).

The scheme established by the Act envisages that in order properly to perform its primary duties, the Regulator will become a hub of technical and practical expertise. Information, knowledge and know-how from all those involved in the built environment industry will be passed to the Regulator, in the hope that it will be subjected to an informed and joined-up evaluation. The Act therefore requires the Regulator to establish various mechanisms to facilitate the acquisition of or access to that information, knowledge and know-how. BSA 2022, s.8 requires the Regulator to make arrangements for a person to establish and operate a voluntary occurrence reporting system, defined as a system to facilitate the voluntary giving of information about building safety to the person who operates the system. This is intended to give the Regulator insights into incidents that might be occurring on the ground. This voluntary occurrence reporting system will be in addition to the obligation (created by BSA 2022, s.87) on the AP to give prescribed information to the Regulator.

---

27 The relevant provisions of BA 1984 are considered in **Chapter 3**.

28 As defined in BA 1984, s.58A. See **Chapter 3** for more detail.

With effect from 28 April 2022, BSA 2022, s.9 abolished the existing Building Regulations Advisory Committee for England established under BA 1984, s.14, and obliged the Regulator to establish a new committee to be known as the 'Building Advisory Committee', pursuant to its powers under the Health and Safety at Work etc. Act (HSWA) 1974, s.11A(3). This committee is to give advice and information to the Regulator about matters connected with any of the Regulator's building functions[29] except its functions relating to the competence of persons in the built environment industry and/or registered building inspectors.

BSA 2022, s.10 requires the Regulator to establish a second committee pursuant to its powers under HSWA 1974, s.11A(3). This second committee is to be known as the 'Committee on Industry Competence' and is to be concerned with the competence of persons in the built environment industry ('industry competence'). This committee is to have the following functions (and any other function that the Regulator considers appropriate): (a) monitoring industry competence; (b) advising the Regulator in relation to industry competence; (c) advising persons in the built environment industry in relation to industry competence; (d) facilitating persons in the built environment industry to improve industry competence; (e) providing guidance to the public (or a section of the public) about ways of assessing the competence of persons in the built environment industry; and (f) carrying out analysis and research in connection with a function mentioned in any of paragraphs (a) to (e).

BSA 2022, s.11 requires the Regulator to establish a third committee pursuant to its powers under HSWA 1974, s.11A(3). This third committee is to be known as the 'Residents' Panel' and is to consist of 'such residents of higher-risk buildings as the regulator considers appropriate', and 'such relevant persons (if any) as it considers appropriate' (s.11(2)). In particular, the Regulator must take all reasonable steps to ensure that the Residents' Panel includes one or more residents of an HRB who are disabled, or a body that represents, supports or promotes the interests of any description of disabled people that includes residents of HRBs, or a member of such a body (s.11(3)). The Residents' Panel is to provide the Regulator with a residents' perspective on such matters connected with the Regulator's building functions and relating to HRBs as the Regulator may specify (s.11(4)). It is the mechanism by which residents will have a voice in the work of the Regulator and, in particular, can give their views on resident engagement, how residents might escalate safety concerns to the Regulator, the Regulator's strategic plan (as to which see below), and any other matters that affect them.

The Regulator must formally consult the Residents' Panel before issuing or revising guidance or regulations on specific matters that concern residents: namely (a) guidance to residents of HRBs about any of their rights or obligations

---

29 As defined in BSA 2022, s.3(5): '(a) any function of the regulator under, or under an instrument made under, this Act or the Building Act 1984; (b) any prescribed function of the regulator; (c) any function of the regulator under Health and Safety at Work etc. Act 1974 so far as relating to a function within paragraph (a) or (b).'

under HSWA 1974, Part 4, (b) guidance relating to any duty under regulations made under BSA 2022, s.89 to give information or documents to residents of HRBs or owners of residential units in such buildings and/or guidance relating to the duties, or (c) guidance relating to or regulations made under BSA 2022, ss.91–93 (relating to the obligation upon a PAP to engage with residents) or s.95 (the duties of residents in HRBs) (s.11(5)).

The Regulator has also established a Joint Regulators' Group (JRG) in order to help develop and pilot new approaches to regulation and to assist with the transaction to the new regulatory framework. The JRG will include senior representatives from the HSE, the Local Government Association, local authority building control, the National Fire Chiefs Council and other organisations as required.

In order to ensure that the Regulator will have such assistance from local authorities or local fire authorities as it might require, BSA 2022, s.13 entitles the Regulator to direct local authorities or local fire authorities to provide it with assistance in its regulation of HRBs; and entitles any local authorities and local fire authorities from whom assistance is requested to provide that assistance. The section expressly extends to the provision by local authorities of support to the Regulator, when the Regulator is acting as a building control authority for a non-HRB (notably in a mixed development including an HRB) (s.13(8)(b)). There are, however, safeguards which are intended to ensure that the Regulator will not issue such directions lightly. Before making a direction, the Regulator must first make a formal, written request to the local authority or fire and rescue authority setting out the reason why the assistance is being requested (s.13(6)(a)). The local authority or fire and rescue authority must be given the opportunity to consider the request and either provide the requested assistance, or make written representations as to why it cannot do so and/or should not be required to do so. The Regulator is required to take any such written representations into account (s.13(6)(b)), and must also obtain the consent of the Secretary of State (s.13(5)), before issuing a direction.

Where an HRB might be Crown premises, BSA 2022, s.14 enables the Regulator to call for assistance from Crown Premises Fire Safety Inspectors, appointed by the Secretary of State under art.25(1)(e) of the Regulatory Reform (Fire Safety) Order 2005, SI 2005/1541, as 'FSO authorised persons'; and ensures that the said Safety Inspectors have the legal power to provide the assistance requested by the Regulator. Section 14 does not include a power to require assistance by direction, nor any of the safeguards that are to be found in BSA 2022, s.13 because Crown Premises Fire Safety Inspectors are themselves Crown servants and it is therefore anticipated that, in the absence of agreement, a request can be made directly to the Secretary of State (see para.204 of the Explanatory Notes to the Act).

The provisions of BSA 2022, s.15 supplement those in ss.13 and 14. They impose a duty on the local authority or fire and rescue authority that provides assistance pursuant to a request or direction to ensure that the person or person(s) providing that assistance have 'the appropriate skills, knowledge, experience and behaviours' (s.15(2)). They also make provisions to facilitate the reimbursement of local authorities or fire and rescue authorities of their costs of providing assistance to the Regulator.

BSA 2022, s.16 entitles the Regulator to issue guidance to local authorities or fire and rescue authorities or Crown Premises Fire Safety Inspectors about their provision of assistance to the Regulator and compels those local authorities, fire and rescue authorities or Crown Premises Fire Safety Inspectors to have regard to that guidance when providing assistance pursuant to BSA 2022, ss.13 or 14.

1.4.1 Transparency: the Regulator's obligation to publish a strategic plan and regular reports

BSA 2022, s.17 requires the Regulator to prepare a 'strategic plan', setting out how the Regulator proposes to carry out its building functions in the period to which the plan relates, and to submit it to the Secretary of State for approval. Before submitting the strategic plan for approval, the Regulator must consult with the Residents' Panel and such other persons as it considers appropriate.[30] The Secretary of State may approve the plan either with or without modifications, but must consult with the Regulator before approving the plan with modifications. Once approved, the Regulator must publish the plan and act in accordance with it. BSA 2022, s.18 supplements s.17 and permits the Regulator to revise its plan during its term and to submit that revised plan to the Secretary of State for approval.

BSA 2022, ss.19–21 require the Regulator to issue reports on various of its functions. Section 19 requires the Regulator to prepare and publish a report, as soon as practicable after the end of each financial year, about the information provided to it during that year pursuant to the mandatory reporting requirements.[31] Section 20 requires the Regulator, at least once each financial year, to publish a statement about its engagement with the Residents' Panel, residents of HRBs, owners of residential units in HRBs, and bodies that represent, support or promote the interests of any such people. Any such statement must, in particular, include information about the Regulator's engagement with residents of HRBs who are disabled. Pursuant to s.21, the Regulator must by 28 April 2025 carry out a cost-benefit analysis of making regular inspections of, and testing and reporting on, the condition of electrical installations in relevant buildings; and consider what further provision in BA 1984 or in guidance under that Act, may be made about (i) stairs and ramps in relevant buildings, (ii) emergency egress of disabled persons from relevant buildings, and (iii) automatic water fire suppression systems in relevant buildings, in order to improve the safety of persons in or

---

30 This reflects the Government's view that 'residents are intended to be at the heart of the new regulatory system' – see para.215 of the Explanatory Notes to the Act.

31 The 'mandatory reporting requirements' are (a) the reports received from accountable persons pursuant to BSA 2022, s.87, together with (b) any provision of building regulations that is prescribed by the regulations for the purposes of this section – see BSA 2022, s.19(2).

about relevant buildings, and must carry out a cost-benefit analysis of the making of that provision (s.21(1)). The Regulator must prepare reports about its analyses (s.21(2)) and provide those reports to the Secretary of State, who must then publish them (s.21(3)).

1.4.2 Authorised officers of the Regulator

BSA 2022, s.22 enables the Regulator to appoint suitably qualified persons to act as authorised officers of the Regulator, with the power to exercise the investigatory powers set out in BSA 2022, Sched.2. Those investigatory powers include powers to enter premises for the purposes of inspecting them and taking measurements, samples or photographs, and a power to require any person to provide information or documents to the officer.

1.4.3 Criminal offences relating to dealings with the Regulator

Anyone who intentionally obstructs an authorised officer exercising their building functions commits a criminal offence (BSA 2022, s.23(1)). Similarly, anyone who, with intention to deceive, impersonates an authorised officer commits a criminal offence (s.23(2)). Anyone who provides false or misleading information to the Regulator in purported compliance with a building enactment or a requirement imposed by virtue of such an enactment, or in connection with an application made to the Regulator under a building enactment, or for the purpose of avoiding enforcement action being taken or continued, commits a criminal offence if they know that the information is false or misleading or are reckless as to whether the information is false or misleading (s.24(1)).

1.4.4 Reviewing and appealing decisions of the Regulator

BSA 2022, ss.25 and 26 deal with reviews of and appeals against decisions of the Regulator. Section 25 permits prescribed persons, before the end of a period prescribed for these purposes by regulations, to give a notice to the Regulator requiring it to carry out a review of a prescribed decision. Regulations made pursuant to s.25 prescribe the decisions that can be reviewed, the persons who can request a review, and the time within which they must do so. Only once the Regulator's review confirms the contested decision can that decision then be appealed to the First-tier Tribunal (s.26).

The following regulations prescribe decisions of the Regulator for the purposes of s.25: the Building Safety (Registration of Higher-Risk Buildings and Review of Decisions) (England) Regulations 2023, SI 2023/315 (the 315 Regulations); the Building (Approved Inspectors etc. and Review of Decisions) (England) Regulations 2023, SI 2023/906 (the 906 Regulations); and the Building (Higher-Risk Buildings Procedures) (England) Regulations 2023, SI 2023/909 (the 909 Regulations). These provisions will be considered in those chapters of this book that address the substantive topics concerned.

CHAPTER 2

Overview of Part 3

Richard Granby

2.1 INTRODUCTION

This chapter provides an overview of BSA 2022, Part 3. Part 3 amends BA 1984. As with much of the Act, Part 3 is concerned with amendments that permit the creating of new regulations and it is in that secondary legislation that many of the substantive legal changes are made. At the time of writing the principal regulations published are the 909 Regulations, the 906 Regulations and the Building Regulations etc. (Amendment) (England) Regulations 2023, SI 2023/911 (the 911 Regulations).

The overall purpose of Part 3 is to give effect to the recommendations in the Hackitt Report which recommended, *inter alia*, a 'golden thread' of information, and reform to the building regulations in respect of complex or high-rise buildings. In June 2019, the Government published the 'Building a Safer Future' consultation detailing proposals to achieve long-term reform of the building safety system. In April 2020 the Government published the response to the consultation, and its proposals for what the Government referred to as a rigorous approach to building control applications and oversight during building work.

The overall structure of the reforms is for there to be three 'gateways' in respect of building design and construction. The first gateway is reforms to the system for planning permission concerned with fire safety as it relates to land use. This gateway does not form part of BSA 2022, being implemented through amendments to secondary planning legislation, primarily to the Town and Country Planning (Development Management Procedure) (England) Order 2015, SI 2015/595, and associated legislation. Those changes came into effect on 1 August 2021.

The second 'gateway' replaces the building control deposit of plans stage, before building work starts, for higher-risk buildings (HRBs), and is a requirement that building control approval must be obtained from the Building Safety Regulator before relevant building work starts.

The third 'gateway' occurs when construction is complete. Building control approval must be obtained from the Building Safety Regulator before registering and commencing occupation of an HRB.

There are also requirements during construction imposed on certain people involved with construction and design of a relevant building.

A full description of the building control regime is beyond the scope of this work. The purpose of this chapter is to provide a broad overview of Part 3 to contextualise the other provisions of the Act.

2.2 WHAT IS A 'HIGHER-RISK BUILDING'?

BSA 2022, s.31 introduces s.120D into BA 1984 defining 'higher-risk building' for England (it also introduces a provision in respect of Wales, s.120I). This defines, in England, an HRB as being a building that is at least 18 metres in height or at least seven storeys and of a description specified in regulations by the Secretary of State. This definition differs from those of HRBs elsewhere in the Act in that the definition is not limited to residential buildings.

The Secretary of State has made regulations which came into force on 23 April 2023: Higher-Risk Buildings (Descriptions and Supplementary Provisions) Regulations 2023, SI 2023/275 (the 275 Regulations). These specify the following descriptions of building as being HRBs: a building containing at least two residential units; a care home; and a hospital (reg.2(a)–(c)). The 275 Regulations also provide an extended definition of 'building' and provisions for calculation of the number of storeys of a building (regs.5 and 6). The 275 Regulations also exclude certain categories of building from the definition, namely secure residential institutions; hotels; military barracks; accommodation for His Majesty's forces or a visiting military force; or an international headquarters of a defence organisation (reg.7). This accords with other sections of the Act which broadly exclude application to the military and to prisons.

At the time of writing no equivalent regulations had been made for Wales but the Welsh Government's consultation response suggests that the regime in Wales will mirror that in England save that an HRB may consist of only one residential unit rather than a minimum of two. The Welsh Government has stated an intent to legislate in the autumn of 2023.[1]

The remaining provisions inserted into BA 1984 by BSA 2022, s.31 (i.e. BA 1984, ss.120E–120H) provide for consultation requirements before making regulations, and for the Building Safety Regulator (see **2.3**) to make recommendations for further or amended regulations if satisfied that there is a category of building, not caught by the existing regulations, for which there is an elevated BSR, and (if that risk materialised) there would be potential for a major incident.

1 Welsh Government, *Consultation – Summary of Responses and the Government Response for the consultation on the Building Safety proposed definition of a higher-risk building* (September 2023).

2.3 THE REGULATOR

The new Building Safety Regulator (the Regulator) is covered further in **Chapter 6**. BSA 2022, s.32 introduces ss.91ZA and 91ZB into BA 1984, whereby the Regulator is made the building control authority in relation to any HRB in England or any proposed such building (including work that would cause an existing building to become or cease to be an HRB).

The new BA 1984, s.91ZB creates a mechanism where, in respect of work of a prescribed description that has a prescribed connection with any HRB work (i.e. work for which the Regulator is the building control authority by virtue of s.91ZA), and where the Regulator is not the building control authority in respect of that connected work, the Regulator may become the building control authority by serving a notice jointly with the person proposing to undertake the work on the local authority and the local authority accepting such a notice.

In practice the intention behind s.91ZB is to facilitate ancillary work being brought under a single building control authority rather than having an inefficient split between the Regulator and the local authority. The local authority is bound to accept the notice unless prescribed grounds exist; appeal will lie to the Tribunal (BA 1984, s.91ZC).

At the time of writing, s.32 is only in force for the making of regulations and to make the Regulator the building control authority under s.91ZA.

2.4 BUILDING REGULATIONS

BSA 2022, s.33 introduces extensive amendments to the building regulations by way of amending Sched.1 to BA 1984 (which provides for the building regulations) to permit the making of regulations governing the making of applications, the giving of notices, and giving or receipt of certificates. The amendments permit more extensive powers for building control authorities in respect of imposing requirements; the provision of certificates by members of an approved scheme (in effect permitting private building control services to provide certain certificates); and to make provision as to obtaining, creating and keeping of documents. This final power is the primary legislative underpinning for the 'golden thread' of information envisaged by the Hackitt Report.

Taken together, the new paras.1D and 1E introduced into Sched.1 permit the creating of positive reporting requirements whereby a person may be obliged to notify the Regulator or local authority of prescribed matters.

The substance of the changes introduced by s.33 in England is found in the 911 Regulations and the 909 Regulations, which came into effect on 1 October 2023. These create two parallel regimes: one for HRBs and one for other buildings.

2.4.1 The 911 Regulations

Regulation 4 of the 911 Regulations provides that most of the procedural requirements in the Building Regulations 2010, SI 2010/2214 (the Building Regulations 2010) do not apply in relation to HRBs. (Instead, the procedures set out in the 909 Regulations apply.)

The key regulation of the 911 Regulations is reg.6, which inserts a new Part 2A into the Building Regulations 2010. This new Part sets out the arrangements a client in relation to a project must make, including the appointment in most cases of a principal contractor and a principal designer, and provisions as to the duties and competence of persons working on a project. Regulation 6 also provides that the client must notify the relevant authority when the principal contractor or principal designer in relation to the work changes, and that after completion of the work the client must send a notice to the authority which includes compliance statements as to the work. A more relaxed regime applies in respect of domestic clients whereby the sole or principal contractor will be responsible for compliance.

Regulation 10 of the 911 Regulations makes provision in relation to the procedure for appeals under BA 1984. BSA 2022, Part 3 provides for a number of new rights of appeal, and, in England, moves most appeals from the Secretary of State to the Regulator and from the magistrates' court to the First-tier Tribunal.

Regulation 12 of the 911 Regulations amends regs.20 and 20A of the Building Regulations 2010 to provide that the client for the project must ensure the person carrying out work in relation to an HRB is aware that the building is an HRB.

Regulation 13 of the 911 Regulations amends reg.38 of the Building Regulations 2010 to provide that the responsible person must acknowledge receipt of the fire safety information provided pursuant to reg.38, and the notice to the building control authority as to handover of fire safety information confirms the information was received by the responsible person.

Regulation 15 of the 911 Regulations amends the existing notice of intention to commence works in reg.16 of the Building Regulations 2010 to become a notice of starting work, and inserts a new requirement to give a notice where work is regarded as commenced. It also sets out the definition of what is to be regarded as commencement of work for the purposes of lapse of building control approval.

Regulation 16 of the 911 Regulations updates the list of provisions whose breaches are not an offence (i.e. the exceptions to the general rule that breaches are an offence) to include a number of the new duties inserted by this instrument, and equivalent provision is made for exclusion from compliance notices. Provision is also made for stop notices and the content of compliance notices, and procedures in relation to them.

2.4.2 The 909 Regulations

It is in the 909 Regulations that the second and third gateways described in **2.1** are to be found and the most significant changes to the process for building a tall building in England are introduced.

Regulation 2 of the 909 Regulations defines the term 'HRB work' as follows:

> 'HRB work' means –
>
> (a) the construction of a higher-risk building;
>
> (b) work to an existing building that causes it to become a higher-risk building together with any work to the building carried out at the same time as that work;
>
> (c) such work, if any, which is necessary to ensure a building that undergoes a material change of use to become a higher-risk building complies with the applicable requirements listed in regulation 6 of the [Building Regulations 2010] (requirements relating to material change of use) together with any work to the building carried out at the same time as that work[.]

Part 2 of the 909 Regulations sets out the procedures for applying for building control approval in relation to HRBs. Applications must be submitted to the Regulator giving the information required and accompanied by the plans and documents required. The information required is wide-ranging, from the purely administrative such as contact details, through a description of the building including the number of floors and a scale plan, to technical requirements such as a construction control plan and – as might be expected given the Act's origin in fire risk – a fire and emergency file. Building control approval may, with the applicant's consent, be subject to a requirement, for example, not to progress beyond a specified point without agreement of the Regulator, or that more detailed plans or documents could be approved by the Regulator at a later date.

Part 2 of the 909 Regulations is divided into two Chapters. Chapter 1 deals with the construction of new HRBs, and Chapter 2 deals with works to existing HRBs. Procedurally the requirements are similar where works to an existing HRB are substantial (e.g. changing the internal layout, height or number of residential units in the building – referred to as 'Category A work'). There is also an entirely exempt category consisting of emergency works (of which the Regulator must be notified), work within an approved scheme or exempt work (as defined by reg.57/Sched.2 of the 909 Regulations, principally relatively minor work).

Part 3 of the 909 Regulations sets out the change control process where any document relating to the work which was approved by the Regulator at the application stage (or subsequently under a requirement or a change control) is to be changed. And provision is also made in this Part for change to the client, principal contractor or principal designer; the insolvency etc. of a client; and the variation of a requirement imposed on a building control approval.

Part 4 of the 909 Regulations defines (at reg.31) the 'golden thread' of information – in practice this means the information required by reg.31 in the form of an electronic file and consists of the plans and approvals submitted to and made by the Regulator (which in turn must accord with Part 2 of these Regulations).

Part 4 also provides for a plan for mandatory occurrence reporting (as to which see BSA 2022, s.87) and the handover of information on completion of work.

Part 5 of the 909 Regulations sets out the procedures for applying for a completion certificate in relation to HRBs. Applications must be submitted to the Regulator giving the information required and accompanied by the plans and documents required. Provision is also made for partial completion certificates where it is proposed a building (or part of a building) is occupied before all of the HRB work is completed.

Part 6 of the 909 Regulations sets out provision relating to inspections, testing and sampling; regularisation of unauthorised work; review by the Regulator of its decisions; and appeals in relation to reviewed decisions, and the procedure under BA 1984, s.30A (which provides that a request can be made to the Secretary of State for determination of an application where the Regulator has not made a decision within the time limit prescribed).

2.5 DUTYHOLDERS AND GENERAL DUTIES

BSA 2022, s.34 inserts a new para.5A into Sched.1 to BA 1984, which permits the making of regulations that may impose general duties in respect of building works and additional duties in respect of persons to be appointed in respect of building works. In turn these amendments are given effect by the 911 Regulations, which amend the Building Regulations 2010 to provide (at reg.11J) a general duty on all persons undertaking building works to ensure that works are planned, managed and monitored so as to be in compliance with all relevant requirements. Additional duties are prescribed for designers and contractors as well as the principal designer (who has overall responsibility for the design) and principal contractor (who has overall responsibility for delivery of the construction).

2.6 INDUSTRY COMPETENCE

BSA 2022, s.35 inserts para.5C into Sched.1 to BA 1984, which creates a power for building regulations, in relation to any work, to impose a competence requirement for any appointed or prescribed person, i.e. a requirement relating to the skills, knowledge, experience and behaviours of that person or the capability of a person other than an individual (i.e. a company) to perform its functions under building regulations. The regulations may require an appointed person that is not an individual to give to an individual the task of managing its functions as an appointed person.

In turn these amendments are again given effect by the 911 Regulations which amend the Building Regulations 2010. Regulation 6 introduces, *inter alia*, paras 11F–11I to the Building Regulations 2010, which provide both a general requirement and specific requirements for designers and contractors to have the 'skills, knowledge, experience and behaviours necessary' to carry out their role. This vague description is then subject to a cascade whereby a principal designer or contractor is responsible for ensuring that other designers or contractors, as applicable, also have the 'skills, knowledge, experience and behaviours necessary'.

2.7 LAPSE OF BUILDING CONTROL APPROVAL/INITIAL NOTICE

BSA 2022, s.36 amends BA 1984, s.32 to provide that where an application for building control approval or an initial notice is made and the application is granted and is not commenced within three years, then the approval lapses. Similarly if a public body's plans certificate is accepted and the relevant work does not commence within three years, then the certificate is treated as not being given or accepted.

2.8 DETERMINATION OF CERTAIN APPLICATIONS BY SECRETARY OF STATE OR WELSH MINISTERS

BSA 2022, s.37 introduces a s.30A into BA 1984, which provides for determination by the 'appropriate national authority' of prescribed applications if made within a prescribed period. Such an application may not be made if the building control authority has already determined the application and no determination may be made by the building control authority once such an application is made. In England the appropriate national authority is the Secretary of State; in Wales, the Welsh Ministers. Appeal from the Secretary of State lies to the Tribunal in England and the magistrates' court in Wales.

In England the process to be followed is governed by the 909 Regulations. Regulations 50–56 provide that the Secretary of State may hear applications if they have not been determined by the Regulator within the time prescribed by the building regulations (if not extended by agreement). In determining the application the Secretary of State will, however, consult with the Regulator. In practice it is likely that decisions will be made by a person designated by the Secretary of State in accordance with reg.54.

2.9 COMPLIANCE AND STOP NOTICES AND OFFENCES

BSA 2022, s.38 introduces new ss.35B–35D to BA 1984, providing for compliance and stop notices to be served by the building control authority. A compliance notice may be given where a person appears to the authority to be contravening or be likely to contravene a relevant provision of the building regulations, or a requirement imposed by virtue of such a provision. A compliance notice is a notice requiring the recipient to take specified steps within a specified period or to remedy the contravention or matters giving rise to it within a specified period. A person who breaches such a provision is liable for imprisonment for a term of up to two years or a fine (or both) and in either case on summary conviction to a further fine not exceeding level 1 on the standard scale for each day on which the default continues after the initial conviction (currently £200).

A stop notice is a notice prohibiting either immediately or from a specified time, the carrying out of specified work until the occurrence of either the taking of specified steps, the occurrence of specified circumstances or the remedying of a specified contravention or the matters giving rise to it. A stop notice may only be given if it appears to the building control authority that the carrying out of the work would contravene a provision of the building regulations prescribed, a compliance notice relating to the work has been contravened or the work contravenes a provision of building regulations (i.e. any requirement) or a requirement imposed by virtue of such a provision and the use of the building in question without the contravention having been remedied would be likely to present a risk of serious harm to people in or about the building.

Breach of a stop notice is punishable to the same extent as a failure to comply with a contravention notice. Breach of a stop notice is *prima facie* a strict liability offence but is subject to a specified defence in BA 1984, s.35D(6), namely that it is a defence for a person charged with an offence under s.35D to prove that the person took all reasonable precautions and exercised all due diligence to avoid the contravention of the stop notice.

The provisions for which a stop notice may be given without the additional requirement of a risk of serious harm are defined by reg.61 of the 909 Regulations and are:

> (a) regulation 3 (HRB work not to be started before approval);
> (b) regulation 7(12)(b) (HRB work not to proceed until approval under a requirement is received);
> (c) regulation 11 (specified work to an existing HRB not to be started before approval);
> (d) regulation 15(12)(b) (work to existing HRB not to proceed until approval under a requirement is received);
> (e) regulation 18(6) (major change not to be carried out before approval);
> (f) regulation 24(11)(a) (major change not to proceed until approval under a requirement is received) but only in relation to a major change …

These provisions are essentially the second and third gateways described above.

Appeals lie to the Tribunal. A compliance notice is suspended automatically on the making of an appeal; a stop notice is not automatically suspended but the Tribunal has a power to suspend the notice pending the appeal.

2.10 GENERAL OFFENCE

BSA 2022, s.39 substitutes BA 1984, s.35 and expands the existing offence of contravening building regulations (save for those excepted) so that it also covers requirements imposed under building regulations. The example given in the Explanatory Note to the Act is requirements imposed at the time of granting building control approval, such as provision of revised plans.

BSA 2022, s.40 introduces a new s.122A to BA 1984, which provides that where an offence under BA 1984 is committed by a body corporate with the consent or connivance of a director, manager or secretary, that person is also liable for the offence.

2.11 REGULATION OF BUILDING CONTROL PROFESSION

BSA 2022, ss.42–53 introduces a substantial overhaul of the regime for the regulation of the building control profession by the insertion of a new Part 2A into BA 1984. The regulatory body for the building control profession in England is the Regulator (i.e the same Regulator as provides approvals for HRBs) and in Wales is the Welsh Ministers. Most, but not all, of the provisions of this section came into effect on 1 October 2023 and the new regime will be phased in between April and October 2024.

The background to this reform is that prior to the Act coming into force the regime of building control in England and Wales was essentially privatised, with most functions in respect of complex projects being carried out by private approved inspectors (in practice, mostly organisations). A body designated by the Secretary of State in England and Welsh Ministers in Wales, CICAIR Ltd, maintained and operated the Construction Industry Council Approved Inspectors Register (CICAIR). CICAIR Ltd in turn was a wholly owned subsidiary of the Construction Industry Council (CIC) and the approval process led to registration as an approved inspector. Approved inspectors registered with CICAIR Ltd were in turn qualified to undertake building control work in accordance with Part II of BA 1984 and the Building (Approved Inspectors etc.) Regulations 2010, SI 2010/2215.

The reforms are extensive. A full description is beyond the scope of this work (the Explanatory Notes to s.42 of the Bill alone run to over 3,000 words, with much of the detail to be provided in secondary legislation). The substance is, however, that the Regulator and each local authority and each registered building control approver will be required, before exercising specified building control functions (such as approving plans or submitting an initial notice), to obtain and consider advice from a 'registered building inspector'; registered building inspectors will also be required to carry out specified tasks such as building control inspections.

Registered building inspectors are in turn subject to what is essentially a full, statutory, professional regulatory regime including standards of competence, a disciplinary process and statutory appeals.

An existing approved inspector will, if they register and meet the appropriate standards, be likely to become a 'registered building control approver' (which will enable them to carry out some of the same functions as they did as approved inspectors but, crucially, not in respect of HRBs). Registered building control approvers are also subject to a regime of statutory control enabling the Regulator to intervene or remove registration in the event of unsatisfactory performance.

Unlike under the pre-Act regime, HRBs will be overseen directly by the Regulator.

2.12 APPEALS

BSA 2022, Sched.6, given effect by BSA 2022, s.56, amends many of the provisions in BA 1984 as to appeals. The essence of the amendments is that most of the appeals that lay to the Secretary of State (i.e. from decisions of local authorities) will now be to the Regulator and appeals that lay to the magistrates' court will now be to the Tribunal.

CHAPTER 3

Building safety risks

Richard Alford

3.1 INTRODUCTION

BSA 2022, Part 4 deals with HRBs. A key aim of the Act is to reduce or mitigate the impact of BSRs in occupied buildings by the creation and maintenance of a so-called 'golden thread' of information. The intention is to ensure that the right people have the right information at the right time to ensure buildings are safe, and BSRs are managed throughout the building's lifecycle. This includes compelling APs to obtain certification that a building is built or converted to a safe standard; to monitor, review, prevent and mitigate potential BSRs; and to ensure that information is shared with residents and passed efficiently to those who later assume responsibility for the management of the building.

The provisions of Part 4 are discussed in Chapters 3–8 of this book. This chapter discusses which 'building safety risks' (BSRs) are within the scope of the Act, and **Chapter 4** explores the definition of 'higher-risk building' (HRB). **Chapters 5** and **6** look at the identity of the 'accountable persons' (APs) responsible for building safety and the extent of their duties. **Chapter 7** discusses the duties of residents. **Chapter 8** deals with the enforcement of the provisions in Part 4.

3.2 WHAT IS A 'BUILDING SAFETY RISK' UNDER THE ACT?

3.2.1 The statutory definition

BSA 2022 does not apply or seek to regulate the safety of buildings in general, but instead focuses on specific safety risks deemed by Parliament to be of primary concern, with scope for the Secretary of State to define additional risks in future. BSA 2022, s.62(1) defines 'building safety risk' as follows:

> a risk to the safety of people in or about a building arising from any of the following occurring as regards the building –
>
> (a) the spread of fire;

(b) structural failure;
(c) any other prescribed matter.

BSA 2022, s.63 empowers the Regulator (see **1.4** on BSA 2022, Part 2) to make recommendations to the Secretary of State to add additional categories of risk if the Regulator considers that such matters have 'the potential to cause a major incident' (i.e. an incident resulting in a significant number of deaths or serious injury to a significant number of people – s.63(8)). The definition of HRB may also be extended in relation to any such category of risk if necessary.

BSA 2022, s.62(2) confirms that any further categories of risk may be prescribed in regulations by the Secretary of State. Before making any such regulations the Secretary of State must consult with the Regulator, unless the new regulations are themselves in response to a recommendation made under s.63 or arising from advice sought from the Regulator by the Secretary of State under BSA 2022, s.64.

3.2.2 Who must be at risk?

The definition in BSA 2022, s.62(1) includes risks to people in the vicinity of the building as well as occupiers or residents of the building itself. Therefore, any matter relating to structural failure or the spread of fire that might endanger a passer-by on the street or any contractor or visitor to the building should also be considered. The most obvious example of a potential risk to a passer-by would be a structural failure resulting in an object or component falling from the building into the street or grounds below.

3.2.3 The type of risk

The definition refers specifically to *spread of* fire, as opposed to a risk of fire generally. Of course, any combustible component in the building is likely to facilitate the spread of fire as well as potentially being the source of ignition. The Explanatory Notes published with the Act suggest that the Act is concerned with the spread of fire between different compartments of a building, rather than spread within any individual flat or unit.

The Act is not concerned with uses of the building or behaviour within the building that may lead to an increased risk of fire. This remains the province of other health and safety legislation.

Cladding and other materials used in the building's construction and upholstering will be the subject of scrutiny, as well as the architectural design and construction of the building, the inclusion of appropriate fire-breaks, insulation systems and fire doors, etc.

'Structural failure' is not defined in the Act. The Explanatory Notes published with the Act refer to situations where the 'structural integrity of the building fails

[and] in doing so poses a risk to the safety of people'. They also state that 'this is likely to manifest as part or all of the building collapsing'.

Case law in relation to LTA 1985, s.11 has defined the structure of a dwelling house as consisting of 'those elements of the overall dwelling house which give it its essential appearance, stability and shape', but not necessarily only the parts that are load bearing (*Irvine's Estate* v. *Moran* [1991] 1 EGLR 261). If a similar approach were taken to the concept of structural failure in BSA 2022, it is likely to extend to any failure of building's walls, foundations, supporting structures and roof structures. The definition may not extend to internal partitions that do not play a structural role, or to windows or glazing that do not comprise part of the wall structures.

3.2.4 The degree of risk

The definition in BSA 2022, s.62(1) does not specify any threshold for the seriousness of risk posed to people in and around the building. For example, it does not specify risk of 'serious injury or death' or similar wording such as is found in BSA 2022, s.63. A fire or structural failure in any large building will almost certainly involve some risk of serious injury or death to people in the vicinity, but if the definition is later expanded by the Secretary of State to include other safety risks, it may be necessary for the Act to specify a threshold for the seriousness of the risk posed.

CHAPTER 4

Higher-risk buildings

Ceri Edmonds

4.1 INTRODUCTION

This chapter deals with the definition of a 'higher-risk building' (HRB) in England.

One of the main recommendations in the Hackitt Report (see **Chapter 1**) was that higher-risk residential buildings (HRRBs) should be subject to a more stringent regulatory regime. The Act addresses this in two ways; firstly, by imposing new requirements for the design and construction of new buildings; and secondly by introducing a system of rules on managing building safety risks (BSRs) once buildings are occupied.

BSA 2022, Part 3 and Sched.5 introduce a series of amendments to BA 1984. By BSA 2022, s.31, a definition of an HRB is inserted into BA 1984 via a new s.120D, with the aim that new regulatory requirements will apply to design and construction works, as well as to refurbishment works on existing buildings.

BSA 2022, Part 4 sets out a system of rules on managing BSRs in occupied HRBs. This includes stringent requirements in relation to registration, certification and safety assessments.

The question of whether a building falls within the definition of an HRB (and an occupied HRB) is therefore of considerable importance.

In this chapter, the phrase 'HRBs under construction' refers to HRBs within the definition of BA 1984, s.120D. 'HRBs post-construction' refers to HRBs within BSA 2022, Part 4.

As discussed below, there is considerable overlap between the definition of an HRB under construction and the definition of an HRB post-construction. However, the definitions are entirely independent of one another, so that any amendment to BA 1984, s.120D would not affect the definition of an HRB under BSA 2022, Part 4, and vice versa. It is therefore possible that the definitions could evolve differently over time or be interpreted differently.

4.1.1 HRBs in Wales

Although BSA 2022, s.4, and the new provisions in BA 1984, apply to Wales, the definitions of an HRB under construction and post-construction only apply to buildings in England. BA 1984, s.120I expressly confers power on the Welsh Ministers to define an HRB under construction in Wales.

Following a consultation, the Welsh Government has confirmed plans for the definition of an HRB under construction. The definition is set out in draft regulations, published at the same time as the initial consultation document. The key proposed difference from the definition of an HRB in England is that HRBs under construction in Wales will include buildings that contain at least one residential unit, rather than a minimum of two such units (Building Safety (Definition of Higher-Risk Building) (Design and Construction Phase) (Wales) Regulations 2023 (draft)).

The reform of the building safety regime during the occupation phase in Wales is being taken forward separately. The Welsh Government has stated that it may define HRBs post-construction differently from HRBs under construction, and may include different categories of buildings.[1] See **Chapter 22** for a more detailed discussion of how the Act will apply in Wales.

4.2 THE DEFINITION

4.2.1 Overview

The definition of an HRB post-construction is set out in BSA 2022, ss.65–70, as supplemented by the 275 Regulations.

In summary, a building will be an HRB post-construction if and only if:

- it is at least 18 metres in height or has at least seven storeys;
- it contains at least two residential units;
- it is not an 'excluded' building as described by regulations; and
- (for an 'occupied' HRB), there are residents of more than one residential unit in the building.

The 275 Regulations set out in more detail how a building is to be measured, including how to count the number of storeys. This is discussed in **4.3**.

The definition only applies to buildings in England (BSA 2022, s.65(1)).

A mixed-use building can be an HRB if it meets the criteria. A residential unit is given the very broad definition in BSA 2022, s.115, namely a dwelling or any other unit of residential accommodation. An example of other units of living accommodation would be student accommodation where basic amenities, such

[1] Welsh Government Consultation Document no. WG46800: Building Safety proposed definition of higher-risk building consultation, 17 February 2023.

as cooking facilities, a toilet and personal washing facilities, are shared with others in the building.

A similar definition is used for HRBs under construction. It is set out in the new BA 1984, s.120D, inserted by BSA 2022, s.31, and is also supplemented by the 275 Regulations. An HRB under construction must be:

- at least 18 metres in height or have at least seven storeys; and
- of a description specified in regulations, namely (by the 275 Regulations, reg.2):
  - a building that contains at least two residential units;
  - a care home; or
  - a hospital.

There is a crucial difference between this definition and that of an HRB post-construction, namely that it includes care homes and hospitals, whether or not they contain at least two residential units, whereas such buildings cannot be HRBs post-construction, as discussed at **4.2.3**.

A building that is at least 18 metres in height or has at least seven storeys and which contains two or more residential units will, if it is not an 'excluded building', be an HRB under construction and post-construction. It will therefore be subject to the more stringent statutory regime both during the design and construction phase, and during the period of occupation.

There is a broad power for the Secretary of State to amend the definitions of an HRB under construction and post-construction, although there are a number of consultation requirements before any such amendments. Detailed provisions as to the process for amending the definition are set out in BSA 2022, ss.65–70 (and in BA 1984, ss.120D–120H). The definition could therefore be broadened in the future to include buildings below 18 metres in height, and categories of buildings could be added to or removed from the list of buildings that cannot be HRBs. The Explanatory Notes that accompany the Act explain the need for the Government to amend the definition in the future in light of critical new information emerging or experience of operating the new regime. The future definition could be made with reference to a building's size, design, use, purpose or other characteristic.

4.2.2 What is a 'building'?

As noted above, the 275 Regulations apply to HRBs both under construction and post-construction. A 'building' for the purposes of the 275 Regulations is defined at length in reg.4. In summary, a 'building' includes:

- a structure (defined as a roofed construction with walls) that is not attached to any other structure;
- a set of two or more structures that are attached;
- for buildings where construction has finished, an independent section of a structure/set of attached structures.

An independent section is a part of a structure that:

- has its own access, other than emergency access, for people to enter and exit the 'wider building' (i.e. the structure or attached set of structures); and
- either has no access to any other section of the wider building, or only has access to another section which does not contain a residential unit.

By way of example, if a building contains a ground floor commercial unit with its own separate access, and a front door at street level leading to six upper floors, then the commercial unit will be an independent section as it has its own entrance. But if the six upper floors contain offices on the first and second floors, and flats on floors three to six, all leading from the same staircase, then the offices will not be an independent section. Rather, the upper floors in their entirety will be an independent section (and, potentially, an HRB).

It is not entirely clear whether, for the purposes of the regulations, both the whole of the wider building and an independent section within it can be considered as a 'building'. But it appears not. The provision that a detached structure is a building is 'subject to' the provision that each independent section within it is a building. The natural inference is that, where a detached structure or set of structures contains one or more independent sections, the statutory requirements for occupied HRBs in BSA 2022, Part 4 will only apply to those independent sections that meet the statutory definition of an HRB, and not to the wider building.

Where a building is an independent section of a wider building, any plant room containing equipment for the provision of services to that independent section is to be considered as part of the building (275 Regulations, reg.4(9)). There is no requirement for any such plant room to be located within the independent section, and a plant room could be considered part of more than one independent section.

4.2.3 Buildings that cannot be HRBs

BSA 2022, s.65 contains enabling provisions for regulations that exclude specified types of buildings from the definition of an HRB post-construction. There is a similar provision in BA 1984, s.120D(4) for HRBs under construction.

At present, the following buildings are excluded from the definition of an HRB under construction and post-construction by the 275 Regulations, regs.7 and 8:

- a building comprised entirely of:
    - a secure residential institution;
    - a hotel;
    - military barracks.
- a building that contains living accommodation:

- provided by the Ministry of Defence;
- provided for His Majesty's forces;
- provided for any visiting force[2] or for an international headquarters or defence organisation.[3]

In addition, the following exclusions apply to an HRB post-construction but not an HRB under construction:

- a building comprised entirely of:
  - a care home within the meaning of the Care Standards Act 2000, s.3;
  - a hospital.

So the regulatory regime for HRBs will apply to care homes and hospitals during the design and construction phase, and during periods of refurbishment works, but not otherwise.

A secure residential institution is defined in the 275 Regulations, reg.1 as an institution used for the provision of secure residential accommodation, including a prison; young offenders institution; detention centre; secure training centre; custody centre; short-term holding centre; or secure local authority accommodation.

It is notable that for some categories – such as army accommodation – a building will be excluded from being an HRB if any part of it is used for those purposes, while for others it is only excluded from being an HRB if it consists *entirely* of a hotel/barracks/prison etc.

This needs to be considered together with the definition of a 'building', discussed in **4.2.2**. It would appear that, where a building includes a hotel, say, on some floors and privately-owned flats on other floors, then the exclusion will not apply and the whole building could potentially be an HRB. But if the hotel has a separate entrance from the flats, so that both parts could be considered an 'independent section', then the hotel will not be an HRB but the part containing the flats will be.

4.2.4 Is the building occupied?

Most of the regulatory regime for HRBs post-construction will only apply to HRBs that are occupied. This is defined in BSA 2022, s.71(2), which provides that an HRB is occupied if there are residents of more than one residential unit in the building. As discussed elsewhere in this book, 'resident' is not currently defined (see **6.3.2**). However, there is a power for the Secretary of State to create

---

2 Under the 275 Regulations, reg.1(3), 'visiting force' has the same meaning as it does for the purposes of Part 1 of the Visiting Forces Act 1952. See s.12 of that Act.

3 As designated for the purposes of the International Headquarters and Defence Organisations Act 1964 (see 275 Regulations, reg.8(c)(ii)).

a definition of a 'resident' in the future, as well as to amend the definition of an HRB being occupied.

4.3 HOW TO MEASURE A HIGHER-RISK BUILDING

The 275 Regulations set out in more detail how a building is to be measured, for the purposes of HRBs both under construction and post-construction.

4.3.1 Measuring the height of a building

Regulation 5 of the 275 Regulations describes how the height of a building is to be measured:

- Height is measured from ground level to the top of the floor surface of the top storey of the building (reg.5(1)).
- For these purposes any storey which is a roof-top machinery or roof-top plant area or consists exclusively of roof-top machinery or roof-top plant is ignored (reg.5(1)).

Where the building sits on uneven ground, such as on a slope, the height is measured from the lowest part of the ground directly adjacent to the building (reg.5(2)). See **Figure 4.3** for an illustration.

As discussed in **4.2.2**, in some cases the 'building' is an 'independent section' of a wider building, such as in the case of a group of flats with their own separate entrance located above a self-contained commercial unit. The requirement to measure from the ground floor up means that the height of the lower, non-residential floors is still included in the calculation. However, there is no provision for non-residential independent sections that are located on top of residential units to be included in the height measurement.

4.3.2 Calculating the number of storeys

Regulation 6 of the 275 Regulations sets out how the number of storeys is to be determined, and provides that the following are to be ignored:

- any storey below ground level;
- any storey which is or consists exclusively of a roof-top machinery or roof-top plant area; and
- any storey consisting of a gallery with an internal floor area that is less than 50 per cent of the internal floor area of the largest storey vertically above or below it which is not below ground level.

So, effectively, basements and roof-top machinery will not count towards the number of storeys in a building. Nor will galleries and internal mezzanines, if they extend less than halfway across the building. See **Figure 4.3**.

A storey is treated as below ground level if any part of the finished surface of the ceiling of the storey is below the ground level immediately adjacent to that part of the building (reg.6(3)). So basement storeys that are entirely below ground will be excluded, but lower ground floors could be included.

As set out above, in some cases a 'building' will be an 'independent section' of a wider building. In such cases, any storey directly beneath the 'building' is to be counted in determining the number of storeys (reg.6(2)). So, for example, where a building contains a self-contained residential section that has four floors of flats above three floors of offices, the 'building' will be considered to have seven floors and so will be an HRB. This does not mean that the requirements for an HRB will necessarily apply to the lower floors.

The rules for measuring an HRB are best explained by illustration. **Figure 4.3** shows how a building on a slope is to be measured, and how the storeys are to be counted.

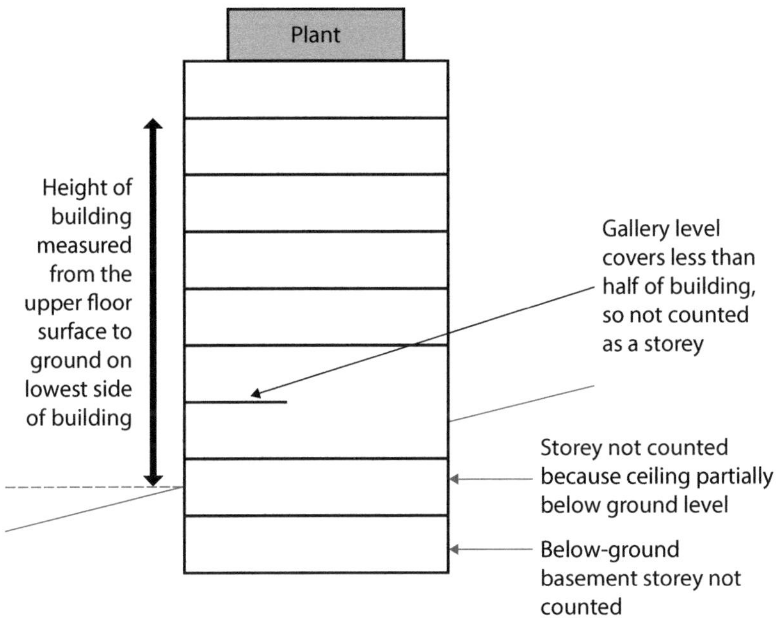

Figure 4.3: Measuring a higher-risk building on a slope

In **Figure 4.3**, the roof-top storey is excluded, as it contains only a plant room. The lowest storey is also excluded, as it is entirely below ground level, as is the storey above, because the ceiling on one side is below the ground adjacent to the building. The mezzanine floor is not counted, as it covers less than the half the floor area of the floors below or above. Thus, the building in **Figure 4.3** has six storeys.

The height is measured from the lowest point of the ground, up to the floor of the storey below the roof-top plant.

There are further helpful illustrations available in Government-published guidance.[4] The guidance states that it only applies to HRBs post-construction, but the same rules apply to measuring HRBs under construction.

4 *Criteria for determining whether a building is a higher-risk building during the occupation phase of the new higher-risk regime* (Department for Levelling Up, Housing and Communities, published 21 June 2023 and amended 19 October 2023).

CHAPTER 5

Who is an 'accountable person'?

Mattie Green

5.1 INTRODUCTION

This chapter concerns the meaning of 'accountable person' (AP) and 'principal accountable person' (PAP) within BSA 2022, Part 4.

APs and PAPs are responsible for managing the building safety risks (BSRs) in occupied higher-risk buildings (HRBs). What is meant by 'building safety risk' and 'higher-risk building' has been considered in **Chapters 3** and **4**. The duties of APs are dealt with in **Chapter 6**.

While there may be multiple APs in relation to an HRB, there will only be one PAP.

By defining who is an AP and who is the PAP, the Act attempts to avoid the risk of residents becoming 'piggy in the middle' while landlords, management companies and developers argue about who is responsible for managing BSRs.

5.2 ACCOUNTABLE PERSON

The definition of 'accountable person' is given by BSA 2022, s.72. As will be seen, the AP is generally the person liable to repair the common parts as defined by s.72(6).

Subject to limited exceptions and special rules for commonhold land, an AP is defined as an individual or a company:

- who holds a legal estate in possession of any of the common parts (s.72(1)(a)); or
- who does not hold a legal estate in any part of the building but who is under a relevant repairing obligation in relation to any part of those common parts (s.72(1)(b)).

Neither the Act nor the Explanatory Notes to the Act provide any guidance as to what is meant by 'a legal estate in possession'. Following the terminology used in the Law of Property Act 1925, s.1, the phrase is likely to mean a freehold or leasehold interest which is not subject to any demise giving an immediate right to possession of the land, such as a lease or sub-lease. A legal mortgagee is also conventionally said to have a legal estate in possession (see e.g. *West Penwith Rural District Council* v. *Gunnell and another* [1968] 1 WLR 1153).

'Common parts' is a defined term. Pursuant to s.72(6), for the purpose of s.72 it means:

- the structure and exterior of the building, except so far as included in a demise of a single dwelling or of premises to be occupied for the purposes of a business; or
- any part of the building provided for the use, benefit and enjoyment of the residents of more than one residential unit (whether alone or with other persons).

'Structure and exterior' is not defined within the Act. Exterior is likely to include the external walls and external parts, such as balconies that are not demised to a tenant. The term 'structure' is capable of a range of meanings. At one end of the spectrum, it could mean all the constituent physical parts of a building. At the other end, it could be taken to be limited to those parts of the building which are essential to the physical integrity of the building, such as the load-bearing walls, foundations and roof. In the context of the Act, the structure is likely to be taken to mean those parts of the building that are essential to the physical integrity of the building.

Persons likely to be an AP pursuant to s.72(1)(a) include the landlord or freehold management companies. Persons likely to be an AP under s.72(1)(b) include a management company in a tripartite lease.

Section 72(1)(a) is subject to an exception in s.72(2) which provides that a person (i.e. 'the estate owner') who would otherwise qualify as an AP under s.72(1)(a) is not an AP if:

- *each* long lease of which the estate owner is lessor provides that a particular person, who does not hold a legal estate in any part of the building, is under a relevant repairing obligation in relation to *all of the relevant common parts* (s.72(2)(a)); or
- *all repairing obligations* relating to the relevant common parts which would otherwise be obligations of the estate owner are functions of a Right to Manage (RTM) company (s.72(2)(a)).

Section 72(2)(a) will apply where all of the leases of which the estate owner is lessor are tripartite leases and provide that a management company is liable to repair all of the relevant common parts. However, it will be necessary to ensure that each and every long lease of which the estate owner is lessor satisfies the requirements of s.72(2)(a) in order to be confident that the estate owner is not an AP.

Section 72(3) and (4) provide, in relation to complex chains of leases, that the person with the relevant repairing obligations in relation to the relevant common parts is the AP. For example, this would apply where an estate owner is an AP pursuant to s.72(1)(a); s.72(2) does not apply; and the estate owner's superior landlord is responsible for repairing the relevant common parts in the superior lease.

Section 72(1) does not apply to commonhold land. In relation to commonhold land, the commonhold association is the AP (s.72(5)).

The Secretary of State may amend the definition of an AP by regulations (s.72(7)). However, no regulations have been made pursuant to s.72(7) at the time of writing.

5.3 PRINCIPAL ACCOUNTABLE PERSON

As stated above, unlike the AP, only one person will be the PAP in relation to any given building.

Where there is one AP in relation to an HRB, then by virtue of s.73(1)(a) that person will be the PAP. However, where there is more than one AP responsible, the PAP is the AP who:

- holds a legal estate in possession in the relevant parts of the structure and exterior of the building (s.73(1)(b)(i)); or
- is within s.72(1)(b) because of a relevant repairing obligation (within the meaning of that section) in relation to the relevant parts of the structure and exterior of the building.

The 'relevant parts of the structure and exterior' of a building means the structure and exterior except so far as included in a demise of a single dwelling or of premises to be occupied for the purposes of a business (s.73(2)).

Section 73(1)(b) is subject to the powers of the First-tier Tribunal (FTT) to determine who is the PAP where more than one AP is within s.73(1)(b).

5.4 APPLICATIONS TO THE FIRST-TIER TRIBUNAL

If there is uncertainty as to the identity of the APs or the PAP for an HRB, or the part of the building for which any AP for the building is responsible, an interested party may apply to the FTT for a determination (s.75(1)). This is considered in more detail in **Chapter 21**.

For the purposes of s.75(1), 'interested person' means:

- the Regulator;
- a person who holds a legal estate in any part of the common parts (or who claims to hold such an estate); or
- a person who is under a relevant repairing obligation in relation to any part of the common parts (or who claims to be under such an obligation).

CHAPTER 6

Duties of accountable persons

Richard Alford

6.1 INTRODUCTION

This chapter considers the duties of 'accountable persons' (APs). See **Chapter 5** for the definition of 'accountable person' and 'principal accountable person' (PAP) and who holds the responsibility in any particular building. APs are responsible for fulfilling the statutory obligations that make up the building safety regime. The duties are extensive and the regulations that support them are very detailed. This chapter will divide the duties into six broad categories:

- certification;
- registration;
- display of information;
- assessment and management of BSRs;
- information and reporting;
- engagement with residents and others.

It will be noted that some duties are expressed to apply to the PAP. These are generally the duties that apply to the whole building, such as displaying information or compiling a 'safety case'. The duties that are expressed to apply to the AP are capable of applying to a particular part of the building for which an accountable person may be responsible where there are multiple APs in one building but will equally apply to a building as a whole where there is only one AP. Where there is only one AP for a building, that person is naturally the PAP (i.e. the *principal* accountable person).

The obligations discussed in this chapter relate only to occupied (or soon-to-be occupied) higher-risk buildings (HRBs).

6.1.1 A note on delegation

BSA 2022, Part 4 does not contain any provisions that expressly permit APs to delegate their duties. When coupled with the fact that a failure to observe any of the obligations under Part 4 may lead to criminal sanctions against the AP, this suggests that APs are not able to do so. However, it is posited that there is nothing in the Act that would prevent the delegation of *the performance* of these duties to, say, a third-party managing agent while the ultimate responsibility for ensuring performance remains with the AP themselves.

It remains to be seen whether the engagement of a fully competent managing agent to fulfil a particular duty under Part 4 would provide the AP with the statutory defence of 'reasonable excuse' in the event that the agent failed to comply with the relevant duty, but this must be considered unlikely in light of the fact that a key part of the policy behind the Act was to establish clear lines of accountability for building safety.

6.2 CERTIFICATION

6.2.1 Requirement for completion certificate before occupation

The Act adopts a system of gateways to ensure that HRBs are built to the appropriate safety standard. The third and final gateway is the issue of a 'completion certificate', confirming that the building complies with building regulations under BA 1984, s.1(1). Whereas it is not necessarily the responsibility of the AP to apply for and obtain a completion certificate – this usually being a function of the building contractor or the developer – an AP is guilty of an offence if the AP permits a residential unit in the part of the building for which the AP is responsible to be occupied before a completion certificate has been obtained (BSA 2022, s.76). Therefore, it is essential that APs ensure that a completion certificate has been issued before the building is occupied.

The requirement for a completion certificate and the potential to commit an offence is triggered in three scenarios:

- when an HRB is newly constructed;
- when any additional residential units are constructed within an existing HRB; and
- when works to a building that cause it to become an HRB are carried out.

The offence created by s.76 is subject to a potential statutory defence if the AP charged can show the AP had a 'reasonable excuse' for the residential unit being occupied before the completion certificate was issued, but it is difficult to imagine the circumstances in which this defence might apply.

An offence under s.76 is triable either way. On summary conviction, the guilty party may be imprisoned for a term of up to 12 months and/or receive an unlimited fine. On conviction on indictment, the potential sanctions are imprisonment for up to two years and/or an unlimited fine.

6.2.2 Direction to apply for a building assessment certificate

BSA 2022, s.79 empowers the Regulator to direct a PAP for an occupied HRB to apply to the Regulator for a 'building assessment certificate'.

If such a direction is given, the PAP must make the application within 28 days. If such an application is not made timeously without reasonable excuse, the PAP commits an offence triable either way and subject to the same sanctions as the offence created by s.76 (see **6.2.1**), save that the PAP will be liable to a further fine on summary conviction (not exceeding level one on the standard scale) for each day on which the default continues after the initial conviction.

When an application is made, the Regulator will conduct an assessment of whether the relevant duties under Part 4 are being complied with (namely, the duties in BSA 2022, ss.83 to 85, 87(5), 89 and 91). Such an assessment may include an inspection of the building in question (BSA 2022, s.81).

Naturally, a certificate will not be granted unless the Regulator is satisfied that the duties are being properly observed. If not so satisfied, the Regulator may give a notice to the PAP specifying a period to remedy any contraventions before a building assessment certificate can be issued.

The Explanatory Notes published with the Act state that this provision is intended to provide a mechanism for the Regulator to assess whether dutyholders are fulfilling their obligations under the Act and provide a transparent outcome for such an assessment. As will be seen below, it is mandatory for the PAP to display the most recent building assessment certificate (if any) in a conspicuous place within the building.

6.3 REGISTRATION

6.3.1 The requirement to register HRBs

Before any part of an HRB is occupied, the PAP must register the building on the register of HRBs maintained by the Regulator.

BSA 2022, s.77 creates a criminal offence if an HRB is occupied when not registered (subject to a 'reasonable excuse' defence). An offence under s.77 is triable either way (the potential penalties are the same as under s.76, see **6.2.1**).

BSA 2022, s.78 empowers the Regulator to register the building on application by a PAP. The maintenance of the register and applications to the same are governed by the 315 Regulations. These regulations set out detailed requirements for applications to register an HRB.

6.3.2 Meaning of 'occupation'

BSA 2022 somewhat nebulously provides that 'a residential unit is occupied if there is a resident of it' (s.76(5)). 'Resident' is not currently defined for the purposes of Part 4. BSA 2022, s.71 provides the Secretary of State with power to make such a definition, but this has not yet been acted upon. In the absence of a more technical definition, a person is likely to be considered a resident if they are occupying the unit with a degree of permanence, as opposed to being a merely transitory visitor. The precise degree of permanence required may well give rise to arguments in future.

6.3.3 Timing of application

The Explanatory Notes accompanying the Act provide that:

> for new buildings, the Principal Accountable Person will be required to register their building before it becomes occupied. … For existing occupied buildings, the Principal Accountable Person will be required to register their building within a transitional period following the new regulatory regime coming into force.

BSA 2022, ss.76 and 78 came into force on 1 October 2023 (reg.2(q) and (r) of the Building Safety Act 2022 (Commencement No.5 and Transitional Provisions) Regulations 2023, SI 2023/993). Therefore, the PAP in relation to any existing HRB that is not already registered is currently liable to be charged under s.76. The register of HRBs is now available to search online at **www.gov.uk/guidance/find-a-high-rise-residential-building**.

6.3.4 Content of application

An application to register an HRB in England can currently be made using the online portal at **www.gov.uk/guidance/register-a-high-rise-residential-building**. The regulations do not however mandate the use of that service.

An application to register an HRB must include the following:

1. If there is only one AP for the building:
   (a) their name;
   (b) an address in England and Wales at which notices (including notices in proceedings) may be served on them;
   (c) their email address;
   (d) their telephone number (315 Regulations, reg.11).
2. If there is more than one AP for the building:
   (a) confirmation of who is the PAP;
   (b) details for which part of the building each AP is responsible; and
   (c) the details in (1) above, for each of the APs for the building (315 Regulations, reg.12).
3. If the PAP is not an individual, what type of organisation it is. In particular, the applicant must state whether it is one of the following:
   (a) a local authority;

(b) a private registered provider of social housing;
(c) a registered provider of social housing;
(d) a commonhold association;
(e) a resident management company (defined as a body corporate which is party to a lease of a building where (a) the body corporate is limited by guarantee and the members of that body are leaseholders, or (b) the majority of the shares of the body corporate are held by leaseholders);
(f) a Right to Manage (RTM) company (315 Regulations, reg.13);

or, if it is not one of the above, details of what type of organisation it is.

4. The name and address and confirmation of authority for any person making the application on the PAP's behalf (315 Regulations, reg.14).
5. The name and address of an individual to serve as a single point of contact (if the PAP or the person making the application on its behalf is not an individual) (315 Regulations, reg.15).
6. A description of the building, comprising:

(a) the address, postcode and, if applicable, name of the building;
(b) the number of residential units (i.e. a dwelling or any other unit of living accommodation) it contains;
(c) the height, in metres, of the building as determined in accordance with regulations made under BSA 2022, s.65(2);
(d) the number of storeys on or above ground level as determined in accordance with regulations made under BSA 2022, s.65(2); and
(e) the year in which the building was completed (315 Regulations, reg.16).

7. In relation to a building completed before 1 October 2023:

(a) the date of the building certificate for the completed building;
(b) the reference number of the certificate; and
(c) the name of the building control body who gave the certificate,

or, if the PAP does not hold any of the above information, an explanation to the Regulator setting out the steps that the PAP has taken to obtain the information (315 Regulations, reg.17).

8. In relation to a building completed on or after 1 October 2023 that falls within the transitional provisions (i.e. the previous building regulatory regime applies):

(a) the date of the building certificate issued in relation to the building;
(b) the reference number of the certificate;
(c) the name of the building control body who gave certificate; and

(d) a copy of the certificate (if multiple certificates have been issued for the same part of the building, the most recent will suffice) (315 Regulations, reg.18).

9. In relation to a building completed on or after 1 October 2023 that is not a building that falls within the transitional provisions:

   (a) the reference number for the building, issued by the Regulator; and
   (b) the date that the building certificate was issued (315 Regulations, reg.19).

6.4 DISPLAY OF INFORMATION

BSA 2022, s.82 provides that the PAP for an occupied HRB must ensure that the following are displayed together in a conspicuous position in the building:

- a notice in prescribed form containing prescribed information about the APs for the building;
- the most recent building safety certificate (see **6.2.2**), unless the building is in 'special measures' (discussed in **8.4**);
- any relevant compliance notice (issued under BSA 2022, s.99, discussed in **8.2**).

Section 82 must be read alongside the Higher-Risk Buildings (Management of Safety Risks etc) (England) Regulations 2023, SI 2023/907 (the 907 Regulations). Regulation 3(8) and (9) in those regulations specify that the notice containing information about APs mentioned above must:

- be in written form and legible when displayed; and
- state the address, telephone number and email address of the PAP and any other AP for the building.

Where a special measures order (see **8.4**) is in force, the PAP has a positive duty to ensure that no building assessment certificate relating to the building is displayed in the building (s.82(2)(b)).

It is an offence for a PAP to contravene either s.82(1) or (2). The offence is triable either way. On summary conviction, the guilty party may be imprisoned for a term of up to 12 months and/or receive an unlimited fine. On conviction on indictment, the potential sanctions are imprisonment for up to two years and/or an unlimited fine. Furthermore, if the default is not remedied by the time of conviction, the PAP will be liable to a further fine (not exceeding level one on the standard scale) for each day on which the default continues after the initial conviction.

6.5 ASSESSMENT AND MANAGEMENT OF BUILDING SAFETY RISKS

Arguably the core obligations on PAPs and APs are to be found in BSA 2022, ss.83–86.

Section 83 requires an AP to assess the BSRs in their part of the building. Section 84 compels the AP to take steps to manage those risks. Section 85 draws together the two previous provisions by mandating the PAP to prepare a 'safety case report' containing the assessments carried out under s.83 and a summary of the steps taken under s.84. Section 86 requires the PAP to notify the Regulator when the safety case report is prepared or modified and to provide a copy of the safety case report to the Regulator as soon as practicable on demand.

Sections 83–86 should be read alongside the 907 Regulations. These provide detailed guidance on the extent of the relevant duties, as set out below.

6.5.1 Assessment of BSRs

An AP's duty to assess the part of the building for which they are responsible commences from the time that the building is occupied (BSA 2022, s.83(1) and (4)).

As soon as reasonably practicable after occupation, the AP must assess the BSRs in their part (if more than one AP) or the whole (if they are the only AP) of the building. At this juncture, it is worth revisiting the definition of 'building safety risk' under the Act, which is limited to the spread of fire and structural defects; the AP's duty under the Act is to assess those risks in particular and not to assess safety risks in general.

The AP's duty to assess BSRs is continuous. Further assessments must be made at regular intervals, as well as 'at any time that the accountable person has reason to suspect that the current assessment is no longer valid' (s.83(2)(b)) and 'at the direction of the regulator' (s.83(2)(c)).

The formulation 'reason to suspect that the current assessment is no longer valid' begs the question of what factors might invalidate a previous assessment. Examples of when this subsection could be engaged might be when there has been a material change to the common parts, structure or exterior of the building that may impact upon the risk of spread of fire or collapse; material developments in safety products or technology; or when a particular construction product or material is revealed to be defective.

An AP is also obliged to conduct an assessment as soon as reasonably practicable after they become the AP, for example if they acquire or take responsibility for a part or all of an existing HRB (s.83(1) and (4)).

The assessment must be suitable and sufficient for the purposes of enabling the AP to comply with their duties to avert, manage and mitigate BSRs under BSA 2022, s.84.

6.5.2 Management of BSRs

BSA 2022, s.84(1) provides as follows:

> An accountable person for an occupied higher-risk building must take all reasonable steps for the following purposes –
>
> (a) preventing a building safety risk materialising as regards the part of the building for which they are responsible;
> (b) reducing the severity of any incident resulting from such a risk materialising.

This is a broad, general duty revolving around the twin obligations of prevention and mitigation. The remainder of the section and the related regulations provide more detail as to what is required.

Section 84(2) makes clear that an AP is expected to carry out works to the part of the building for which they are responsible if necessary (s.84(2)).

Section 84(4) provides that any steps must be taken promptly.

Section 84(5) spells out that the AP must take a long-term and reflective approach to their duties: they must 'make and give effect to arrangements for the purpose of ensuring the effective planning, organisation, control, monitoring and review of steps taken under this section'.

Section 84(3) specifies that, when taking steps under s.84, the AP must act in accordance with prescribed principles. These are set out in the 907 Regulations, reg.4 as being to:

> (a) avoid building safety risks;
> (b) evaluate building safety risks that cannot be avoided, including identifying the proportionate measures required to address, reduce, mitigate and control the risks;
> (c) combat building safety risks at source by introducing proportionate measures to address, reduce, mitigate and control the risk at the earliest opportunity;
> (d) ensure suitable and proportionate systems are in place for the effective inspection, testing and maintenance of the efficacy of measures taken;
> (e) give collective protective measures priority over individual protective measures;
> (f) adapt to technical progress;
> (g) where reasonable to do so, replace the dangerous with the non-dangerous or less dangerous;
> (h) consider the impacts on residents and carry out engagement with residents;
> (i) give appropriate instructions and information to employees and persons working on or in the building;
> (j) ensure that any person responsible for or assisting with compliance with a duty in or under Part 4 of the 2022 Act has the relevant competence.

With regard to principle (j), the 907 Regulations, reg.4(2) provides that:

> A person has the relevant competence –
>
> (a) where the person is an individual, if that person has the skills, knowledge, experience and behaviours necessary to perform the functions for which they are responsible in a satisfactory manner;

(b) where the person is not an individual, if that person has the organisational capability to ensure that the functions for which it is responsible are performed in a satisfactory manner.

and under reg.4(3) provides that:

> An individual who is in training is deemed to have the relevant competence for a function if that individual is adequately supervised by a person with the relevant competence when performing the function.

It will be seen that the principles focus on a proactive approach to reducing risks; the need for prompt action; reviewing and testing preventative measures; adapting to advances in technology; and replacing dangerous elements or components. The AP should also prioritise collective protective measures and liaise and engage with residents in relation to any steps taken.

The principles, and whether they have been observed, will be a key consideration when the Regulator is considering enforcement action or prosecution.

6.5.3 The safety case report

The PAP is responsible for preparing the safety case report (BSA 2022, s.85). This document brings together the assessment(s) carried out by the AP under BSA 2022, s.83 and the steps taken under BSA 2022, s.84. In larger buildings with multiple APs, the safety case report will bring together in one document the various assessments and steps for the constituent parts of the building.

The PAP must compile a safety case report as soon as reasonably practicable after the building is occupied and when the PAP becomes the PAP in respect of an existing building.

The safety case report must be kept under review and be revised whenever there is a further assessment under s.83 or any further steps are taken under s.84.

The 907 Regulations, reg.5(1) stipulates that the following information must be included in the safety case report:

(a) the registration number given to the building on the register;
(b) a brief description of the building and its wider environment;
(c) a description of the possible scenarios of building safety risks that have been identified by each AP through the risk assessment process under section 83 of the 2022 Act, the likelihood of those risks materialising and the assessment of the likely consequences if they do materialise;
(d) a description of how the steps taken by each AP demonstrate compliance with the obligations under section 84 of the 2022 Act;
(e) a description summarising the system for managing safety for the building including but not limited to details of –

    (i) how safety measures are tested and maintained,
    (ii) the policies and procedures in place for managing works to the building, including for assuring the competence of designers and contractors appointed, quality of materials used and assessment and management of building safety risks whilst works are in progress;

(f) a description of emergency plans in place for the building including but not limited to –

 (i) a description of equipment in place to allow emergency services to respond to an emergency,
 (ii) details of the information provided to emergency services to support their emergency response planning,
 (iii) a description of the expectation with regard to residents and how they are to respond to emergency situations.

Regard should be had to the mandatory contents for the safety case report in reg.5 by all APs when considering and implementing steps to manage risks under s.84.

The safety case report must be kept in electronic form (907 Regulations, reg.5(2)).

The Regulator must be informed whenever a safety case report is prepared or updated (BSA 2022, s.86(1)). When notifying the Regulator of a revision in a safety case report, the PAP must include (a) an overview of the main revisions to the safety case report and (b) an explanation of why the revision has been made (907 Regulations, reg.5(3)).

A copy of the safety case report must be provided to the Regulator as soon as reasonably practicable if so requested (BSA 2022, s.86(2)).

The Regulator may also issue a direction as to the way in which a notification in relation to a safety case report or a copy of the same should be provided to the Regulator. Any such direction must be published on its website and made available for inspection at its offices (907 Regulations, reg.5(4) and (5)).

6.6 INFORMATION AND REPORTING

Part of the policy intention behind the Act was to ensure that information is effectively kept, shared and passed on between those persons with an interest in HRBs. BSA 2022, ss.87–90 set down requirements in relation to information reporting, record keeping and dissemination. Section 87 makes provision for mandatory reporting to the Regulator. Section 88 deals with record keeping. Section 89 deals with providing information to others, including residents. Section 90 deals with passing information on to successor APs and/or PAPs.

6.6.1 Reporting information to the Regulator

BSA 2022, s.87(1) provides that an AP for an occupied HRB must give information to the Regulator 'in prescribed circumstances … by the prescribed time and in the specified way'. Regulation 6 of the 907 Regulations prescribes that an AP must provide both a notice and a report to the Regulator following any 'safety occurrence', more precisely 'an incident or situation relating to the structural integrity of, or spread of fire in, a higher-risk building that meets the risk condition' (907 Regulations, reg.6(2) and 6(5)).

When a safety occurrence takes place, the AP's first duty is to provide a notice to the Regulator containing a brief description of the nature of the safety occurrence and the address of the building in which it took place (907 Regulations, reg.6(2)(a)) as soon as reasonably practicable after the incident has taken place (907 Regulations, reg.6(3)(a)).

In addition, within a period of 10 days beginning with the day of the safety occurrence coming to the AP's attention (907 Regulations, reg.6(3)(b)), the AP must provide to the Regulator a report containing (reg.6(2)(b)):

- the date and time of the safety occurrence;
- the date and time the safety occurrence was first notified to the Regulator;
- the date of submission of the report to the Regulator;
- the address of the building at which the safety occurrence took place;
- the name, address, telephone number and email address of the AP making the report;
- the details of the safety occurrence, including:
    - whether any persons were injured or killed as a result of the safety occurrence;
    - details of any recent building work;
    - details of how the safety occurrence was discovered;
- a description of the measures taken to mitigate or remedy the safety occurrence; and
- details of any wider impact or other considerations.

It should be noted that the time period for the provision of the report begins on (i.e. includes) the day of the incident coming to the AP's attention. Also, the provision does not specify 'working days'. Therefore, if an incident comes to the AP's attention on, say, 10 January, the report must be provided to the Regulator by 19 January.

A person who, without reasonable excuse, does not provide the prescribed information in the prescribed manner or within the prescribed timeframe is liable to summary conviction (BSA 2022, s.87(4)).

6.6.2 'Mandatory occurrence reporting system'

In order to facilitate the prompt reporting of incidents pursuant to BSA 2022, s.87(1), the PAP for the building must establish a 'mandatory occurrence reporting system'. This must be a robust and accessible system for the reporting of information to APs to enable them to provide the above-mentioned notice and report to the Regulator within the required timeframe.

As per the regulations (907 Regulations, reg.6(4)), the PAP must ensure the following:

- there is a single reporting system for the building;
- the system is accessible to all residents *and* other users of the building;
- the system enables:
  - the reporting and recording of incidents and situations by individuals to the AP;
  - the recording of incidents and situations identified by the AP;
  - the timely assessment of reports or records of incidents and situations to determine whether they constitute a safety occurrence;
  - the notification and reporting of safety occurrences to the Regulator within the required periods;
- there are regular reviews of the system to ensure that it remains effective.

6.6.3 Keeping information on HRBs

BSA 2022, s.88 requires APs to assemble and keep up-to-date prescribed information and documents relating to HRBs. The information and documents must be kept in an electronic format which ensures that it is capable of being transferred to other persons without loss or corruption. The information kept must be accurate (907 Regulations, reg.7).

The data kept must be 'intelligible to intended readers of the data' and a key should be provided if necessary. In many cases, the intended readers will be owners or residents, so the information will need to be stored with that in mind.

The information and documents must be secure from unauthorised access, but also kept in such a manner so that it can be provided on request in accordance with BSA 2022, s.89.

The information and documents that are to be kept under s.88 is the so-called 'golden thread'. The precise scope of the golden thread information is defined by reg.4 of the Higher-Risk Buildings (Keeping and Provision of Information etc.) (England) Regulations 2024, SI 2024/41 (the 41 Regulations).

Golden thread information: information that must be kept by APs

The information that must be kept by APs under BSA 2022, s.88 is that set out in paras.2–4 of Sched.1 to the 41 Regulations and the documents that must be kept by APs are those set out in paras.16–31 those Regulations. Together, this is known as the 'golden thread' information (41 Regulations, reg.4).

The information that APs (or, in some cases as indicated below, PAPs only) need to keep pursuant to the 41 Regulations is as follows:

1. In relation to work to the HRB that consists only of work suitable for self-certification or third-party certification schemes under the Building Regula-

tions 2010, the fire safety information which the client of that scheme work is required to give to any responsible person (RP) (i.e. the responsible person under the Regulatory Reform (Fire Safety) Order 2005, SI 2005/1541, art.3) for that HRB pursuant to the 909 Regulations (Sched.1, para.2).

2. (PAPs only) Where an HRB has been registered, the most up-to-date registration information for that building (Sched.1, para.3).
3. (PAPs only) The key building information that is given by the PAP to the Regulator pursuant to the Higher-Risk Buildings (Key Building Information etc.) (England) Regulations 2023, SI 2023/396 (the 396 Regulations), regs.19 and 21 (only applicable where an application to register the HRB has been made and 28 days have since elapsed. The 396 Regulations and the definition of 'key building information' are discussed in **6.6.4**) (Sched.1, para.4).
4. (PAPs only) Where an application has been made for a building assessment certificate in relation to an HRB:
   (a) the information that is contained in the most recent application made, pursuant to BSA 2022, s.80 (applications for building assessment certificates) or regulations made under that section; and
   (b) any information that the PAP provides further to a request by the Regulator, following receipt of that application, to support the Regulator's assessment under BSA 2022, s.81 (building assessment certificates) (Sched.1, para.5).
5. A list identifying each fire safety management measure, and a record of where each of those measures is located (Sched.1, para.6).
6. Where an evacuation strategy has been produced in relation to a building, the evacuation strategy and evacuation information for the part of the HRB for which the AP is responsible (Sched.1, para.7(1)(a)). In this context 'Evacuation information' means information for a person in an HRB about the steps to take to prevent and mitigate risks to themselves and other persons in relation to the spread of fire or structural failure in any part of that building which includes:
   (a) a description of the procedures to be followed and steps to be taken by persons in the building;
   (b) a description of when and in what circumstances a person should evacuate the building; and
   (c) information about any fire safety management measure that may assist a person to evacuate the building.
7. (PAPs only) Where an evacuation strategy has been produced in relation to a building, the evacuation strategy and evacuation information for the HRB as a whole (Sched.1, para.7(1)(b)).

8. Any information required under reg.4(3)(a) and (b) of the Fire Safety (England) Regulations 2022 (relating to construction materials and building plans).
9. A list identifying each structural safety measure in the building. A structural safety measure means a measure taken in relation to risk of structural failure in respect of the building or any part of it that has been put in place for the purpose of preventing or reducing the severity of any structural failure in the building and has not been provided by a resident for their own use.
10. The schedule of any maintenance and repairs that are planned in relation to any equipment, device or materials (whether or not a fixture or part of the fabric of the building), by or on behalf of any AP for the building pursuant, whether in full or in part, to complying with s.84(1) (management of BSRs – see **6.5.2**) (Sched.1, para.10(a)).
11. Where an inspection has been undertaken in relation to any BSR and a report of the outcome of the inspection has been produced, the most recent report (Sched.1, para.10(b)).
12. Any information recorded as part of the planning, design or construction of the HRB (or part of the building), which relates to the approach taken in designing the building (or part of the building), including in particular:

    (a) any design code applied, as provided for in the National Planning Policy Framework (published on 27 March 2012 and as updated on 20 July 2021);
    (b) any British or International building standard applied to and complied with in its construction;
    (c) any description as to the intention of the design used in its construction.

13. In relation to a report under a mandatory occurrence reporting system for the HRB where no more than seven years have passed since the day that the AP created or received the report:

    (a) any information provided to the Regulator by the AP in accordance with BSA 2022, s.87(1) (mandatory reporting requirements) of the Act or regulations made under that section; and
    (b) a description in summary of any steps taken by the AP in response to that report.

14. The following information relating to the prevention and mitigation of BSRs:

    (a) A summary, which is to include an evaluation of the level of risk to residents of the HRB, of the most up-to-date fire risk assessment for each part of the HRB.

(b) A summary of the safety case report which must include the following information:

(i) a description of any assessment of a BSR in the report;
(ii) a description of the steps taken or planned to be taken to manage any identified BSR; and
(iii) an evaluation of how effectively any identified BSR is being or is planned to be managed.

(c) The following information:

(i) how a resident and owners of residential units may take active steps in relation to their residential unit to:

– prevent a BSR materialising; and

– reduce the severity of any incident resulting from the risk materialising;

(ii) how and to whom a resident or owner of a residential unit may report a BSR relating to their building, and
(iii) the duties on residents and owners of residential units under BSA 2022, s.95 (duties on residents and owners).

(d) Information in relation to an HRB setting out:

(i) the location of any fire escape routes, fire doors and other aids (e.g. fire or smoke alarms, emergency lighting etc., and anything else provided by the AP or the responsible person (RP) for the primary purpose of assisting evacuation);
(ii) a list of the fire and smoke control equipment for that building, save for that provided by a resident for their own use;
(iii) where the fire and smoke control equipment is located;
(iv) instructions for use of the fire and smoke control equipment by residents, where it is intended for use by residents;
(v) evacuation information for the building.

15. The following information relating to the dutyholders, the Regulator and other persons:

(a) A summary explaining the role and duties of each of the following persons in relation to the HRB:

(i) the Regulator;
(ii) the PAP for the HRB;
(iii) the AP responsible for the part of the HRB in which the resident's or owner's residential unit is located;
(iv) any RP (under the Regulatory Reform (Fire Safety) Order 2005) responsible for any part of the HRB; and

(v) any person the PAP has appointed for administrative purposes as a single point of contact in regard to resident communication.

(b) An explanation of how the responsibilities of each of those relevant persons differ.
(c) The name and telephone number of each of those relevant persons.
(d) The email address and a postal address in England and Wales at which notices (including notices in proceedings) may be served on each of those relevant persons.

16. The following information and documents relating to the rights of residents and owners of residential units:

(a) The most up-to-date version of the residents' engagement strategy.
(b) An up-to-date list of the information and documents that an AP is required to provide to a resident of a residential unit and an owner of a residential unit in accordance with BSA 2022, s.89 (see **6.6.4**) and any regulations made under that section.
(c) Details of the information and documents copies of which a resident or an owner of a residential unit may request in accordance with BSA 2022, s.92 (see **6.7.2**), including:

(i) a list of information that may be requested;
(ii) a list of the documents copies of which may be requested; and
(iii) the procedure that the resident or owner must follow when making a request.

(d) Information to explain the AP's legal duty to provide requested information and requested copies of documents in a form that is accessible.
(e) Where information or a copy of a document is requested pursuant to BSA 2022, s.92(1) (see **6.7.2**) but is not provided by the AP, the reason for not providing the information or a copy of the document.
(f) The up-to-date complaints system procedure established and operated for the HRB by the PAP pursuant to BSA 2022, s.93 (complaints procedure operated by PAP) of the Act (see **6.7.3**), setting out:

(i) the circumstances in which a relevant complaint to the PAP may be made;
(ii) the procedure for making a complaint;
(iii) what steps the PAP is required to take to resolve any issues raised in a complaint;
(iv) how the person making a complaint ('the complainant') will be kept informed of the steps being taken by or on behalf of the PAP to resolve any issue raised in their complaint; and

(v) what further action the complainant may take if they are not satisfied that the steps taken by the PAP have resolved an issue raised in their complaint.

(g) A summary of the circumstances in which a resident or owner may make a relevant complaint to the Regulator and any policy the Regulator has published in relation to its complaints procedure established pursuant to BSA 2022, s.94 (complaints procedure operated by the Regulator).

17. In relation to a relevant complaint made to a PAP where no more than seven years have passed since the day that the PAP received the complaint, a description, in summary of:

(a) the information contained in the complaint;
(b) any steps taken by any AP for the HRB in response to the complaint;
(c) any involvement of the Regulator in relation to or in response to the complaint; and
(d) the outcome of the complaint.

Golden thread information: documents that must be kept

The documents that the AP will be required to preserve are as follows:

1. Any completion certificates or partial completion certificates in relation to the building (Sched.1, para.16).
2. Any self-certification or third-party certification building certificates issued under the Building Regulations 2010 (Sched.1, para.17).
3. (PAPs only) The most recent building certificate for any particular part of the building filed as part of the registration application for a transitional building (i.e. required during the registration process pursuant to the 315 Regulations) (Sched.1, para.18).
4. (PAPs only) Any documents that that accompanied any application for a building assessment certificate pursuant to BSA 2022, s.80 or were subsequently provided as part of any assessment by the Regulator under BSA 2022, s.81 (Sched.1, para.19).
5. (PAPs only) Any notice given by the Regulator under BSA 2022, s.81(3)(b) (i.e. a notice that the application for a building assessment certificate has been refused) within the previous seven years (Sched.1, para.20).
6. (PAPs only) The most recent building assessment certificate (issued under BSA 2022, s.81) (Sched.1, para.21).
7. The most recent version of any document created or received by an AP, in relation to the part of the HRB for which it is responsible, where that document was created for the purpose of complying with art.9 of the Regulatory Reform (Fire Safety) Order 2005, SI 2005/1541 (i.e. a risk assessment carried out by the RP under that Order identifying the general fire precautions

that need to be taken and ensuring compliance with the Order) and managing the risk of fire spread in any part of the HRB (Sched.1, para.22).

8. Where regs.5 or 6 of the Fire Safety (England) Regulations 2022, SI 2022/547 impose a requirement in relation to an HRB, the latest version of:
   (a) the record of the design and materials of the external walls required by reg.5 of those Regulations; and
   (b) the floor plans (including the single page building plan) required by reg.6 of those Regulations (Sched.1, para.23).
9. The latest version (provided that the same contains sufficient information for an AP to perform its duties to assess and manage BSRs under BSA 2022, Part 4 – if not, previous versions must also be kept) of:
   (a) any statement or report giving an assurance that an assessment of structural risks for an HRB, whether for the whole or any part of the building is not necessary;
   (b) any statement, assessment or report evaluating the structural risks to the HRB, where any assessment of structural risks to an HRB has been undertaken, whether for the whole or any part of the building (Sched.1, para.24).
10. Any report that contains an up-to-date assessment of any BSR to the HRB as a whole or to any part of that building for which the AP is responsible (Sched.1, para.25).
11. Insofar as the same relates to a BSR that affects parts of the building for which the AP is responsible:
   (a) the safety case report for the building (as defined in BSA 2022, s.85(1) – see **6.5.3**);
   (b) a record of any maintenance of and any repairs undertaken to any equipment, device or materials (whether or not a fixture or part of the fabric of the building), which were planned by or on behalf of any AP for the building to comply with BSA 2022, s.84(1) (management of BSRs) (see **6.5.2**), where no more than seven years have passed since the day on which the record was created; and
   (c) the most recent version of any document, relating to a BSR, that was created for the purpose, whether in full or in part, of enabling the effective planning, organisation, monitoring, control and review of steps taken with regard to managing BSRs in the HRB pursuant to BSA 2022, s.84(5) (Sched.1, para.26).
12. Any plan of:
   (a) the current construction of the building;
   (b) the building when it was first constructed (Sched.1, para.27).

13. Any report received or created pursuant to the mandatory occurrence reporting system (see below) in the previous seven years (Sched.1, para.28).
14. Any documents that the AP is required to give to a resident or an owner of a residential unit in an HRB as part of the residents' engagement strategy (see item (16) in the list of information to be kept in **6.6.3**) (Sched.1, para.29).
15. Any log that records details of recurring complaints where no more than seven years have passed since the day that the most recent complaint was received by the PAP (Sched.1, para.30).
16. Any contravention notice given by an AP pursuant to BSA 2022, s.96 (contravention notices) (i.e. to a resident or an owner of a residential unit) where no more than five years have passed since the day that the notice was given.

6.6.4 Provision of information to others

BSA 2022, s.89 confers upon the Secretary of State broad powers to require APs to provide prescribed information and documents to various categories of person, namely (s.89(1)):

- the Regulator;
- another AP for the building;
- residents of the building;
- owners of residential units in the building; or
- any other prescribed persons.

At the time of writing there are three statutory instruments that include provisions relevant to s.89:

- the 396 Regulations;
- the 907 Regulations; and
- the 41 Regulations.

The 396 Regulations provide self-contained requirements for APs to provide designated 'key building information' to the Regulator and to any PAP (if that is a different person). The 907 Regulations and the 41 Regulations set out the requirements to provide information to persons in the other categories in s.89(1), including residents, owners of residential units, persons conducting building work in the building, and local fire and rescue authorities etc.

Regulation 8 of the 907 Regulations sets down timescales for the provision of information and documents prescribed under s.89 and the form in which such information and documents are to be provided.

Regulation 8 must be read together with the 41 Regulations, which provide the detail of what information and documents must be provided to each particular category of person under s.89 and define the information and documents that will form the so-called 'golden thread' information.

At first blush, these provisions appear onerous, mandating the sharing of a significant amount of information with those with an interest in or residents of the building as well as the Regulator, with the AP required to keep the information updated and provide information to new residents and owners as soon as practicable after they move into or acquire a residential unit in the building.

The obligation to provide copies of information and documents under BSA 2022, ss.89, 90 and 92 and the 41 Regulations is subject to various exceptions in relation to information with commercial sensitivity (reg.17) and including personal data (reg.18). Regard should be had to those regulations if an AP is concerned about sensitive or personal data that they may be required to provide.

The following paragraphs will consider an AP's duties to provide information and/or documents to each of the categories in s.89(1).

The Regulator

KEY BUILDING INFORMATION

Under the 396 Regulations, the PAP (or a person authorised to do so on their behalf) must provide to the Regulator specified 'key building information' within 28 days of the application to register any HRB (396 Regulations, regs.19, 20 and 23).

When there is a change to any of the key building information, the PAP must notify the Regulator within 28 days of becoming aware of the change.

The said information must be provided to the Regulator in electronic form as directed by the Regulator (396 Regulations, regs.24 and 25). The provisions contemplate that the Regulator may in due course require the information to be uploaded via a website address.

Key building information is broken down into seven categories:

- use;
- materials;
- fixtures on external walls;
- structure;
- storeys and staircases;
- energy;
- emergency planning.

The table below sets out the information (some of which is highly technical in nature) that must be provided under each of those categories.

Table 6.6: Key building information to be provided.

Category	Information to be provided
Use	The principal use* of: (a) the HRB; (b) any ancillary building; (c) any outbuilding; (d) any storey below ground level in the HRB (reg.4). Any subordinate use (any other use than the principal use) of the same (save for any outbuilding) (reg.5). Whether there has been a change in the principal use since construction (reg.6). * Use must be described by using one of the following categories, which are extracted from Approved Document B (Fire Safety) volume 1: Dwellings 2019 edition (as amended in 2020 and 2022): (a) residential (dwellings); (b) residential (institutional); (c) residential (other); (d) office; (e) shop and commercial; (f) assembly and recreation; (g) industrial; or (h) storage and other non-residential (reg.7).
Materials	With regard to the external wall of the HRB: (a) a description of the material used in its composition; and (b) if there is more than one material, what percentage of the whole each material constitutes (reg.8). If there is insulation of the external wall: (a) a description of the material used in the composition of that insulation; and (b) if there is more than one material, what percentage of the whole does each material constitute (reg.9). With regard to the roof of the HRB: (a) the main material used in the composition of the part of the roof that provides a waterproof covering; (b) whether there is a separate layer of insulation; and (c) whether the roof plane is pitched or flat or a combination of both (reg.10).
Fixtures on external walls	With regard to any fixture attached to the external wall or roof of the HRB: (a) the type of fixture; and (b) the main material from which the fixture is composed.
Structure	With regard to the structure of the HRB: (a) the main material used; and (b) the type of structural design the building has in order to comply with Part A (Structure) of Sched.1 to the Building Regulations 2010.
Storeys and staircases	The number of storeys below ground level that are in the HRB. In relation to staircases – (a) the number of staircases that the HRB has; and (b) how many of those staircases serve, as part of the same flight of stairs, the storey at ground level and every storey above it.

Category	Information to be provided
Energy	The type of energy supply to the HRB (reg.15). The type of energy storage system of the HRB (reg.16).
Emergency planning	A description of the type of evacuation strategy that is in place for the HRB (reg.17). A list of the fire and smoke control equipment within the HRB, save for that provided by a resident for their own use; and where in the building that equipment is located (reg.18).

Regulation 22 provides that where there is more than one AP for an HRB, each AP is responsible for notifying the PAP of any change in the Key Building Information for their part of the building within 28 days of becoming aware of the change, or as soon as practicable following any request from the PAP.

The 907 Regulations and the 41 Regulations

Regulation 8(1) of the 907 Regulations deals with an AP's obligations to the Regulator. The prescribed information and documents must be provided to the Regulator 'as soon as reasonably practicable after the information or document has been created or updated, or where there is a requirement for the recipient to request the information or document, as soon as reasonably practicable after the request is made'.

In addition to the duties under the 396 Regulations above, under reg.5 of the 41 Regulations an AP must provide certain information to the Regulator whenever a specified third-party is appointed to oversee or conduct its affairs.

The relevant appointments that trigger this obligation are:

1. The appointment of a monitor in relation to a moratorium that has taken effect pursuant to the Insolvency Act 1986, Part A1.
2. The appointment of a supervisor in relation to a voluntary arrangement that has been approved pursuant to the Insolvency Act 1986, Part 1 or 8.
3. The appointment of an administrator pursuant to the Insolvency Act 1986, Sched.B1.
4. The appointment of a receiver under the Insolvency Act 1986, Part 3 or the Law of Property Act 1925, s.109.
5. The appointment of a liquidator under the Insolvency Act 1986, Part 4 or 5 (which make provision regarding winding up).
6. The appointment of a trustee in bankruptcy pursuant to the Insolvency Act 1986, Part 9.
7. The appointment of a housing administrator pursuant to the making of a housing administration order under the Housing and Planning Act 2016, s.99.

As soon as reasonably practicable after any such appointment, the AP must provide to the Regulator the following information:

- their own name and the address of each HRB for which they are responsible as an AP;
- where the AP is a company, the company registration number;
- the name and description of the appointment of that office-holder or person appointed; and
- a postal address, and a telephone number or email address for that office-holder or person appointed.

Any other APs in the building

Where there is more than one AP for a building, each AP for that building must provide to every other AP in the building the golden thread information and documents that the AP is required to keep for that building (41 Regulations, reg.6).

For the list of the golden thread information and documents that the AP is required to keep (see **6.6.3**, summarising Sched.1 to the 41 Regulations).

The information or documents do not need to be provided to an AP who has confirmed in writing that they already have access to the said information and documents (41 Regulations, reg.6(2)).

Pursuant to 907 Regulations, reg.8(1), the relevant information and documents must be provided to the other APs 'as soon as reasonably practicable after the information or document has been created or updated, or where there is a requirement for the recipient to request the information or document, as soon as reasonably practicable after the request is made'.

Residents

An AP for an HRB must provide to each resident aged 16 in the part of the building for which that AP is responsible the information and/or documents set out in the 41 Regulations. These are set out above at paras.(14)–(16) of **6.6.3** (41 Regulations, reg.7).

The relevant information and documents must be provided to any resident of an HRB as soon as reasonably practicable after any of the following occurs:

1. The HRB becomes occupied or the time when the person became an AP for the building.
2. A new resident moves into the building, in which case the new resident should be given the prescribed information and documents.
3. The AP becomes aware that information previously given has become out of date (907 Regulations, reg.8(7)).

The obligation to provide information and/or documents does not apply in respect of a person that the AP is not aware resides in their part of the building having taken all reasonable steps to make themselves aware of who resides in the residential units in their part of the building (41 Regulations, reg.7(2)).

Information and documents must be provided to residents electronically (907 Regulations, reg.8(5)) in writing and 'in a form which allows the recipients to understand the content and aims of the information or document given, including explanations of technical language used, or with plain English summaries of complex or technical provisions' (907 Regulations, regs.8(9)(a) and (b)).

Owners of residential units

An AP for a higher-risk building must *take all reasonable steps* to provide each owner of a residential unit in the part of the building for which that AP is responsible with the same information and documents that must be provided to residents (see *Residents* above).

Note that an AP's obligations in respect of *owners* of residential units is to take all reasonable steps, whereas the duty owed to *residents* of which the AP is aware or should be aware is absolute (41 Regulations, reg.7).

Any non-resident owner of a residential unit must be provided with the relevant information and documents as soon as reasonably practicable after any of the following occurs:

1. The AP becomes aware that the person has taken ownership of a residential unit within the building.
2. The AP becomes aware that the information previously given is out of date.

In circumstances where a resident in a residential unit has received a contravention notice (see **7.4**), the notice must be provided to the non-resident owner of that unit as soon as practicable after such notice has been given (907 Regulations, reg.8(8)).

Information and documents must be provided to owners electronically (reg.8(5)), in writing and 'in a form which allows the recipients to understand the content and aims of the information or document given, including explanations of technical language used, or with plain English summaries of complex or technical provisions' (907 Regulations, regs.8(9)(a) and (b)).

Relevant landlords

Paragraph 8(1) of the 41 Regulations provides that a so-called 'relevant landlord' is a person prescribed under BSA 2022, s.89(1)(e). 'Relevant landlord' means the owner of a residential unit in an HRB where an AP for that building has given a contravention notice to any person residing in that residential unit (41 Regulations, reg.2; for contravention notices, see **7.4**).

A relevant landlord will also fall within the scope of draft reg.7 as a 'non-residential owner', so it is not clear what this category adds. Regulation 9(2) of the 41 Regulations clarifies that all the AP must do is 'take all reasonable steps to provide a copy of [the] notice to the relevant landlord'. This must be done 'as soon as reasonably practicable after the information or document has been created or updated, or where there is a requirement for the recipient to request the information or document, as soon as reasonably practicable after the request is made' (907 Regulations, reg.8(1)).

It bears repeating that, in circumstances where a resident in a residential unit has received a contravention notice (see **7.4**) a copy of the notice itself must be provided to the non-resident owner of that unit as soon as practicable after such notice has been given (907 Regulations, reg.8(8)).

'Client'

A 'client' is a person for whom a 'project' (i.e. building work including any related planning, design or management work) is being conducted in relation to the building (907 Regulations, reg.8(3) and (4)).

The AP must give the prescribed information and documents to any client as soon as possible after the client gives notice to the AP that a project is taking place in the building and provides a name, address and email address for the supply of prescribed information and documents (907 Regulations, reg.8(2)).

Regulation 10 of the 41 Regulations provides that the AP must provide a client for a project relating to their part of the building with any golden thread information relevant to that part of the building and concerning:

- fire safety management (Sched.1, para.6);
- structural risks (Sched.1, para.9);
- management of BSRs (Sched.1, para.10);
- building design (Sched.1, para.11).

The AP must also provide the client with a copy of any document that the AP must keep as part of the golden thread information relating to their part of the building and concerning:

- fire safety management (Sched.1, para.22);
- structural risks (Sched.1, para.24);
- plans (Sched.1, para.27(a)) (41 Regulations, reg.10(3)).

There is no obligation to provide documents or information to a client who is also an AP for the building to which the project relates or who has not provided their name, address and email address for the supply of prescribed information and documents.

The obligation to provide information on 'structural risks' does not apply where the material is 'security sensitive' within the meaning given in the 41 Regulations, reg.15. Material is said to be 'security sensitive' when it relates to a relevant safety item within the building (an item in the common parts that is intended to improve the safety of people in or about the building in relation to a BSR – BSA 2022, s.95(4)) and discloses how the item operates or how to interfere with its intended function.

Responsible persons (under the Regulatory Reform (Fire Safety) Order 2005)

An AP must provide information and documents for the part of the building for which they are responsible to the RP for the building pursuant to the Regulatory Reform (Fire Safety) Order 2005, SI 2005/1541.

The information and documents that an AP must provide to the RP is any golden thread information that the AP must keep pursuant to BSA 2022, s.88 and the 41 Regulations, Sched.1 relating to:

- fire safety management (see Sched.1, paras.6(1) and 22);
- evacuation of the part of the building for which the AP is responsible (see Sched.1, para.7(2)); and
- plans (see Sched.1, para.27) (41 Regulations, para.11(2)).

The PAP must also provide to each RP:

- a copy of the safety case report; and
- the evacuation strategy and information for the building as a whole (41 Regulations, reg.11(3)).

Any information and documents are to be provided as soon as reasonably practicable after the information or document has been created or updated, or, where there is a requirement for the recipient to request the information or document, as soon as reasonably practicable after the request is made (907 Regulations, reg.8(1)).

Fire and rescue authorities

A PAP must provide to the fire and rescue authority for the area in which the building is situated a copy of:

- the key building information (as defined in **6.6.4**);
- the evacuation strategy and plan;
- where applicable, details of any refusal of an application for a building certification certificate; and
- the safety case report for the building.

An AP must provide to the local fire and rescue authority a copy of:

- the evacuation strategy and plan for the part of the building for which they are responsible;
- the information that the AP is required to keep under the Fire Safety (England) Regulations 2022, SI 2022/547, reg.4; this consists of information that must be kept in or provided to the local fire and rescue authority in relation to a 'secure information box';
- details of the building design that are kept as part of the golden thread information;

- fire safety regulation information in respect of the design and materials of the external walls and floor plans;
- any plans of the current construction of the building and the building when it was first constructed;
- any contravention notice (see **7.4**) given by an AP under BSA 2022, s.96 (to a resident of the building) within the previous five years;
- any document or information that is kept as part of the golden thread information, when requested by the fire and rescue authority.

Any information or documents are to be provided as soon as reasonably practicable after the information or document has been created or updated, or where there is a requirement for the recipient to request the information or document, as soon as reasonably practicable after the request is made (907 Regulations, reg.8(1)).

6.6.5 Display of information in the common parts of the building

The regulations that support BSA 2022, s.89 also provide that certain information must be displayed in the common parts of the building. Namely:

1. Details of the process for reporting a BSR as regards the building.
2. Instructions as to how to make a relevant complaint.
3. The identity of and the address, telephone number and email address of:
   (a) the PAP for the building;
   (b) any other AP for the building;
   (c) any person who is an RP within the meaning of the Regulatory Reform (Fire Safety) Order 2005, SI 2005/1541, art.3 in relation to the building.
4. The details of any person the PAP has appointed for administrative purposes as a single point of contact in regard to resident communication to contact to request further building safety information.
5. A list of types of further information that a resident can request and the process for making such a request (907 Regulations, reg.8(9)).

Regulation 8(10) of the 907 Regulations clarifies that the public display of information within the building does not satisfy any requirement to provide prescribed information to residents under BSA 2022, s.29. This duty is also separate and in addition to the duty to display information regarding the accountable person and certification under BSA 2022, s.82.

6.6.6 Handover of information

BSA 2022, s.90 provides that where an AP ceases to be responsible for all or any part of a building it must give certain prescribed information and a copy of any prescribed documents to its successor, any other APs in the building and the Regulator.

The prescribed information and documents are the golden thread information that the outgoing AP was, immediately before the relevant time, required to keep under BSA 2022, s.88 and the 41 Regulations, reg.4 (see **6.6.3**) (41 Regulations, reg.13).

The prescribed information and documents must be given to the successor and any other APs in the building as soon as reasonably practicable after the cessation of the AP's responsibility (907 Regulations, reg.9(1)).

The prescribed information and copy documents must be given in electronic form, without data loss or corruption in a form intelligible to the recipient (with a key if necessary) (907 Regulations, reg.9(2)).

Furthermore, the following information must be provided to the Regulator as soon as reasonably practicable after the AP ceases its duties:

- the outgoing person's name;
- the building or part of the building for which the outgoing person was responsible;
- the registration number given to the building on the register;
- the date that the outgoing person ceased to be responsible for the building or part of the building; and
- the name, address, telephone number and email address of any person who has become responsible for the building or part of the building for which the outgoing person has ceased to be responsible and a description of the part of the building for which any such person is responsible (907 Regulations, reg.9(3)).

The Regulator may give directions as to the manner or format in which this information is to be provided.

It is an offence to fail, without reasonable excuse, to provide the prescribed information to the successor, other APs and the Regulator. The offence is triable either way. On summary conviction, the guilty party may be imprisoned for a term of up to 12 months and/or receive an unlimited fine. On conviction on indictment, the potential sanctions are imprisonment for up to two years and/or an unlimited fine. Furthermore, if the default is not remedied by the time of conviction, the AP will be liable to a further fine (not exceeding level one on the standard scale) for each day on which the default continues after the initial conviction.

6.7 ENGAGEMENT WITH RESIDENTS AND OTHERS

6.7.1 Residents' engagement strategy

The core obligation

The PAP for an HRB must prepare a *residents' engagement strategy*, the purpose of which is to promote the sharing of information and a dialogue on building safety decisions with residents (16 years of age and over) and the owners of residential units. The PAP must prepare such a strategy as soon as practicable after the building is occupied or they become the PAP for the building.

A building safety decision is defined in BSA 2022, s.91(2) as a decision by an AP about the management of the building made in connection with the performance of a duty of an AP pursuant to BSA 2022, Part 4.

Review

Having prepared the strategy, the PAP must act in accordance with that strategy and, at prescribed times, must:

- review the strategy as set out below; and
- consult residents, residential unit owners and any other APs in the building in relation to any such review.

The strategy must be reviewed:

- at least every two years and within a reasonable period following the conclusion of a consultation;
- within a reasonable period after any *mandatory occurrence report* (see **6.6.1**) is made to the Regulator;
- within a reasonable period after the completion of significant material alterations to the building, unless these alterations have already been considered as part of a review in the circumstances above (907 Regulations, reg.10(1)).

Significant material alterations that will trigger the need to review the strategy include the following:

1. Work which increases or decreases the external height or width of the building.
2. Work which changes the number of storeys the building has (including adding or removing a mezzanine or gallery floor).
3. Work which changes the number of residential units contained in the building.
4. Work which changes the number of, or width of, the staircases in the building or which changes the number of, or width of, any other escape routes within the building.

5. Work to the external wall of the building, but excluding work which consists only of materials of a description specified in the Building Regulations 2010, reg.7(3) becoming part of the wall (this is a lengthy list of materials, for which reference should be had to the relevant building regulations).
6. Work which changes the internal layout of the building (907 Regulations, reg.10(1)).

Consultation

A consultation with residents and the owners of residential units must take place whenever:

- a new residents' engagement strategy has been prepared; or
- there has been a revision to the residents' engagement strategy (except a revision made in consequence of responses to an earlier consultation).

Any such consultation must:

- continue for a reasonable period;
- use 'appropriate and reasonable methodologies', which may include digital, postal or in-person events, to canvas views; and
- take reasonable steps to ensure that any relevant person likely to be affected is aware of the consultation (907 Regulations, reg.10(8)).

When a building is first occupied in stages, 907 Regulations, reg.10(4) grants the PAP a discretion to carry out the consultation when they consider appropriate so that the majority of residents and owners are able to participate.

Distribution of copies

As soon as reasonably practicable after the strategy has been prepared or revised each AP must give a copy of the strategy to:

- each resident of the building who is aged 16 or over who resides in a residential unit in the part of the building for which the AP is responsible (unless the AP is not aware of such a resident having taken all reasonable steps to make themselves aware of persons who reside in their part of the building);
- each owner of a residential unit in that part of the building; and
- any other AP with responsibility for part of the building (907 Regulations, reg.10(6)).

Mandatory contents of the strategy

A residents' engagement strategy must contain the following (907 Regulations, reg.10(7)):

1. A requirement that the PAP must inform residents when works resulting from a building safety decision will be carried out, and the purpose of those works.
2. Unless works are required to commence on an emergency basis and it would be impracticable to consult relevant persons, where works taking place for a period of more than one day arising from a building safety decision will limit access to any part of a building, or otherwise cause a nuisance to residents, a requirement that the PAP must consult relevant persons about:
   (a) the days and times when works are to take place, and
   (b) how to mitigate disruption to relevant persons from the works.
3. A requirement that the PAP must give due consideration to the responses to any consultation.
4. Provision for the keeping of records of reviews carried out by the PAP.
5. Provision for setting out in writing to residents how consultations are to be carried out on the residents' engagement strategy and on building safety decisions.

6.7.2 Requests for further information

Where an owner of a residential unit or a resident who is aged 16 or over makes a request to an AP to give them prescribed information or a copy of a prescribed document, the AP must respond as soon as is reasonably practicable. Any information or copies requested must be provided in writing and 'in a form which allows the recipients to understand the content and aims of the information or document given, including where reasonable to do so, explanations of technical language used, or with plain English summaries of complex or technical provisions' (BSA 2022, s.92 and the 907 Regulations, reg.11).

The information or documents that may be requested under this provision are set out in the 41 Regulations, Sched.3. The information that must be provided on request is as follows:

1. Where any information is set out partially in the safety case report, the full information to which that partial information relates.
2. Any assessment in the safety case report of the BSRs made under BSA 2022, s.83 (assessment of BSRs) an AP for the HRB.
3. Any information in relation to steps taken under BSA 2022, s.84 (management of BSRs) by an AP for the HRB.
4. A summary of any representations made to the most recent consultation carried out pursuant to BSA 2022, s.91(1)(c) (residents' engagement strategy).

The documents that must be provided on request are as follows:

1. Up-to-date fire risk assessments for each part of the HRB.
2. The most up-to-date version of the safety case report for the building.
3. Where in the most up-to-date version of the safety case report:
    (a) an extract of any evidence is relied on in the report, the document containing the whole of that evidence;
    (b) any document is referenced in the report, that document.
4. A copy of any order and written reasons of any determination made by the First-tier Tribunal in relation to any PAP for the HRB, pursuant to BSA 2022, s.75(1)(b) and (2) (determinations by the tribunal).
5. Any record of a decision, together with reasons for the decision, about whether to revise the resident engagement strategy pursuant to BSA 2022, s.91(1)(b) (residents' engagement strategy).

The obligation to provide further information on request does not apply in relation to certain categories on information or documents where the material is 'security sensitive' within the meaning given in the 41 Regulations, reg.16. Material is said to be security sensitive when it relates to a relevant safety item within the building (an item in the common parts that is intended to improve the safety of people in or about the building in relation to a building safety risk (BSR) – BSA 2022, s.95(4)) and discloses how the item operates or how to interfere with its intended function. The categories of information or documents which may fall within this exception are:

- completion and partial completion of works at the building;
- structural risks;
- the BSR assessment;
- the management of BSRs; and
- the plans of the building.

6.7.3 Establishing a complaints procedure

The PAP must establish and operate a system for the investigation of complaints relating to BSRs and the performance by an AP for the building of any duty under BSA 2022, Part 4 (BSA 2022, s.93). This must be done as soon as reasonably practicable after the building is occupied or the PAP assumes that position for the building.

Regulation 12 of the 907 Regulations contains detailed and highly prescriptive provisions in relation to the establishment and operation of such a policy.

The PAP must publish a complaints policy containing prescribed information (see the 907 Regulations, reg.12(2)).

The complaints system introduced by the PAP must secure the following aims, namely that:

1. Any complaint which is a relevant complaint, made to any AP for the building, is dealt with under the system (907 Regulations, reg.12(3)).
2. There is an effective process for the prioritisation of relevant complaints taking account of the level of risk involved (907 Regulations, reg.12(4)).
3. All complaints are dealt with in an impartial and fair manner under the system (907 Regulations, reg.12(5)).
4. Any question as to whether a complaint is a relevant complaint is determined under the system or, if necessary, referred to the Regulator for final determination of that question (907 Regulations, reg.12(6)).
5. Any person is able to make a relevant complaint (907 Regulations, reg.12(7)).
6. A complaint may be made via any reasonable method, including in particular any method agreed between the PAP and relevant persons, as that expression is defined in BSA 2022, s.91, as to the manner in which complaints should be made (907 Regulations, reg.12(8)).
7. A complainant may be assisted by another person in the making of a complaint and in responding to the investigation of a complaint (907 Regulations, reg.12(9)).
8. A complaint which is a relevant complaint is dealt with under the system, irrespective of whether the complaint identifies that it is a relevant complaint or specifies that it is a matter to be dealt with under the system (907 Regulations, reg.12(10)).
9. Any complaint is acknowledged as soon as reasonably practicable (907 Regulations, reg.12(11)).
10. If a complaint is accepted by the PAP as a relevant complaint, that the complainant is informed of that fact (907 Regulations, reg.12(12)).
11. If a complaint is not accepted by the PAP as a relevant complaint, that the complainant is given reasons for that decision and informed of the right to take the issue to the Regulator for final determination (907 Regulations, reg.12(13)).
12. A relevant complaint may be rejected for consideration under the system if it consists of a complaint which has already been determined or which is under consideration following a complaint by the same complainant (907 Regulations, reg.12(14)).
13. All complaints are dealt with in a timely manner and the complainant is given information about the timeframe for responding to and taking action in response to the complaint, including details of any changes to the timeframe communicated, with reasons for any such changes (907 Regulations, reg.12(15)).
14. A procedure exists for reconsidering the first substantive response to a relevant complaint where the complainant requests reconsideration (907 Regulations, reg.12(16)).
15. All responses to a complaint include details of how that response may be challenged including:

(a) in the case of a first substantive response to a relevant complaint, details of how the complainant may ask the PAP to reconsider that response; and
(b) in the case of any subsequent substantive response to a relevant complaint, details of the right to refer the complaint to the Regulator, and how the complainant can do so (907 Regulations, reg.12(17)).

16. A procedure exists for referral of a complaint to the Regulator where:

(a) there is an absence of agreement between the PAP and any APs for the building as to the appropriate response to the complaint; and
(b) the complainant consents to the referral (907 Regulations, reg.12(18)).

17. All responses to the complainant are in writing and in a form which allows the recipient to understand the content of the information given, including explanations of technical language used, or with plain English summaries of complex or technical provisions (907 Regulations, reg.12(19)).
18. A substantive response to a complaint:

(a) addresses all material points relating to the relevant complaint;
(b) gives reasons for decisions;
(c) gives details of any action undertaken;
(d) gives details of any action planned, including a timeframe for that action to begin and be completed (907 Regulations, reg.12(20)).

BSA 2022, s. 94 provides that the Regulator will establish a complaints procedure to deal with relevant complaints that are made directly to it or referred by a complaints system operated by a PAP under s.93.

6.8 GENERAL SANCTIONS

Indications have been given throughout this chapter where the duties of PAPs and APs give rise to potential criminal sanctions if they are not observed. **Chapter 8** deals more fully with the enforcement of the duties of APs and residents under BSA 2022, Part 4.

However, it should be mentioned at this point that a failure to comply with *any* of the obligations under Part 4 or the regulations issued under it could potentially give rise to a criminal sanction if contravened without reasonable excuse *and* such contravention places one of more people in the building at a significant risk of death or serious injury arising from a BSR (BSA 2022, s.101).

Any such offence is triable either way. On summary conviction, the guilty party may be imprisoned for a term of up to 12 months' imprisonment and/or subject to an unlimited fine. On conviction on indictment, the potential sanctions are imprisonment for up to two years and/or an unlimited fine. If the default is not addressed following conviction, the offender will be liable upon summary conviction to a further fine not exceeding level 1 on the standard scale for each day on which the default continues.

6.9 FIRE SAFETY

BSA 2022, s.156 contains provisions amending the Regulatory Reform (Fire Safety) Order 2005, SI 2005/1541. This includes the addition of new arts.22A and 22B. Article 22A provides that the identity of any AP for the building must be included in the 'relevant fire safety information' maintained and shared by the RP under the Regulatory Reform (Fire Safety) Order 2005. Article 22B requires the RP to cooperate with each AP for the building for the purpose of the AP carrying out their duties under the Act.

While these new provisions do not necessarily confer any further duties on APs, APs should be aware that they will be expected to cooperate and are entitled to expect the cooperation of the RP under the Regulatory Reform (Fire Safety) Order 2005.

CHAPTER 7

Duties of residents

Andrew Butler KC

7.1 INTRODUCTION

The final section of the 'waterfall' of duties by which the Act seeks to achieve the safety of higher-risk buildings (HRBs) is the imposition of certain duties on residents and owners. These provisions are found in ss.95–97.

These provisions were brought into force by the Building Safety Act 2022 (Commencement No.6) Regulations 2024, SI 2024/40 (the 40 Regulations) with effect from 16 January 2024.

7.2 ON WHOM ARE THE DUTIES IMPOSED?

There are two categories of person on whom duties under this set of sections are to be imposed: (i) residents of residential units in an occupied HRB who are aged 16 or over; and (ii) owners of residential units in such a building (BSA 2022, s.95(1)). These are the same categories of people who will be required to be provided with an engagement strategy under BSA 2022, s.91(4) and, indeed, who can make a request for further information to an accountable person (AP) under BSA 2022, s.92(1).

These categorisations merit a couple of comments.

As to (i), it might be said that there is an element of tautology about 'residents of residential units in occupied HRBs' but, in fairness to the drafter, the inclusion of the reference to 'residential units' probably clears up confusion which might otherwise have existed about the position of commercial tenants. As it is, it is clear that commercial tenants are not under the duties imposed by this section. And the reference to 'occupied' HRBs is also necessary because, of course, under BSA 2022, s.71(2) an HRB is not occupied for the purposes of the Act unless there are residents of more than one residential unit.

As to (ii), 'owner' is defined by BSA 2022, s.115 as meaning the person for the time being receiving the rackrent of the premises in question, whether on the person's own account or as agent or trustee for another person, or who would so receive it if those premises were let at a rackrent. ('Rackrent' is, to all intents and purposes, synonymous with 'market rent'.)

It would appear from this definition that if a person (X) is or would be receiving rent as agent or trustee for another (Y), it is X who is the owner for the purposes of this section, and not Y. Less clear is the answer to the question of who is the owner where there is a chain of tenancies, meaning that more than one person is in receipt of rackrent (or would be if one were payable). It is thought likely that each such person will come within the definition of 'owner'. The only suggestion that this is not what the Act contemplates is the fact that the definition in s.115 refers to 'the' person, rather than 'a' or 'any' person. Despite that, however, if a person comes within the definition, it would be prudent for them to observe the duties.

7.3 WHAT ARE THE DUTIES?

BSA 2022, s.95(2) sets out the three duties to which those persons will be subject:

- they must not act in a way that creates a significant risk of a building safety risk (BSR) materialising (s.95(2)(a));
- they must not interfere with a relevant safety item (s.95(2)(b)); and
- they must comply with a request, made by the appropriate accountable person (AAP), for information reasonably required for the purposes of a duty under BSA 2022, ss.83 or 84 (s.95(2)(c)).

Given the range of people who will be subject to these obligations, including residents as young as 16, they are doubtless intended to be readily comprehensible, and, by and large, they are.

7.3.1 Creating a significant BSR

The first obligation – not to act in a way that creates a significant risk of a BSR materialising – harks back to BSA 2022, s.62, in which BSRs are defined. They are risks to the safety of people in or about a building arising from any of the following occurring as regards the building: (a) the spread of fire; (b) structural failure; and (c) and other prescribed matter (at the moment, there are none). While, again, there is a whiff of tautology here (in that the provision effectively introduces the concept of a 'risk of a risk'), it is reasonably self-explanatory. It would obviously extend to, for example, removing or damaging a structural support within the building, or deciding to host an impromptu barbecue on one's living room floor. Closer to the line might be a barbecue on a balcony (much might depend on the circumstances there) or – given the need for a BSR to be something which occurs 'as regards the building' – activities that risk fire in the vicinity of the building, but perhaps not in the building itself. Setting light to something outside, such as foliage, rubbish or a car, whatever criminal liability it could attract, may nevertheless not come within the definition of a BSR.

As to the requirement that the risk be 'significant', the Act does not define this term. It begs the question: by whom is 'significance' to be judged? This question is best answered by reference to the enforcement provisions which are considered in greater detail below. Since a contravention notice is to be issued by the AAP 'where it appears to [that person]' that a contravention has occurred (BSA 2022, s.96(1)), the answer, in the first instance, is that it is the opinion of the AAP which matters. However, the notice is given teeth only by the power of the county court to enforce it, which in turn depends (*inter alia*) on a judge being satisfied both that the contravention has occurred, and that it is necessary to make the order (s.96(7)). This acts as a check against the possibility of an officious AAP issuing contravention notices in respect of actions which do not merit them, because they do not give rise to a significant risk of a BSR.

Finally, there would appear to be no requirement that the action be deliberate. So, accidentally covering over an electrical device, falling asleep while smoking in front of the television, or damaging a structural pillar in a basement parking area by reversing one's car into it, might all constitute contraventions of BSA 2022, s.95(2)(a). Indeed, even non-negligent actions (such as bringing onto the property a product which the owner does not know and could not reasonably have known to be a fire hazard) would also appear to be covered by the section.

7.3.2 Interfering with a relevant safety item

The second duty is not to interfere with a relevant safety item. BSA 2022, s.95 elaborates on both elements of this duty.

First, interfering with a thing is defined by s.95(3) as damaging something, removing something, or doing anything to or in relation to a thing which interferes with its intended function. The use of the phrase 'to or in relation to' suggests that the interference need not physically affect the item itself. Thus the duty might be engaged by, for example, teenagers covering over a smoke detector to allow them to smoke without detection, or somebody placing a bookcase or other piece of furniture in front of a fire alarm in a communal area.

The damage, removal, or interference with function must be 'without reasonable excuse'. It is difficult to anticipate what might constitute a reasonable excuse, but disabling an irritatingly over-active fire alarm or sprinkler pending its repair might perhaps come within that phrase.

Second, 'relevant safety item' is defined by s.95(4) as something which (i) is in, or forms part of, the common parts as defined by BSA 2022, s.72; and (ii) is intended to improve the safety of people in or about the building in relation to a BSR.

The definition of common parts in s.72 covers both 'the structure and exterior of the building, except so far as included in a demise of a single dwelling or of premises to be occupied for the purposes of a business' and 'any part of the building provided for the use, benefit and enjoyment of the residents of more than one residential unit (whether alone or with other persons)'. So it seems that removing a fire extinguisher from a private residence within an HRB would not be a contravention of the duty under s.95(2)(b) (although it might no doubt create a significant risk of a BSR under s.95(2)(a)). But removing one from a communal part of an HRB would be.

Section 95(4)(b) provides that the phrase 'relevant safety item' means 'any other prescribed thing', but no provision has yet been made extending its meaning.

7.3.3 Compliance with requests made by AAPs

The third and final duty to which residents are subject is the duty to comply with requests made by AAPs for 'information reasonably required' for the purposes of a duty under BSA 2022, ss.83 and 84. The duties under ss.83 and 84 relate to the assessment and management of BSRs and are described in **Chapter 6**. By virtue of s.95(4), the AAP is the AP who is responsible for the part of the building comprising the residential unit in question.

There is no prescribed requirement for the request to be in writing and it would appear that an oral request will suffice.

In theory, this duty requires the person who is subject to it (a) to know who the AAP is; (b) to know whether a person making a request is properly authorised by the AAP; (c) to know what the duties are under ss.83 and 84; and (c) make an assessment of what information is reasonably required for the purposes of those duties. This assessment would probably test many lawyers, let alone 16-year-old residents of HRBs, and it might therefore be said with some force that this is an unwelcome departure from the simplicity which characterises most of the provisions relating to residents' duties. Nevertheless, in practice, a request will probably be made in writing and with a certain degree of formality; a person who makes it will need to satisfy a county court judge that it was made with due authority, and was for information reasonably required, and a person who receives it will similarly run the risk that a judge will be so satisfied. In most cases, it is thought that the answer to these questions will be fairly obvious.

In assessing what information is reasonably required, however, a balance will no doubt need to be struck between considerations of privacy, and considerations relevant to communal safety. Asking whether anyone in a particular household smokes, and if so what precautions are taken within the household against the outbreak and spread of a fire started by discarded cigarettes, might well be regarded as reasonable; asking whether residents own, for example, items of furniture or clothing made out of particularly flammable types of material would appear to be more obviously intrusive, and therefore less capable of justification.

It must also be borne in mind that contravention notices arising out of a failure to give information will only be enforced if and in so far as a judge considers enforcement 'necessary'. More is said about this in **7.4**.

7.4 ENFORCEMENT OF THE DUTIES

As alluded to above, enforcement of the residents' duties is in the first instance by contravention notice. The provisions regarding contravention notices are contained in BSA 2022, s.96.

7.4.1 When, how and by whom is a contravention notice given?

BSA 2022, s.96(1) provides that the section applies where it appears to the AAP that a 'relevant person' 'has contravened or is contravening' one of the residents' duties. As might be expected, a 'relevant person' for these purposes means a person who is subject to the residents' duties (see s.96(10)).

It should be noted that it will not be enough for the AAP to fear that a duty may be contravened in the future. For the giving of a contravention notice to be possible, it is necessary for the contravention to have happened, or to be ongoing.

If the condition for the application of the section is met, the AAP may give a contravention notice to the relevant person. The AAP can no doubt act through a duly appointed agent for this purpose, but no one other than the AAP may give a contravention notice. So, for example, neither a neighbour nor landlord (unless they happen also to be the AAP, or the AAP's agent) can properly give such a notice.

As with many of the provisions under the Act requiring the giving (or provision) of a document, nothing is said about the mode of giving, although by virtue of s.96(6) the Secretary of State is given the power to make regulations about this. Pending the making of such regulations, it is thought that any means of giving which is effective in bringing the notice to the intended recipient's attention will suffice. For a contravention notice to be enforced, one of the matters of which a judge needs to be satisfied is that the notice 'has been given' (see s.96(7)(a)), and the more room for doubt there is about this, the more likely it is that enforcement proceedings will be unsuccessful. Leaving a notice affixed to a door, sending it by email, or leaving it with a fellow resident, may well not be considered effective if it does not come to intended recipient's attention. Properly evidenced personal service will be the most effective way.

7.4.2 What must a contravention notice contain?

BSA 2022, s.96(3) provides that a contravention notice is a notice that:

- specifies the alleged contravention;

- specifies any steps which the AAP considers that the relevant person (see **7.4.1**) should take in order to remedy the contravention (and a reasonable time for taking those steps);
- specifies anything which the AAP considers that the relevant person should refrain from doing to avoid further contravention of the duty; and
- contains an explanation of the steps which the AAP may take under s.96 if the notice is not complied with.

It would seem to follow that a document which fails to meet any of those requirements is simply not a contravention notice for the purposes of the Act. An omission cannot therefore be cured by the sending of a supplemental document, unless that document also fulfils all the other requirements of s.96(3).

Furthermore, if the allegation is one of non-compliance with the duty under s.95(2)(b) (i.e. interfering with a relevant safety item), the contravention notice may require the relevant person to pay to the AAP a sum specified in the notice (s.96(4)). The sum may be specified only if (a) it is necessary to repair or replace the relevant safety item as a result of the contravention; and (b) the sum specified does not exceed the reasonable cost of so doing (s.96(5)).

It is not necessary for a contravention notice to contain that information – it is a matter of choice for the AAP. Furthermore, if the contravention notice does contain that information, but in some way fails to comply with s.96(5) (perhaps because repair or replacement cannot be said to be 'necessary', or the sum demanded exceeds the reasonable cost of repair/replacement), the author's view is that this does not invalidate the notice; rather, it may affect enforcement (see further **7.4.3**).

As well as empowering the making of provision about how a contravention notice is to be given, s.96(6) contains provision for the Secretary of State to make regulations about their form, and further provision (beyond that set out in s.96(3)) about their content. Such a regulation has been made – see the 907 Regulations, reg.13. This came into force at the same time as the 40 Regulations, namely 16 January 2024. Regulation 13(1) provides that a contravention notice must contain:

(a) details of any statutory provision which it is alleged the relevant person has contravened;
(b) details of any previous communication between the [AAP] and the relevant person relating to the alleged contravention;
(c) details of any guidance issued by the regulator which is relevant to the alleged contravention;
(d) where any steps are specified under section 96(3)(b) of the 2022 Act, an explanation why the [AAP] considers that the steps should be taken;
(e) where a sum is specified under section 96(4) of the 2022 Act, an explanation why the sum is required and evidence of the amount specified;
(f) details of the complaints procedure operated by the PAP under section 93 of the 2022 Act available to the relevant person to dispute all or part of the contravention notice;
(g) the name and contact details of the AP giving the contravention notice.

By reg.13(2), the regulations also provide that a contravention notice must be

(a) in writing; and
(b) in a form which allows the relevant person to understand the content and aims of the notice, including explanations of technical language used, or with plain English summaries of complex or technical provisions.

It is not clear how reg.13(2)(b) will be satisfied if the relevant person is illiterate, or does not read English.

7.4.3 Application to the county court

BSA 2022, s.96(7) provides that the county court may, on an application made by the AAP, make an order under s.96 if three conditions are satisfied. Those are that:

- a contravention notice has been given;
- the contravention alleged in the notice occurred; and
- it is necessary to make the order.

Comment has been made above about the need for the notice to have been 'given' (and how that requirement might be satisfied). The question of whether the contravention alleged in the notice occurred will be a simple question of fact (although it should be noted that there is no scope for the court to act on the basis of a contravention which might be proven to have occurred, but which is not alleged in the notice).

The final requirement is that the court must be satisfied that it is necessary to make the order. Some care is needed here. It is suggested that the court should be careful not to apply the test of necessity in deciding whether a contravention occurred. So (for example) a request for information does not have to be for information that is necessary, merely for information that is 'reasonably required'. Accordingly, if a court is of the view that it is *necessary* to make an order in order to get a tenant to respond to a request for information *reasonably required*, an order should be made. Furthermore, while the court is the ultimate arbiter of what is necessary, in deciding what is reasonable it will presumably give an appropriate degree of respect to the AAP's view, rather than simply substituting its own view.

One rather surprising omission from the list of conditions which must be met before an order can be made is any provision requiring the notice not to have been complied with. If follows from this that an order can in theory be made even if the notice has been complied with. Ordinarily, a court may not consider that an order is necessary in those circumstances. However, it is possible to imagine a recalcitrant tenant complying with a contravention notice the day before an application is due to be heard, in circumstances where there was a concern that this was being done for expedience and that the contravention would be repeated as soon as the hearing was over. In those circumstances, despite the contravention notice having been complied with, the court might well still regard it as necessary to make the order.

An order made under s.96 can do one or more of several things, namely:

- require a relevant person (see **7.4.1**) to provide specified information, or do a specified thing, by a specified time;
- prohibit a relevant person from doing a specified thing; or
- where a contravention notice includes a request for payment of a sum of money, require a relevant person to pay the AAP a specified sum (s.96(8)).

The sum which the county court may order to be paid may be less than the sum sought in the contravention notice, but it may not exceed it. No doubt the sum ordered by the county court may take into account factors such as the relevant person's age and means, as well as the cost of the repair or replacement.

It is at least arguable that if a contravention notice can be shown to have requested a sum in circumstances where repair or replacement is not necessary, or a higher sum than is reasonable, that is not a proper request within the scope of s.96(4), with the consequence that the pre-condition for an order for payment being made by the court is not met.

7.5 ACCESS TO PREMISES

While not expressed in the terms of a resident's duty as such, the last of this trio of sections confers a power on the county court to allow an AP to have access to a resident's premises in certain limited circumstances.

7.5.1 When does this power arise?

BSA 2022, s.97(1) provides that the section applies where four conditions are satisfied:

- an AP for an occupied HRB makes a request to an RP to enter relevant premises;
- the request is made for the purpose of (i) facilitating the performance of a duty under BSA 2022, ss.83 or 84, or (ii) determining whether a duty under BSA 2022, s.95 has been contravened;
- the request complies with various formal requirements set out in s.95(2); and
- entry to the premises is not given.

The phrase 'relevant premises', in the first bullet point above, is defined by s.97(5) to mean any premises in the part of the building for which the AP is responsible that are occupied or controlled by (i) a resident of a residential unit in the building, or (ii) an owner of a residential unit in the building. This definition gives rise to two points.

First, while the Act reverts in this section to use of the phrase 'accountable person' (AP) rather than 'appropriate accountable person' (AAP) (which is the phrase used in ss.95 and 96), this does not in fact broaden the class of people who can seek access; the definition of 'relevant premises' limits the power to make a request to the AP responsible for the premises in question (and so does the work done by the word 'appropriate' in ss.95 and 96).

Second, the definition goes beyond a person's home, and extends to any other part of the building which they might control; for example, a storage area or parking space. Correspondingly, the definition of a 'relevant person' is broader for the purposes of this section than it is for those of ss.95 and 96. In s.97, a 'relevant person' is not only (i) a resident who is aged 16 or over or (ii) an owner of the premises (as it is in the other sections) but also (iii), where premises are 'controlled but not occupied', a person controlling those premises.

It is notable that, by contrast to what is required for the service of a contravention notice under s.96, there is no requirement for an AP to suspect that a contravention has occurred or is occurring before an access request is made. Such a request can be made simply for the purpose of facilitating performance of a duty under ss.83 or 84. Even the alternative purpose for seeking access, namely to determine whether there has been a contravention, does not require reasonable grounds for suspicion that there has.

As with many other comparable provisions of the Act, no guidance is given as to how a request is 'made'. However, one of the formal requirements of an access request (see further **7.5.2**) is that the time at which access is requested must be at least 48 hours after the request is made. This may shed some light on how a request should be considered to have been made. It cannot sensibly be when the request is sent (as that may well be more than 48 hours before receipt, particularly if the request is by post), nor when the recipient actually receives it (as that would obviously be outside the knowledge of the AP making the request). It is more likely to be the case that a request is treated as 'made' when the recipient might reasonably be expected to have received it. It would therefore be sensible (if circumstances permit) for the AP to make allowance for the likely time of receipt in setting the time at which access is required. How much of an allowance will obviously depend on the mode of delivery which is used.

7.5.2 What form must the request take?

As stated above, the third condition for the engagement of the county court's power to order access is that the request complies with various formal requirements. Those requirements are set out in BSA 2022, s.96(2). They are that:

- the request is in writing;
- it sets out the purposes for which it is made;
- it contains an explanation of why it is necessary to enter the premises for that purpose;

- it requests access to the premises at a reasonable time; and
- (as mentioned in **7.5.1**) it is made at least 48 hours before the time at which access is required.

These requirements are considered self-explanatory. Notably, there is no prescribed form, nor any power for the Secretary of State (or anyone else) to make regulations prescribing a form.

7.5.3 What order may the AP seek if access is not given?

If access is not given, the AP may seek an order requiring the relevant person (see **7.5.1**) to allow the AP, or a person authorised by the AP, to enter the relevant premises at a reasonable time for the purpose mentioned in the request. The order may also, if it is necessary for that purpose, authorise the taking of measurements, photographs, recordings or samples by the AP or person authorised by the AP.

The grant of these ancillary powers suggests that no other functions may be performed during the visit. It would not, for example, be possible to use these powers in order to interview the relevant person about activities on the premises (notwithstanding that the relevant person might be in breach of a duty under BSA 2022, s.95 for failing to give that information).

7.5.4 What are the court's powers?

If application is made, the court may make an order granting the relief sought if it is satisfied that such an order is 'necessary' for the purpose mentioned in the request. As with orders enforcing contravention notices (see **7.4.3**), it is suggested that some care is required with the test of necessity. A request must be made for the purpose of 'facilitating' performance of a BSA 2022, ss.83 or 84 duty; this of itself does not mean that access is necessary, merely that it will make performance easier or more convenient in some way. So, it is suggested, the court is similarly not concerned with whether access is necessary; it is only concerned with whether making an order is necessary for the purpose of facilitating performance of a duty.

If the court makes an order, it must specify a date on which, or a period within which, the AP or person authorised by the AP may enter the relevant premises for the purpose in question.

7.5.5 Human rights considerations?

It is not difficult to imagine that a human rights challenge to the BSA 2022, s.97 power, based in particular on the European Convention on Human Rights, Article 8 right to respect for privacy and family life, might at some stage be advanced. Any power involving the giving of access to a person's home is likely to be scrutinised with considerable care. However, and without wishing to opine on the likely success of such a challenge, it does seem that by building in safeguards into s.97 (including the need for formal notice, a period of not less than 48 hours before access is sought, and an obligation to grant access only at a reasonable time), Parliament has struck a balance between Article 8 rights, and the countervailing right to enable APs to inspect premises as a means of facilitating compliance with their own duties. For these reasons, and because of the unquestionable importance of making HRBs safe for everyone living there, it is likely that a challenge to a s.97 order based on Article 8 rights would (at the very least) face formidable difficulties.

CHAPTER 8

Enforcement

Ceri Edmonds

8.1 INTRODUCTION

This chapter deals with the mechanisms by which the Regulator can enforce compliance with the duties of an 'accountable person' (AP) in relation to a higher-risk building (HRB), as well as the mechanisms by which an AP can enforce the duties of residents. They only apply to England and Wales. This chapter covers:

- compliance notices;
- contravention notices;
- requests for access;
- special measures orders (SMOs);
- criminal offences;
- appeals.

For a detailed discussion of who the AP is and their duties see **Chapters 5** and **6**. A more detailed discussion of contravention notices is in **Chapter 7**.

8.2 COMPLIANCE NOTICES

8.2.1 What is a compliance notice?

Compliance notices are notices requiring the recipient to take specified steps or to remedy a breach of any requirements in relation to building safety. They have been introduced by BSA 2022, s.38 (which introduces a new s.35B into BA 1984 for breaches of building regulations) and s.99 (for breaches of the requirements in BSA 2022, Part 4). They are aimed at enforcing compliance with various requirements for HRBs, and more generally with building regulations.

For both BSA 2022 and BA 1984, a compliance notice can be served as either a remedial or preventative measure to remedy a breach or avoid a contravention. A compliance notice can either require the recipient to take specified steps or simply require the recipient to remedy the breach or the matters giving rise to it, without specifying the manner in which this is to be done. Either way it will specify the period for compliance. At present there are no rules about how long that period should be.

Whereas compliance notices under BSA 2022, s.99 can only be given in relation to HRBs, compliance notices under BA 1984, s.35B (for breaches of building regulations) can be given in relation to any building. For HRBs, compliance notices are given by the Regulator (in England, the UK Health & Safety Executive (HSE)). This applies both to notices under BSA 2022 and notices under BA 1984, s.35B. Compliance notices under BA 1984, s.35B in respect of non-HRBs are given by the building control authority.

Under BSA 2022, s.100(4), the Regulator must take reasonable steps to notify the local authority and fire and rescue authority when it serves a notice under s.99.

Section 99 (and, in England, BA 1984, s.35B) came fully into force on 1 October 2023 by virtue of the Building Safety Act 2022 (Commencement No.5 and Transitional Provisions) Regulations 2023, SI 2023/993, regs.2(h), 2(i) and 2(s)–(u). Other provisions only came into force on 16 January 2024 by virtue of the 40 Regulations, including the duty on the Regulator to enforce the provisions of the Act in relation to HRBs. In addition, BSA 2022, s.38 (and the new BA 1984, s.35B) is not yet in force in Wales.

8.2.2 The form of compliance notices

BSA 2022 provides for regulations to be made about the form, content and giving of notices (BSA 2022, s.100 and BA 1984, s.35D, inserted by BSA 2022, s.38). On 9 August 2023 the Secretary of State made the 907 Regulations. These give some guidance about the form and content of notices under BSA 2022, s.99, but there are three preliminary points to note. Firstly, the regulations do not apply to notices under BA 1984, s.35B. Although it is likely that many of the same requirements will apply, there are not yet any regulations governing the form and content of such notices. Secondly, the 907 Regulations only apply to notices in England, and there are currently no regulations setting out the requirements for compliance notices in Wales. Thirdly, the 907 Regulations, reg.1(2) provides that they will come into force at the same time as BSA 2022, s.83. This only came into force on 16 January 2024.

Now that the published regulations are finally in force, a compliance notice under s.99 in England will have to:

- be in writing;
- state that it is a compliance notice given under BSA 2022, s.99;
- specify the date on which the compliance notice is given;
- specify the time for compliance;

- include the name and address of the AP to whom the compliance notice is given;
- state which statutory duties the AP is alleged to have contravened;
- give details of the nature of the contravention;
- specify the building or part of the building in which the contravention of the relevant requirement is alleged to have occurred;
- for urgent action notices under BSA 2022, s.99(4), specify that it is an urgent action notice and give the reasons why the Regulator considers an urgent action notice is appropriate;
- state the consequences of contravention of the compliance notice;
- state that the compliance notice may be withdrawn by the Regulator at any time;
- give details of the right to appeal to the First-tier Tribunal (FTT), including the period within which any appeal must be made, the right to apply to the Tribunal under BSA 2022, s.103(4)(a) for a direction in relation to an urgent action notice, and the right to apply under s.103(5) for an extension of the time period for compliance.

A compliance notice may not relate to the contravention of more than one relevant requirement (907 Regulations, reg.14(2)). It appears therefore that where an AP has breached multiple requirements the Regulator will need to give multiple compliance notices.

The 907 Regulations do not stipulate that a compliance notice must set out the action required from the recipient. It appears from the wording of s.99(2) and s.99(3) that a compliance notice can either specify the steps that the AP is to take to remedy or prevent a contravention, or more generally require them to remedy the contravention or the matters giving rise to it.

A compliance notice under BA 1984, s.35B cannot be given more than 12 months after the alleged contravention occurred. There is no such restriction for compliance notices under BSA 2022, s.99, and it appears that the Regulator can give a s.99 compliance notice at any time after it becomes aware of a contravention.

The 907 Regulations do not give any guidance as to how long the specified time for remedying the breach or taking any specified steps should be. At present, there is no express requirement for that period to be a reasonable amount of time to carry out any necessary works.

8.2.3 To whom is the compliance notice given?

Compliance notices are given to a person 'who appears ... to have contravened, be contravening or be likely to contravene' either a building regulation (for notices under BA 1984) or a requirement under BSA 2022, Part 4 or associated regulations (for notices under BSA 2022, s.99). Under the Act they are served on an AP for an HRB. As discussed in **Chapters 5** and **6**, some buildings will have more than one AP, and so will have a 'principal accountable person' (PAP) and other APs responsible for other parts of the building. Essentially, a compliance notice is 'given to' the party who has breached their duty, but the Regulator must also give a copy to the PAP and all other APs.

The 909 Regulations provide that compliance notices under BA 1984, s.35B are not to be given in relation to breaches of duty by approved inspectors.

8.2.4 Withdrawing a compliance notice

Under the 907 Regulations, reg.14(5), the Regulator may withdraw a compliance notice at any time. Where the Regulator withdraws a compliance notice, the Regulator must as soon as reasonably practicable give written notice of the withdrawal to the recipient of the compliance notice. The 907 Regulations do not specify whether the Regulator is also to send notice of withdrawal to the other APs in the building.

As noted above, this only applies to compliance notices given under BSA 2022, s.99 in England. It remains to be seen if similar provisions will apply in relation to notices in Wales or notices under BA 1984.

8.2.5 Urgent action notices

In the most serious cases, where people are in immediate danger (or will be if the threatened breach occurs), the Regulator can specify that a compliance notice under BSA 2022, s.99 is an 'urgent action notice'. The main relevance of this is that, unlike non-urgent notices, an urgent action compliance notice remains in force pending the outcome of any appeal (see **8.6**).

8.3 CONTRAVENTION NOTICES AND ACCESS TO PREMISES

Contravention notices are notices that an AP can give to a resident who has contravened their duties in relation to an HRB, telling the resident what they must do or must stop doing. They were introduced by BSA 2022, s.96. There may be situations where an AP requires access to a flat in the building in order to better carry out its duties, or to determine whether a resident or lessee has contravened their duties under BSA 2022, s.95 (whether or not the AP intends to give a contravention notice). BSA 2022, s.97 makes provision for the AP to make a written request for access and to apply to the court if the request is refused. These provisions came into force on 16 January 2024.

The responsibilities of APs and residents are discussed in **Chapters 6** and **7** and further consideration of contravention notices can be found in **Chapter 7**, including the content of contravention notices, requests for access, and applications to the county court.

8.4 SPECIAL MEASURES

8.4.1 Overview

In response to the recommendations in the Hackitt Report (see **Chapter 1**), the Act has introduced a special measures regime, allowing the Tribunal to appoint a special measures manager (SMM) who will take on the management of risks in an HRB as a last resort, to keep residents safe from poor management of building safety risks (BSRs).

The provisions in relation to special measures and SMOs are contained in BSA 2022, s.102 and Sched.7. They came into force on 16 January 2024.

8.4.2 When will an SMM be appointed?

BSA 2022, s.102 and Sched.7 empower the FTT to make an SMO appointing a named SMM for a building, to carry out the functions of all APs (BSA 2022, s.102 and Sched.7). The test for making an SMO is set out in Sched.7, para.4(4), namely that the Tribunal will only make such an order where it is satisfied there has been:

- a serious failure by an AP to comply with their duties; or
- a failure on two or more occasions.

The Act does not define what would constitute a 'serious failure' and at the time of writing there is no case law on this. However it seems logical that a serious failure would include acts or omissions which place people in the building in immediate danger. Thus, failure to comply with an urgent action compliance notice would appear to be sufficient grounds for appointing an SMM. But these are not the only circumstances in which an SMO would be made, and there is currently no requirement to issue a compliance notice before applying for an SMO.

The Act provides that the Tribunal 'may' make an order. However, there is no requirement for it to be 'just and convenient' to do so, nor any other such fetter on the Tribunal's discretion as to whether to make an order.

At the time of writing there is no case law or other guidance on how the Tribunal should exercise its discretion. An obvious factor for the Tribunal to consider would be whether an order is necessary or desirable to ensure the safety of residents, as this is the statutory purpose of the special measures regime. It would be logical for this to be a forward-looking exercise, like the decision whether to appoint a manager under the Landlord and Tenant Act (LTA) 1987, s.24. So the jurisdiction to appoint an SMM is triggered by the AP's failures, but the Tribunal will decide on the best way forward and may take account of any proposals by the AP to remedy their failures. But in the absence of a 'just and convenient' test, it would appear that the Tribunal will make an SMO unless the AP can show that the AP has taken sufficient steps so as to make such an order unnecessary.

8.4.3 What will an SMO contain?

The primary function of an SMO is to appoint a named SMM who will undertake the statutory functions of an AP in relation to a building. It appears that the FTT has discretion as to what it can include in an SMO, and the potential measures are wide-ranging. Under Sched.7, para.4(5), an SMO can provide for:

- the AP to compensate the SMM for the relevant expenses incurred, or to be incurred, by the SMO;
- any other matter in relation to the exercise of the SMM's functions; and
- any incidental or ancillary matter.

So, for example, an SMO could provide for an SMM to have access to parts of the HRB as necessary.

There is scope for the Regulator to provide financial assistance to the SMM by way of grants or loans. So far no regulations or other guidance are in place as to what, if any, assistance will be available. But if any monies are provided, their use and any repayment could be set out in the SMO.

8.4.4 The effect of an SMO

While an SMO is in force, any function of an AP under the Act is to be treated as a function of the SMM, except in relation to making an application or an appeal to the Tribunal (BSA 2022, Sched.7, para.5(2)). So the SMM will essentially step into the shoes of the AP. As part of this, the SMM will take on the rights and responsibilities under any pre-existing contracts entered into by the AP in relation to the building (BSA 2022, Sched.7, para.7). This is in direct contrast to the position of a Right to Manage (RTM) company, which does not become a party to contracts previously made by the landlord.

Once an SMO is in force, any s.99 compliance notice ceases to have effect. However this does not mean that an AP will no longer be liable for any contravention of a compliance notice that occurred before the SMO is made (Sched.7, para.5(3)). It follows that even after an SMO is made, an AP could be convicted of an offence under BSA 2022, s.99 or s.101 and subjected to a penalty such as a fine.

The Act imposes a statutory trust on payments made by APs to the SMM (BSA 2022, Sched.7, para.6), similar to the trust imposed on service charges under LTA 1987, s.42. Monies paid by APs are held on trust to defray the expenses incurred in the exercise of the SMM's functions in relation to the HRB, with any residue held on trust for the AP. Where payments have been made by more than one AP, the APs can agree their shares in writing. In default of any agreement, the residue is held in such shares as the Tribunal may direct. There is no express requirement that they will be held on trust in the same proportions as they are paid, presumably because the contributions of the APs are not fungible but are directed towards specific measures for the parts of the HRB for which they are respectively responsible.

8.4.5 The relationship with LTA 1987, s.24

There is already a well-established process for appointing a manager where the Tribunal is satisfied that a building is not being well managed. This is governed by LTA 1987 and applies to most buildings with two or more flats, not just HRBs. A detailed discussion of the appointment of managers under LTA 1987 is outside the scope of this book, but in summary, a leaseholder can apply for an order under LTA 1987, s.24 appointing a manager where the landlord has breached its obligations. The Tribunal will appoint a manager where it is just and convenient to do so.

The functions of a Tribunal-appointed manager and an SMO are not identical, but there is obviously a potential overlap. This is addressed in BSA 2022, Sched.7, which considers three circumstances: first, where there is already a Tribunal-appointed manager in place before an SMO is made; second, where a lessee wishes to apply for a Tribunal-appointed manager after the appointment of an SMO; and third, where the SMM wishes to apply for a Tribunal-appointed manager.

Where the Tribunal has previously appointed a manager under LTA 1987, s.24, a subsequent SMO will not displace that manager, and the order under s.24 will remain in force. However, the Tribunal may amend the s.24 order to avoid any overlap in their functions, so that the SMM and not the Tribunal-appointed manager will be responsible for the functions of the AP in relation to an HRB.

Similarly, the making of an SMO will not prevent an application for a Tribunal-appointed manager. However, once in force, Sched.7, para.8 will introduce new subsections into LTA 1987, s.24, which mean that a s.24 order may not provide for a manager to carry out a function which has already been delegated to an SMM. So the Tribunal-appointed manager can take over responsibility for, say, general management and routine repairs, but not for the functions of the AP in relation to an HRB such as certification or management of BSRs.

In addition, the new LTA 1987, s.24ZA (in force from 16 January 2024) will empower an SMM to apply for a s.24 order where the landlord or any AP is in breach of any obligations owed to the SMO under the SMM. The SMM must first serve a notice under LTA 1987, s.22 on the landlord, any other person with management obligations for the building, and each AP.

8.4.6 The process for making an SMO: initial notice and final notice

An SMO is made on the application of the Regulator (BSA 2022, Sched.7, para.4(1)). There is no provision that allows for any other person, such as a lessee, to apply to the Tribunal for an SMO.

Before applying for an SMO, the Regulator must give an 'initial notice' setting out their intention to apply for an SMO and inviting representations in response. Once the period for making representations has expired, the Regulator will decide whether to proceed with the application and give a final notice setting out its decision.

The initial notice and final notice must be given to each AP, each resident aged 16 and over, each lessee, any managing agent, any recognised tenants' association, any Tribunal-appointed manager, and the local fire and rescue authority and housing authority.

Where the AP is a registered provider of social housing, the Regulator must also give a copy to the Regulator of Social Housing. For mixed-use premises, the Regulator must also give a copy to the responsible person (RP) for the purposes of the Regulatory Reform (Fire Safety) Order 2005, SI 2005/1541 in relation to any commercial unit. This is the employer, in relation to a workplace, or the person who is occupying the commercial premises for the purpose of carrying on a business. Where there is no such person, the RP is the owner.

There is provision for regulations as to the form of the initial notice and the way in which it must be given, and also to amend the list of people to whom it must be given. At the date of writing, no such regulations have been made although Sched.7 does set out what the notices must contain.

There is no power for the Tribunal to dispense with the service of an initial notice or a final notice, but the Regulator only has to notify those persons of whom it has knowledge after taking reasonable steps to identify the recipients. So, for example, if the Regulator is unaware that a residential unit has been sub-divided, the failure to give a notice to the residents of each sub-divided unit would not prevent the Regulator from making the application. The requirement to give a notice to 'each resident' does not, in the author's view, require a separate notice to be given to each resident. This may change with regulations, but there is currently no requirement to include the name of the resident in any notice, and it would be unduly burdensome to expect the Regulator to identify the name (and potentially date of birth) of each occupant of each flat. A notice addressed to 'the residents' of a particular unit would therefore suffice and would fulfil the statutory purpose of the notices.

Schedule 7, para.2(3) sets out the requirements for an initial notice. It must include:

- a statement that the Regulator proposes to apply for an SMO;
- the address of the building;
- the reasons for the proposed application;
- the terms of the proposed order;
- the name and address of the proposed SMM;
- the period in which recipients can make representations in response; and
- an email or postal address to which representations can be sent.

If the Regulator is seeking an order that the AP makes payments to the SMM, it must send a financial management proposal with the initial notice, setting out an estimate of the expenses the SMM is expected to incur, including a reasonable amount for contingencies, and the measures the SMM is expected to take (i.e. what the expenses will be for). Where there is more than one AP, the financial management proposal should include the proposed apportionment of the expenses and the reasons for that apportionment.

There is no guidance as yet as to the length of time for making representations. This may be set out in future regulations but at the time of writing there is no minimum period. Nevertheless the Explanatory Notes accompanying the Act make clear that the affected parties should have the opportunity to comment and provide representations, and that the Regulator should discharge its power to apply for an SMO in a fair and transparent way (Explanatory Notes, para.1566). It is clear therefore that the initial notice should give a reasonable period for representations.

The Regulator must make a decision whether to apply for an SMO after the period for making representations has expired (Sched.7 para.2(5)(a)). It must then serve a final notice to the same categories of persons informing them of its decision and the reasons for that decision. Where the Regulator decides to apply for an SMO, the final notice must specify the terms of the order it is applying for, including the name and address of the proposed SMM. Where the Regulator is seeking an order that the AP make payments to the SMM, it must give a financial management proposal with the final notice. The requirement to make the decision *after* expiry of the period for representations suggests the Regulator cannot issue the final notice immediately. Rather, sufficient time must have elapsed for the Regulator to make its decision – even if only a few hours.

There is no express requirement that the order specified in the final notice should be in the same terms as that indicated in the initial notice. In fact, the requirement for wide-ranging consultation would indicate that the Regulator could amend the draft order, including by strengthening its provisions to address concerns raised by residents. Similarly, it appears that it is open to the Regulator to identify a different SMM in the final notice.

Once the order is made, the Regulator must take all reasonable steps to notify the same categories of people to whom it sent the initial and final notice. This requirement also applies when an SMO is discharged or varied.

8.4.7 Varying or discharging an SMO

At any time that an SMO is in force, the Regulator, an AP or the SMM can apply to the Tribunal for further directions (BSA 2022, Sched.7, para.11), or to vary or discharge the order (Sched.7, para.14(1)). There is no provision for a resident or lessee to make such an application. The Regulator has a positive obligation to review the SMO at least once a year and to apply to have it varied if necessary.

Before making any application to vary an SMO the Regulator must give an initial notice and then a final notice. The rules for these notices are set out in Sched.7, para.13 and are similar to those discussed in **8.4.6** in relation to notices given before the SMO is first applied for. They must be given to the same categories of people, set out the order sought and the reasons for it, and (for the initial notice) specify a time period and correspondence address for making representations.

There is no requirement for any such notice where an SMM or an AP applies to vary or discharge an SMO. Nor is there any express requirement for the Regulator to serve a notice where it intends to apply to discharge, rather than vary, an SMO. This is in contrast to the requirement in Sched.7, para.15 for the Regulator to notify people of 'the making, variation or discharge' of an SMO, discussed above.

In considering whether to discharge or vary an order the Tribunal must have regard to:

- the risk of problems recurring; and
- whether it is just and convenient to do so in all the circumstances (Sched.7, para.14(3)).

These factors apply whether the application is made by the Regulator, an AP or the SMM. Again, this appears to be a forward-looking exercise, but with a requirement to consider whether it is just and convenient. The case law on orders under LTA 1987, s.24 may therefore be of some assistance.

An application to change the named SMM can only be made by an AP (or the SMM) if the Regulator, other APs and the SMM (as the case may be) agree to the change. In the absence of any such agreement, only the Regulator can apply to change the SMM. The requirement for the SMM's agreement does not apply if the SMM lacks capacity (for example if the SMM has died).

When an order is discharged, the SMM will have to prepare a reconciliation account, setting out receipts and expenses and the payments into and out of any relevant bank accounts, and explaining any differences. The SMM must give a copy to the Regulator and each AP. The Tribunal can order the AP to pay any shortfall to the SMM, or the SMM to refund any surplus. This can be ordered at the time the SMO is discharged or at any time thereafter.

8.5 SERVICE OF NOTICES

Unless and until different provision is made in regulations, the rules on service of contravention notices, compliance notices (under both BSA 2022 and BA 1984), and notices in relation to special measures are governed by BSA 2022, s.29. Notices can be given by hand or left at/posted to the addressee's 'proper address'. This is the registered office for a company, principal office for a partnership, or last known address for anyone else. They can also be sent by email, but only to 'an electronic address at which the person has agreed to receive documents or has agreed to receive the document'.

Where the AP's name and proper address is not known, despite taking reasonable steps to ascertain it, then the compliance notice can be given by addressing it to the AP and fixing it 'to a conspicuous part of the premises or building'.

8.6 APPEALS

The Act provides for appeals to the FTT against compliance notices and/or applications for an extension of time for compliance. Appeals against contravention notices would be dealt with under the PAP's complaints procedure (see **Chapter 6**). It is expected that any objections to a contravention notice would also be considered by the county court in deciding whether to make an order under BSA 2022, s.96(7).

Where a compliance notice is appealed, it is of no effect pending the final determination or withdrawal of the appeal (BSA 2022, s.103(3)(a)). In addition, the specified period for taking the specified steps is 'treated as extended by the period (i) beginning with the day on which the appeal is made, and (ii) ending with the day on which the appeal is finally determined or withdrawn' (s.103(3)(b)). There is an exception however, for urgent action notices (see **8.2.5**). In such cases, the notice remains in force pending the outcome of the appeal, unless the FTT (on an application by the appellant) makes a direction otherwise (s.103(4)).

Appeals against s.99 compliance notices can be on the grounds that 'the person has not contravened, is not contravening, or is not likely to contravene' the requirements and/or 'that it is unreasonable to require the person to do any thing specified to be done in the notice' (s.103(2)). There is no equivalent provision, setting out the potential grounds, in the prospective s.39A covering appeals in BA 1984.

Under BSA 2022, s.106, there is scope for regulations to make provision about the effect of any appeal on other notices given by the Regulator. This would not however apply to contravention notices as such notices are given by the AP.

An appeal to the FTT against a compliance notice will take place by way of rehearing. So the Tribunal must consider the decision afresh, and may take into account new evidence (BSA 2022, s.106(2)). Under s.106(3), when it hears an appeal the Tribunal may confirm, vary or quash the decision of the Regulator. There is no limit on the Tribunal's powers to vary a decision and it would appear therefore that the Tribunal has a wide discretion as to the orders it can make under s.106. This also applies to appeals against other decisions of the Regulator under BSA 2022, Part 4, but would not apply to appeals against contravention notices as these are not decisions made by the Regulator.

If the county court makes an order in relation to a contravention notice, the usual rules about appeals from the county court will apply. Similarly, an SMO is made by the FTT and so the usual rules on appeals from the FTT to the Upper Tribunal would apply.

8.7 CRIMINAL OFFENCES

The Act creates a number of criminal offences in relation to HRBs, including:

1. Contravention by an AP of a relevant requirement which places one or more people at critical risk (BSA 2022, s.101).
2. Contravention of a s.99 compliance notice (s.99(4)).
3. Contravention of a compliance notice under BA 1984, s.35B (BA 1984, s.35B(5) inserted by BSA 2022, s.38) (in force in England but not yet in Wales).

Each of these is punishable by imprisonment for up to two years and/or a fine. In addition, the court can impose a further fine of up to £200 per day (at current levels) for each day on which the default continues after conviction. This works out at about £73k per year and is presumably intended as a deterrent to landlords who might decide it was cheaper simply to pay the fine than carry out the remedial works.

Since s.101 came into force, an AP can be convicted (and a fine imposed) even where no compliance notice has been given. It does not appear that s.101 is intended to apply to every breach of any requirement. It will only apply where the contravention has resulted in a significant risk of death or serious injury arising from a BSR. This is discussed further in **Chapter 3**, but would include the spread of fire, structural failure or any other prescribed matter. There is scope for regulations to provide that certain of the requirements will not, if breached, give rise to an offence.

As noted above, it appears that a separate compliance notice is to be given in relation to each separate contravention of the duties in BSA 2022 (or BA 1984). It follows that a separate penalty would apply for each contravention.

There is a 'reasonable excuse' defence, but it is unclear what circumstances would constitute a reasonable excuse. There is of course not yet any case law on what factors the court will take into consideration in assessing the level of any fine, but it is likely that non-compliance with an urgent action notice would attract a higher penalty.

CHAPTER 9

Part 5 and the Schedule 8 exceptions

Daniel Dovar and Richard Miller

9.1 INTRODUCTION

BSA 2022, Part 5 contains provisions about remediation of certain defects, including the creation of four new causes of action in the form of remediation orders (Ros), remediation contribution orders (RCOs), building liability orders (BLOs) and costs contribution orders (CCOs) in respect of construction products. Those are discussed in **Chapters 14** and **15**. This chapter discusses the provisions of BSA 2022, Part 5 which affect recovery of service charges, including BSA 2022, Sched.8, which has effect by BSA 2022, s.116(1). Additional restrictions on recovery are also provided for by amendments to LTA 1985, by BSA 2022, s.112 (see **Chapter 12**). These restrictions are in addition to those set out in this chapter.

Schedule 8 sets out circumstances in which limits are imposed on the ability of certain landlords to recover the cost of remediation work through the service charge from the residential leaseholders. It provides a number of different scenarios where cost recovery is either outright prohibited or limited. In broad terms these divide the focus onto: (1) the work, (2) the landlord, and (3) the tenant. Even if the landlord is able to recover the cost of works from a residential leaseholder, the sums recoverable may be subject to a cap or spread out over a long period of time.

In outline there are limits where:

- the landlord has responsibility for the defect in the first place;
- the landlord and associated companies have a net worth in excess of a certain sum;
- an individual leasehold interest is of low value;
- the works relate to specific types of defect.

9.2 DEFINITIONS

BSA 2022, Part 5 contains definitions which apply to Sched.8, and the latter starts with a paragraph (para.1(1)) dedicated to yet more definitions, some of which have already been explained in the body of the Act, and some of which are new. The most relevant are set out below for ease of refence.

9.2.1 Relevant building

BSA 2022, s.117 defines 'relevant building' for the purposes of BSA 2022, ss.119–125 and Sched.8 as follows:

> 'Relevant building' means a self-contained building, or self-contained part of a building, in England that contains at least two dwellings and –
>
> (a) is at least 11 metres high, or
> (b) has at least 5 storeys.
>
> This is subject to subsection (3).

The Act has an idiosyncratic approach to the measurement of height, and to the counting of storeys; this is discussed in relation to higher-risk buildings (HRBs) in **Chapter 4** (see **4.3**). The same approach is adopted in relation to relevant buildings – see BSA 2022, s.118.

By s.117(3), the definition does not include:

> a self-contained building or self-contained part of a building –
>
> (a) in relation to which a right under Part 1 of the Landlord and Tenant Act 1987 (tenants' right of first refusal) or Part 3 of that Act (compulsory acquisition by tenants of landlord's interest) has been exercised,
> (b) in relation to which the right to collective enfranchisement (within the meaning of Chapter 1 of Part 1 of the Leasehold Reform, Housing and Urban Development Act 1993) has been exercised,
> (c) if the freehold estate in the building or part of the building is leaseholder owned (within the meaning of regulations made by the Secretary of State), or
> (d) which is on commonhold land.

The 711 Regulations, reg.2 provides that, for the purposes of s.117(3)(c), a freehold estate is leaseholder owned where:

- the freehold estate is solely owned by tenants in the building, whether through a corporate structure or otherwise; and
- s.117(3)(a), (b) and (d) do not apply in relation to the building.

Section 117(4) provides that a building is self-contained if it is structurally detached, and s.117(5) that part of a building is self-contained if:

> (a) the part constitutes a vertical division of the building,
> (b) the structure of the building is such that the part could be redeveloped independently of the remainder of the building, and
> (c) the relevant services provided for occupiers of that part –

(i) are provided independently of the relevant services provided for occupiers of the remainder of the building, or
(ii) could be so provided without involving the carrying out of any works likely to result in a significant interruption in the provision of any such services for occupiers of the remainder of the building.

'Relevant services' means services provided by means of pipes, cables or other fixed installations.

This definition will be a familiar one to property lawyers as it is substantially the same as that in the Commonhold and Leasehold Reform Act 2002, s.72 in the context of acquiring the right to manage. For a full discussion of the principles, see Tanfield Chambers, *Service Charges and Management* (5th Edn, Sweet & Maxwell, 2021), 23-06ff.

9.2.2 Relevant defect

BSA 2022, s.120(2) defines 'relevant defect' for the purposes of BSA 2022, ss.122–125 and Sched.8 as follows:

> 'Relevant defect', in relation to a building, means a defect as regards the building that –
>
> (a) arises as a result of anything done (or not done), or anything used (or not used), in connection with relevant works, and
> (b) causes a building safety risk.

Further terms are then defined. Section 120(3) provides that 'relevant works' means any of the following:

> (a) works relating to the construction or conversion of the building, if the construction or conversion was completed in the relevant period;
> (b) works undertaken or commissioned by or on behalf of a relevant landlord or management company, if the works were completed in the relevant period;
> (c) works undertaken after the end of the relevant period to remedy a relevant defect (including a defect that is a relevant defect by virtue of this paragraph).

The 'relevant period' here means the period of 30 years ending with the time this section comes into force.

Section 120(4) clarifies that the reference to anything done (or not done) in connection with relevant works includes anything done (or not done) in the provision of professional services in connection with such works.

Finally, s.120(5) sets out three further definitions for the purpose of the section:

> 'building safety risk', in relation to a building, means a risk to the safety of people in or about the building arising from –
>
> (a) the spread of fire, or
> (b) the collapse of the building or any part of it;
>
> 'conversion' means the conversion of the building for use (wholly or partly) for residential purposes;

'relevant landlord or management company' means a landlord under a lease of the building or any part of it or any person who is party to such a lease otherwise than as landlord or tenant.

9.2.3 Further definitions under Sched.8

Schedule 8, para.1(1) provides a number of definitions, including the following:

'prescribed' means prescribed by regulations made by the Secretary of State; . . .
'relevant measure', in relation to a relevant defect, means a measure taken –

(a) to remedy the relevant defect, or
(b) for the purpose of –

(i) preventing a relevant risk from materialising, or
(ii) reducing the severity of any incident resulting from a relevant risk materialising;

'relevant risk' here means a building safety risk that arises as a result of the relevant defect;
'service charge' has the meaning given by section 18 of the Landlord and Tenant Act 1985 [see **9.4.2**].

The definition of 'relevant measures' is important because this Schedule is concerned with limiting the recovery of the cost of taking a relevant measure.

9.3 CERTIFICATION

The process of landlord certification and qualifying lease certification is labyrinthine and is dealt with in **Chapters 10** and **11**. It can be highly material to the operation of Sched.8 in that failure to adhere to the certification requirements can give rise to presumptions which are adverse to the landlord in terms of service charge recovery.

If the obligation for a landlord to provide certification is not complied with, the contribution condition will be presumed to be met (for which see Sched.8, para.3 discussed at **9.5.2**), and so recovery of the costs of relevant measures under a qualifying lease will be barred. The contribution condition seeks to measure the landlord's wealth. The landlord's certificate (LC) is a means by which the landlord must disclose information from which it should be possible to ascertain the landlord's wealth. It follows that the penalty for failing to give that information is a presumption that the wealth bar is met.

By the 711 Regulations, reg.6(7), a failure to provide the LC will mean that Sched.8, para.2 is treated as having been met in accordance with Sched.8, para.14(2), which would bar recovery under *any* lease (including commercial) for the cost of *any* relevant defect. Paragraph 2 is concerned with the culpability of the landlord for the defect in the first place. Again, the certificate seeks to ensure that the landlord discloses relevant information so that the leaseholder can interrogate that position. It follows that in default of compliance, there is a presumption that the landlord is culpable.

Further, unless the landlord has taken all reasonable steps and any prescribed steps to obtain a leaseholder deed of certificate (LDC) and no such certificate has been provided, another adverse presumption arises: that the ownership conditions for a qualifying lease have been met. All of the limitations, with the sole exception of para.2 imposed by Sched.8, only apply to a qualifying lease.

9.4 BSA 2022, SECTION 119: QUALIFYING LEASES

Schedule 8 (apart from para.2) applies only to 'qualifying leases'.

BSA 2022, s.119(2) provides that a lease will be a 'qualifying lease' if it satisfies the following conditions:

(a) it is a long lease of a single dwelling in a relevant building,
(b) the tenant under the lease is liable to pay a service charge,
(c) the lease was granted before 14 February 2022, and
(d) at the beginning of 14 February 2022 ('the qualifying time') –
    (i) the dwelling was a relevant tenant's only or principal home,
    (ii) a relevant tenant did not own any other dwelling in the United Kingdom, or
    (iii) a relevant tenant owned no more than two dwellings in the United Kingdom apart from their interest under the lease.

The effect of including a specified moment in time as part of the definition is that a lease's status as qualifying or otherwise is fixed for all time. Two illustrations at para.948 of the Explanatory Notes demonstrate this:

Example 5

A person owns a flat which has a qualifying lease. The lease is qualifying because the flat was their principal home on 14 February 2022. They sell the flat on. The leaseholder protections automatically transfer to the future buyer of the flat. The protections transfer irrespective of the identity of the buyer, because the status of the lease as qualifying was determined with respect to the position on 14 February 2022.

Example 6

A person owns a flat which has a non-qualifying lease because on 14 February 2022 they owned nine flats in total in England. They sell it on to a buyer who intends to live in the flat. Even though the flat will be the buyer's principal home, the lease remains non-qualifying because on 14 February 2022 it was not a qualifying lease.

9.4.1 Condition A

BSA 2022, s.119(4)(a) defines 'long lease' as meaning a lease granted for a term of years certain exceeding 21 years, whether or not it is (or may become) terminable before the end of that term.

BSA 2022, s.117(2) defines 'relevant building' as a self-contained building, or self-contained part of a building, in England that contains at least two dwellings and is at least 11 metres high, or has at least five storeys. This definition is subject to s.117(3), which excludes a building or part of a building in respect of which leaseholders have exercised their right of first refusal or collective enfranchisement; or if the freehold is leaseholder owned; or which is on commonhold land.

9.4.2 Condition B

'Service charge' has the meaning set out in LTA 1985, s.18(1), which states:

> In the following provisions of this Act 'service charge' means an amount payable by a tenant of a dwelling as part of or in addition to the rent –
>
> (a) which is payable, directly or indirectly, for services, repairs, maintenance, improvements or insurance or the landlord's costs of management, and
> (b) the whole or part of which varies or may vary according to the relevant costs.

For further consideration of this provision, see Tanfield Chambers, *Service Charges and Management* (5th Edn, Sweet & Maxwell, 2021), 9-02ff.

9.4.3 Condition C

The Government's stated intention with Condition C was to give certainty to leaseholders and prevent unscrupulous landlords from avoiding the provisions of the Act. Unfortunately, as originally enacted, this decision had the unintended consequence of adversely affecting the interests of leaseholders who wished to obtain a new lease.

The Leasehold Reform, Housing and Urban Development Act 1993, s.56(1) states that a leaseholder who exercises the right in Chapter II of Part I acquires a 'new lease' granted 'in substitution for the existing lease', which process operates by way of surrender and regrant. Accordingly, exercising the right to obtain a new lease after 14 February 2022 had the potential to deprive the leaseholder of the protections in the Act.

This lacuna has very recently been resolved by amendments contained in the Levelling-up and Regeneration Act 2023, s.243.[1] Section 243 adds s.119(3A) to BSA 2023, which states:

> A connected replacement lease (see section 119A) is also a 'qualifying lease'.

1 In force 26 December 2023.

Section 243 also inserts s.119A into BSA 2023. Section 119A is a lengthy addition to the Act which introduces more new definitions and concepts. Section 119A(1) sets out the basic definition of 'connected replacement lease':

> For the purposes of section 119 (and this section) a lease (the 'new lease') is a 'connected replacement lease' if –
>
> (a) the new lease is a lease of a single dwelling in a relevant building,
> (b) the tenant under the new lease is liable to pay a service charge,
> (c) the new lease was granted on or after 14 February 2022,
> (d) the new lease replaces –
>
> (i) one other lease, which is a qualifying lease (whether under section 119(2) or (3A)), or
> (ii) two or more other leases, at least one of which is a qualifying lease (whether under section 119(2) or (3A)), and
>
> (e) there is continuity in the property let.

The rest of s.119A then sets out further definitions of the terms above, together with clarifications.

By s.119A(2), the new lease replaces another lease if the term of the new lease begins during the term of the other lease, and the new lease is granted in substitution of the other lease, or the term of the new lease begins at the end of the term of the other lease (regardless of when the lease is granted). The circumstances in which a new lease is granted in substitution of the other lease include a surrender and regrant, a new lease under the Landlord and Tenant Act (LTA) 1954, s.24, the Leasehold Reform Act 1967, s.14 or Sched.1, or the Leasehold Reform, Housing and Urban Development Act 1993, s.56.

By s.119A(4), there is continuity in the property let if the newly let property is exactly the same as the already let property; the newly let property consists of some or all of the already let property, together with other property (whether or not that other property was previously let) (a 'property combination'); or the newly let property consists of some, but not all, of the already let property (but no other property) (a 'property reduction'). Section 119A(5) clarifies that there is no continuity in the property let by virtue of a property reduction if, as respects any lease in the relevant chain of qualifying leases, there was continuity in the property let by virtue of a property combination. Section 119A(7) provides that there is also continuity in the property let if the new lease is granted to rectify any error in the lease, or any lease, which the new lease replaces.

Section 119A(13) contains definitions for 'already let property', 'chain of qualifying leases', 'current connected replacement lease', 'initial qualifying lease', 'new lease', 'newly let property', and 'preceding qualifying lease'.

The Levelling-up and Regeneration Act 2023, s.243(5) backdates the effect of the amendment to 28 June 2022. The retrospectivity of this section means that there is no benefit to a landlord from taking an uncompromising approach to leaseholders who do not have qualifying leases only by virtue of having extended their leases after 14 February 2022.

Section 119A(10) and (11) confer on the Secretary of State the ability to make regulations about the meaning of 'connected replacement lease', including the ability to change the meaning, which may have retrospective effect. Given the length and complexity of s.119A, the power likely exists to allow for fast amendments in the event there are still unintended consequences which would prevent long leaseholders from having the benefit of the protections in BSA 2022, Part 5 and Sched.8.

9.4.4 Condition D

Condition D has three sub-conditions:

(i) the dwelling was a relevant tenant's only or principal home,
(ii) a relevant tenant did not own any other dwelling in the United Kingdom, or
(iii) a relevant tenant owned no more than two dwellings in the United Kingdom apart from their interest under the lease.

These are considered in more detail below.

Condition D, sub-condition (i)

(i) The dwelling was a relevant tenant's only or principal home

The phraseology in sub-condition (i) is familiar and features most notably in the Housing Act 1985, s.85 and the Housing Act 1988, s.1(1)(b). Case law under those provisions is likely to assist in ascertaining whether the sub-condition is satisfied. For discussion, see *Encyclopedia of Housing Law and Practice* (Sweet & Maxwell, looseleaf), P-007.

This sub-condition might cause some difficulty in practice. It must be established at the qualifying time. If a dispute were to arise in, say, 2027 as to whether a lease were a qualifying lease on the basis that the leaseholder as at the qualifying time did not satisfy the sub-conditions, evidence would be needed as to the quality of the leaseholder's occupation as at 14 February 2022. Where leaseholders at that date have subsequently sold their properties, that would involve trying to locate them to take witness evidence. Even if they could be found, there is no incentive for a predecessor-in-title to provide that information.

For that reason it is fast becoming common conveyancing practice for sellers of leasehold interests to be required to provide an LDC (see **9.3**).

Condition D, sub-conditions (ii) and (iii)

(ii) a relevant tenant did not own any other dwelling in the United Kingdom, or
(iii) a relevant tenant owned no more than two dwellings in the United Kingdom apart from their interest under the lease

By BSA 2022, s.119(4)(b), for the purposes of s.119, and therefore sub-conditions (ii) and (iii), 'a person "owns" a dwelling in England, Wales or Northern Ireland if the person has a freehold interest in it or is a tenant under a long lease of it'.

Sub-condition (ii) seems to be redundant; any relevant tenant who satisfied sub-condition (ii) would also satisfy sub-condition (iii); i.e. either they do not own any other dwellings or they owned no more than two in addition to the flat in question. The alternative construction to this section which gives some meaning to both sub-conditions is counter intuitive, in that it advantages those who do not live at the subject property; i.e. either (i) and (ii) must be met, so that when a person lives in the flat in question they cannot own any other property, but if it is not their home and the 'or' is an alternative to sub-conditions (i) and (ii), then they can own up to three properties, including the subject property.

As mentioned above, by Sched.8, para.13, unless the landlord has taken all reasonable steps and any prescribed steps to obtain an LDC and no such certificate has been provided, there is a presumption that the ownership conditions have been met. The leaseholder will nevertheless still have to establish Conditions A to C.

9.5 THE SCHEDULE 8 EXCEPTIONS

The rest of this chapter addresses the Sched.8 exceptions to the payment of service charges relating to relevant measures.

In *Adriatic Land 5 Ltd.* v. *The Long Leaseholders at Hippersley Point* [2023] UKUT 271 (LC),[2] the Upper Tribunal considered whether Sched.8, para.9 was capable of applying to costs incurred before 28 June 2022 and sought from leaseholders on or after that date. Edwin Johnson J considered that BSA 2022, Part 5 and Sched.8 were a self-contained code and concluded at [158]:

> Viewed in this light it does not seem to me to be surprising that Paragraph 9, or for that matter other Paragraphs of Schedule 8 are capable of applying to costs incurred before Schedule 8 came into force. This seems to me to be consistent with the overall scheme of Sections 116–125 and Schedule 8. What might be seen as unfair results are, it seems to me, simply a reflection of life in the new world of the 2022 Act.

Paragraph 8, at least, applies to costs incurred before 28 June 2022, and it may be that, on their particular language, this is also true of other paragraphs.

9.5.1 Schedule 8, para.2: responsibility – landlord focus

Schedule 8, para.2 applies where the relevant landlord (or associated person) is responsible for the 'relevant defect'. That is defined in BSA 2022, s.120(2) as a

2 Under appeal.

defect that arises as a result of anything done (or not done), or anything used (or not used), in connection with relevant works, and causes a BSR.

This is a wide paragraph, and unlike the others, it is not limited to qualifying leases; it applies to a lease of any premises in a 'relevant building' as defined in BSA 2022, s.117, including commercial. This is sufficiently clear from Sched.8, para.2, but, perhaps for the avoidance of doubt, the 711 Regulations, reg.10 explicitly states that para.2 applies to non-residential leases.

Paragraph 2 is absolute in its limitation. If it is engaged, no service charge is payable in respect of a 'relevant measure'. In some respects this is unsurprising if the landlord or its associates are responsible for the defect in the first place.

Four further definitions are provided for in para.2(3) and (4):

- 'Responsible for' a relevant defect means, in the case of an initial defect, if the person was the developer or was in a joint venture with the developer or they undertook or commissioned works relating to the defect, and in any other case, if the person undertook or commissioned works relating to the defect.
- 'Developer' means a person who undertook or commissioned the construction or conversion of the building (or part of the building) with a view to granting or disposing of interests in the building or parts of it.
- 'Initial defect' means a defect which is a relevant defect by virtue of BSA 2022, s.120(3)(a).
- 'Relevant landlord' means a landlord under the lease at the qualifying time or any superior landlord at that time.

As stated above, this paragraph will be deemed to apply if the landlord fails to comply with the requirements to provide an LC (Sched.8, para.14(2) and the 711 Regulations, reg.6(7)).

The concept of 'association' is an important one under the Act and is the subject of separate consideration in **Chapter 18**.

9.5.2 Schedule 8, para.3: contribution condition – landlord focus

Schedule 8, para.3 measures the depth of the landlord's pocket and only applies to restrict payment under a qualifying lease. There is a presumption in Sched.8, para.14 that this condition is met unless the landlord provides a certificate proving otherwise (see **Chapter 10**).

No service charge is payable for a relevant measure relating to a relevant defect if the landlord group at the qualifying time has a net worth in excess of N × £2 million. N is the number of relevant buildings of which the landlord group was a landlord at the qualifying time.

There are two further definitions:

- 'Landlord group' means the relevant landlord and any person associated with the relevant landlord. This is modified by the 711 Regulations, reg.3(2), which states that a person is not to be considered so associated where they would only be so because of BSA 2022, s.121(4) or (5)(a);

- 'Net worth' is valued as per regulations made by Secretary of State. The relevant regulation is the 711 Regulations, reg.5 which, in summary, provides that:

  net worth = total assets – total liabilities – intangible assets.

  These terms are defined in reg.5(3)(a).

As an example, if a landlord company was a subsidiary of another company, and their combined total net worth was £8 million, and together they owned five relevant buildings, they would not meet the contribution condition and this paragraph would not apply. However, if they only owned three relevant buildings, it would be met and therefore they would not be able to recover the costs of any relevant measures through the service charge from any leaseholder holding a qualifying lease.

9.5.3 Schedule 8, para.4: value of leases – tenant focus

Schedule 8, para.4 turns attention to the value of the lease. No service charge for the cost of a relevant measure relating to a relevant defect is payable if the value of the qualifying lease is at the qualifying time worth less than £325,000 in Greater London or less than £175,000 elsewhere.

A lease is to be valued as at 14 February 2022. The 711 Regulations, reg.9 sets out how to determine the value of a qualifying lease. Where the qualifying lease was disposed of after 31 December 2020, the price paid at completion will be the value. Where the most recent disposal was before that date, the value is determined by multiplying 'Vy' (the price paid at completion) by 'My' (the multiplier for the year in which that disposal took place), as set out in the table in Sched.2 to the 711 Regulations.

So, for example, a lease bought in 2000 for £100,000 in Greater London would have a value of £100,000 × 3.10 = £310,000 and no service charge would be payable.

9.5.4 Schedule 8, paras.5–7: other limitations – tenant focus

There is a 'permitted maximum' for a service charge under a qualifying lease for the cost of a relevant measure relating to a relevant defect. This is both backward and forward looking as to what service charges are caught. It starts five years before the provision comes into force (28 June 2022, which is not to be confused with the date of commencement). The amount will vary according to the value of the lease and is then subject to a further reduction in that, under Sched.8, para.7, only one-tenth of that maximum can be charged in any one year.

The permitted maximum is set out in Table 9.5.

Table 9.5: Permitted maximum service charge

Value band of qualifying lease	Permitted maximum
Less than £325,000 in Greater London or less than £175,000 elsewhere	£0
More than the above to less than or equal to £1 million	£15,000 in Greater London or £10,000 elsewhere
Greater than £1 million to £2 million	£50,000
Greater than £2 million	£100,000

Further, in relation to shared ownership leases, where the tenant's total share was less than 100 per cent at the qualifying time –

(a) the value of the qualifying lease at that time is to be determined as if the tenant's total share at that time was 100 per cent;
(b) the permitted maximum is the tenant's total share (as at that time) of what would otherwise be the permitted maximum.

The value of a qualifying lease is to be measured in accordance with the 711 Regulations, reg.9, discussed at **9.5.3**.

9.5.5 Schedule 8, para.8: removal or replacement of cladding – work focus

The next exception looks at the specific works themselves. Where they are directly related to cladding, no cost can be recovered.

No service charge is payable under a qualifying lease for cladding remediation; that is, the removal or replacement of a cladding system that both forms the outer wall of an external wall system and is unsafe.

This will require an analysis of the make up of the cladding system, whether it forms the outer wall, and whether it is unsafe. As to the meaning of 'unsafe', which is not a defined term, the authors expect that will tie in with the various assessments of risk undertaken (i.e. under BSA 2022, Parts 4 and 5 and the BSR).

The intention is to ensure that the cost of this type of remediation does not fall on the leaseholders and that the landlord pursues others for a contribution (either the developer or other landlords), or seeks to obtain the sums from the Building Safety Fund (BSF) (for which see BSA 2022, s.133 and **Chapter 13**).

9.5.6 Schedule 8, para.9: legal or professional service – work focus

No service charge is payable under a qualifying lease for legal or professional costs incurred relating to the liability or potential liability of any person incurred as a result of a 'relevant defect'.

'Relevant defect' is defined by BSA 2022, s.120:

(2) 'Relevant defect', in relation to a building, means a defect as regards the building that –

(a) arises as a result of anything done (or not done), or anything used (or not used), in connection with relevant works, and
(b) causes a building safety risk.

(3) In subsection (2) 'relevant works' means any of the following –

(a) works relating to the construction or conversion of the building, if the construction or conversion was completed in the relevant period;
(b) works undertaken or commissioned by or on behalf of a relevant landlord or management company, if the works were completed in the relevant period;
(c) works undertaken after the end of the relevant period to remedy a relevant defect (including a defect that is a relevant defect by virtue of this paragraph).

'The relevant period' here means the period of 30 years ending with the time this section comes into force [i.e. 28 June 2022].

(4) In subsection (2) the reference to anything done (or not done) in connection with relevant works includes anything done (or not done) in the provision of professional services in connection with such works.
(5) For the purposes of this section –

'building safety risk', in relation to a building, means a risk to the safety of people in or about the building arising from –

(a) the spread of fire, or
(b) the collapse of the building or any part of it;

'conversion' means the conversion of the building for use (wholly or partly) for residential purposes;
'relevant landlord or management company' means a landlord under a lease of the building or any part of it or any person who is party to such a lease otherwise than as landlord or tenant.

The reference to services includes services provided in connection with obtaining legal advice, proceedings before a court or tribunal, arbitration and mediation. The Explanatory Notes at para.1754 state that 'in connection with' is intended to capture a wide range of services and would include, for example, costs incurred in obtaining expert evidence or testimony in court proceedings. In *Adriatic Land 5 Ltd.*,[3] para.9 of Sched.8 was held to encompass the costs of a landlord's dispensation application under LTA 1985, s.20.

In *Adriatic Land 5 Ltd.*, Edwin Johnson J (at [108]) stated that:

> the reference to a liability or potential liability in Paragraph 9 (1) is open ended, in terms of its wording. As such, it may be said to include liabilities arising under the 2022 Act and liabilities arising from other sources.

This suggests a very wide scope.

3 Under appeal.

9.5.7 Miscellaneous

Schedule 8, para.10 prohibits sums being taken from the reserves or being levied where no service charge is payable. Schedule 8, para.11 prevents a landlord topping up any under-recovery from a leaseholder who does not qualify for a reduction. Schedule 8, para.16 precludes a landlord from charging the costs to the leaseholders where prescribed information or documentation is not handed over to the leaseholders. Schedule 8, para.18 voids any attempt to avoid the Schedule.

9.6 THE 859 REGULATIONS, REGULATIONS 3–5: RECOVERY OF AMOUNTS FROM OTHER LANDLORDS

Where a landlord is prohibited from recovering all or part of its costs from leaseholders by reason of Sched.8, the landlord may have recourse to other landlords for a contribution to those costs under the 859 Regulations, regs.3–5.

9.6.1 Schedule 8, reg.3: responsible landlord

Where a landlord is precluded by Sched.8, para.2 (because the landlord is in some way responsible for the defect in the first place: see **9.5.1**) from recovering costs as a service charge, under the 859 Regulations, reg.3, the landlord can seek to recover contributions from other landlords.

Such a landlord is termed a 'responsible landlord', which is defined by reg.3(8) as:

> (a) the person who, at the beginning of 14th February 2022, was the landlord of the tenant referred to in paragraph (1) or any superior landlord and was on that date –
>
> (i) responsible for the particular relevant defect to which the relevant measure relates; or
>
> (ii) associated with a person responsible for that relevant defect; or
>
> (b) the person who, on or after 14th February 2022, became the owner of that landlord's, or superior landlord's, interest.

This envisages that between 14 February 2022, and the time the obligation to take a relevant measure arose and was complied with, the interests superior to that of the occupational lease changed. The new landlord is able to seek a contribution from the old landlord (or any superior landlord) if they were responsible for the 'relevant defect' (as defined in Sched.8, para.2). The sum that they are liable for is termed the 'remediation amount', being the cost of a relevant measure relating to a relevant defect.

In such a case, the new landlord must notify the old landlord of its liability (859 Regulations, reg.3). The recipient can challenge its liability to the First-tier Tribunal (FTT) (859 Regulations, reg.5), but it must do so within 30 days of notification. The recipient can challenge: (i) whether it is actually a responsible landlord as defined by the Act; and/or (ii) the extent of the sum claimed from it (859 Regulations, reg.6). In the absence of a successful appeal to the FTT, the recipient is liable to pay the amount stated in the notice (859 Regulations, reg.2).

9.6.2 The 859 Regulations, reg.4: contributing landlords

Regulation 4 is also concerned with a landlord recovering the remediation amount from other landlords, but this regulation concerns a situation where it is precluded from recovering this amount by way of service charge from the leaseholders by reason of Sched.8, para.3 because of its net worth: see **9.5.2**. In this case the landlord can recover from the 'contributing landlord' which is defined as:

> the person who is the landlord under the qualifying lease referred to in paragraph (1) provided that they met the contribution condition in paragraph 3 of Schedule 8 to the Act on the 14th February 2022.

The same process of notification and appeal to the FTT applies.

9.6.3 The 859 Regulations, reg.5: other cases

Regulation 5 applies where a landlord cannot recover the remediation amount from the leaseholders due to Sched.8, paras.4–9 and 11 (see above). In those circumstances, other landlords under 'any lease in the building' are liable to make a contribution. Quite what that contribution will be depends on the extent of that landlord's interest. There are three types of landlord: Type 1, who has either a freehold interest in the building or a leasehold interest in 90 per cent or more of the storeys; Type 2, who has a leasehold interest in between 41 per cent and 89 per cent of the storeys in the building; and Type 3, who has a leasehold interest in 40 per cent or less of the storeys in the building.

Where a landlord only has a leasehold interest in part of a storey, the landlord is treated as having such an interest in the whole of that storey (859 Regulations, reg.11).

Regulations 5(4)–(6) set out how each type of landlord's contribution is calculated, which is based on the remediation amount divided by a factor corresponding to the number of different types of landlord in the building.

The same notice provisions and appeal process apply as with the 859 Regulations, regs.3 and 4, save that the landlord can also challenge its share of the remediation amount.

CHAPTER 10

The landlord's certificate

Andrew Butler KC

10.1 INTRODUCTION

Certification has proved itself to be one of the most controversial and difficult issues arising under the Act.

This chapter considers the 'landlord's certificate' (LC). It also considers a second, less well-known type of certificate, which must be given by a former landlord to a current landlord to facilitate completion of the LC. This is referred to in this chapter as the 'former landlord's certificate' (FLC). **Chapter 11** then considers the leaseholder deed of certificate (LDC).

10.2 THE LANDLORD'S CERTIFICATE

10.2.1 The statutory framework

To understand the role of the LC, it is necessary to begin with the statutory framework. The starting point is BSA 2022, s.122, which introduces Sched.8 in the following terms:

> **Remediation costs under qualifying leases etc**
>
> Schedule 8 –
>
> (a) provides that certain service charges amounts relating to relevant defects in a relevant building are not payable, and
> (b) makes provision for the recovery of those amounts from persons who are landlords under leases of the building (or any part of it).

The concepts introduced by this deceptively simple provision (relevant defects and relevant buildings) are discussed at **9.4**.

Turning to BSA 2022, Sched.8 itself, the first provision to consider is para.2. This provides:

> 2 (1) This paragraph applies in relation to a lease of any premises in a relevant building.

(2) No service charge is payable under the lease in respect of a relevant measure relating to a relevant defect if a relevant landlord –

(a) is responsible for the relevant defect, or
(b) is associated with a person responsible for a relevant defect.

This provision, which will be referred in this chapter to as 'the para.2 limitation', is unique within Sched.8, because unlike all the other substantive limitations on the recovery of service charges which are introduced by that Schedule, it applies to 'a lease of any premises' and not, as the others do, only to qualifying leases. (As to what a qualifying lease is, see **Chapter 9**.) It apparently applies even to commercial leases as well as residential ones.

Schedule 8, para.3 then introduces another limitation, which prevents the recovery of service charges in respect of a relevant measure relating to any relevant defect if the landlord under the lease as at 14 February 2022 met 'the contribution condition'. This will be referred to in this chapter as 'the para.3 limitation'. The para.3 limitation, like those which follow it, relates only to qualifying leases. The 'contribution condition' is essentially a measure of the landlord's wealth; it is fulfilled if the group's net worth, as at 14 February 2022, exceeds £2,000,000 for each building containing a lease in respect of which a member of the landlord's group was the landlord at that date.

The LC is relevant to both the para.2 and para.3 limitations. It is introduced by Sched.8, para.14, which contains two deeming provisions, relating to the para.2 and para.3 limitations respectively. In relation to the para.3 limitation, Sched.8 provides, at para.14(1), that:

> The person who was the landlord under a qualifying lease at the qualifying time ('the relevant landlord') is to be treated for the purposes of this Schedule as having met the contribution condition (as defined by paragraph 3) *unless the landlord under the lease provides to the tenant under the lease a certificate, complying with any prescribed requirements, that the relevant landlord did not meet that condition* [emphasis added].

Then it provides at para.14(2) (in relation to the para.2 limitation) that:

> The Secretary of State may by regulations provide that (in some or all cases) the condition in paragraph 2(2) is to be treated for the purposes of this Schedule as met in relation to a lease to which paragraph 2 applies *unless the landlord under the lease provides to the tenant under the lease a certificate that complies with any prescribed requirements* [emphasis added].

The certificates contemplated by these two paragraphs have been amalgamated into the LC.

It will be seen that both these provisions are, to some extent, dependent on secondary legislation. Paragraph 14(1) goes further than para.14(2), in that it actually creates the fiction with which it is concerned. By contrast, para.14(2) merely empowers the Secretary of State to make regulations creating the fiction. However, para.14(1) contemplates that regulations might be made setting out the requirements of the LC.

10.2.2 The 711 Regulations

The relevant regulations for the purposes of both para.14(1) and 14(2) of Sched.8 are the 711 Regulations.

The 711 Regulations, reg.6 introduces the LC. The LC is the document required to prevent either the para.2 or para.3 limitations from arising by default.

The 711 Regulations have themselves been substantially amended by the Building Safety (Leaseholder Protections etc.) (England) (Amendment) Regulations 2023, SI 2023/895 (the 895 Regulations). The 895 Regulations came into force on 5 August 2023.

Both the 711 Regulations and the 895 Regulations are expressed to extend to England and Wales, but only apply in England. There are no regulations relevant to the LC in force in Wales; nor is BSA 2022, s.122 in force there.

10.2.3 Who is required to give the LC?

The LC must be given by 'a current landlord' – see the 711 Regulations, reg.6(1). This term was initially defined under the 711 Regulations as meaning 'a person who is the landlord under a qualifying lease of that building' (see the 711 Regulations, reg.1(3)). This was, to put it mildly, a flawed piece of drafting, for two reasons. First, qualifying leases are not of buildings, but of dwellings within buildings. Second, the definition seemed to contemplate that only landlords under qualifying leases were required to serve an LC. That presented something of a conundrum, because the para.2 limitation (which, it will be recalled, is automatically engaged by a failure to provide an LC) applies to both qualifying and non-qualifying leases.

The definition of 'current landlord' has now been changed by the 895 Regulations to 'a person who is the landlord under a lease of premises in a relevant building'.

While the position is not entirely clear, it is suggested that where there is a chain of tenancies of a dwelling in a building, every landlord in the chain must give a certificate to its immediate tenant. This is because:

- the empowering provision in Sched.8, para.14(2) empowers the Secretary of State to make regulations 'in relation to a lease to which paragraph 2(2) applies', and para.2(2) applies to 'a lease of any premises in a relevant building';
- there is nothing in the definition of 'current landlord' to suggest that what is contemplated is only the landlord of a qualifying lease.

One consequence of this might be that, in a situation where A is a freeholder, B is an intermediate landlord, and C is a sub-tenant, A might certify correctly to B, but B certify incorrectly (or not at all) to C. The effect of that would be that B could not recover relevant service charge from C, but A could recover it from B.

Conversely, if A certified incorrectly, B could in theory recover relevant service charge from C, but might not be liable to pay it to A.

The position is somewhat anomalous, because there is little doubt that the para.3 limitation only applies to landlords under qualifying leases, so only they (and not superior landlords) need therefore certify that they do not meet the contribution condition. But the position appears to be different in respect of the para.2 limitation. In that context, the safer view is that every landlord of a lease of a dwelling in a relevant building, under which service charge is payable, must certify.

10.2.4 When must the LC be given?

The 711 Regulations, reg.6(1) provides that a current landlord:

> must provide a certificate (a 'Landlord's Certificate') to a leaseholder in each of the following circumstances –
>
> (a) when the current landlord makes a demand to a leaseholder for the payment of a remediation service charges;
> (b) within four weeks of receipt of notification from the leaseholder that the leasehold interest is to be sold;
> (c) within four weeks of becoming aware (either themselves or by notification from another person) of a relevant defect not covered by a previous [LC]; or
> (d) within four weeks of being requested to do so by the leaseholder.

The 895 Regulations introduced a fifth occasion for service of an LC, being:

> (e) within four weeks of becoming aware of a new [LDC] . . . which is in relation to a lease of a dwelling in the building of which the current landlord is the landlord and which contained information that was not included in a previous [LC].

The use of the phrase 'in each of the following circumstances' suggests that an LC must be given on every occasion that any of the five trigger events occurs; it is therefore insufficient for a landlord to provide an LC to a leaseholder on just one occasion.

While undoubtedly cumbersome, there is logic to requiring repeated certificates in relation to the para.2 limitation, because landlords may be responsible for more than one defect. However, it is harder to detect any logic to it in regarding the para.3 limitation. This is because a landlord will either have met the contribution condition as at 14 February 2022 or will not have done so, and that will never change. Additionally, Sched.8, para.14(1) refers to the need for the landlord to provide a tenant with 'a certificate' certifying that it does not meet the contribution condition, suggesting the provision of one certificate is enough to stop the para.3 limitation from arising by default.

The five occasions for providing an LC are referred to in this chapter as 'trigger events'. Some comment on each one is required.

The first trigger event is whenever a landlord makes a demand to a leaseholder for payment of a remediation service charges. This is defined as 'a service charges which includes a charge in respect of a relevant measure relating to any relevant defect' (711 Regulations, reg.1(3)). 'Service charges', 'relevant measure' and 'relevant defect' are all defined terms under the Act and are discussed in **Chapter 9**.

This is the only trigger event which requires the provision of a certificate on the occasion of the trigger event itself. The other trigger events allow the landlord four weeks from the date of the event. This is logical, as it is the only trigger event entirely within the landlord's control.

The second trigger event is four weeks from the receipt of notification by the leaseholder that the leasehold interest is to be sold. There are at least two points of potential difficulty here.

First, it is clear that notification must come from the leaseholder rather than anyone else. In this respect, the provision differs from an otherwise very similar provision regarding the LDC – see **Chapter 11**. However, the provision gives no guidance on how the notification is to be given, or who within the landlord's organisation is its effective recipient. Given the potentially significant consequences flowing from notification, it would be sensible to require a certain level of formality. A request made to an appropriate representative of the landlord (say, a receptionist or relevant housing officer) in the course of their duties should suffice, as should a communication delivered to the landlord's office. But an oral request made to an employee who has no responsibility for the relevant dwelling, or made on a chance meeting or social occasion to an employee who does, should not do so.

Second, there is no guidance as to the meaning of the phrase 'is to be sold'. Several possibilities present themselves: Does this mean (a) that the leaseholder intends to put the property on the market; (b) that the leaseholder has put it on the market; (c) that terms with a buyer have been agreed; or (d) that contracts have been exchanged? The author's untested view is that, as a matter of the ordinary use of language, scenario (c) best reflects the meaning of this elusive phrase. It would feel a little premature to say that the property 'is to be sold' in scenarios (a) and (b); (d) is possible, but there are practical considerations at play here, since a buyer will presumably want to know whether an LC has been served (and what it says) before committing to a purchase. Additionally, had it been the drafter's intention to start time running from the date of exchange of contracts on a conveyance of the leasehold interest, it would have been easy enough to say so explicitly.

The third trigger event is a landlord becoming aware of a relevant defect not covered by a previous certificate. Again, this provision is fraught with difficulty, for several reasons.

First, assuming the landlord is a corporation, attributing an individual's knowledge to a corporation of which they are part is a notoriously difficult area of the common law. This may make it difficult to say when a corporate landlord has become aware of a defect. To quote the leading work on agency, *Bowstead and Reynolds on Agency* (23rd Edn, Sweet & Maxwell, 2023) at para.8-209:

> It is always necessary to consider the context of the particular legal issue to which imputation of knowledge might be pertinent. There is no overarching principle that a principal is deemed to know at all times and for all purposes that which an agent knows.

But, as a general rule, knowledge acquired by an agent while carrying out tasks for the principal will be imputed to the principal.

Second, it may also be difficult to say even when a natural person 'becomes aware' of a relevant defect. While this is easy enough where the information is provided by a third party (say, a notification from a leaseholder), it will be less easy if the defect is discovered incrementally (say, by a process of intrusive works at the property over a period of several days or weeks).

Third, it is unclear exactly what the landlord must be aware of. Is it the existence of the defect, or must it also be aware that it is a relevant defect (as defined in BSA 2022, s.120(2)) – or indeed that it is a relevant defect which is not the subject of a previous LC? Any of these widely differing interpretations of the 711 Regulations, reg.6(1)(c) is supportable by reference to language and syntax. This is unsatisfactory, given the potentially serious consequences of failing to serve an LC on time.

It is the author's view that, in order for time to run, the landlord must be aware both that there is a defect and that it is a relevant defect. However, the landlord does not also need to be aware that the defect has not been covered by a previous LC. Otherwise, a landlord could stop time running simply by declining to check prior LCs. In practice, it is likely a landlord will know immediately whether the defect is relevant, and the subject of a previous certificate, as soon as they are notified of its existence, but they may not always know.

The fourth trigger event is a request by a leaseholder to provide an LC. By comparison to the other trigger events, this is reasonably clear. However, there are a couple of issues which need to be considered. The first is whether an oral request suffices. While it may be more difficult to prove such a request was made, there is no reason to think that a proven oral request is insufficient. The second, mirroring the difficulties surrounding the concept of 'notification' regarding the second trigger event or 'becoming aware' regarding the third one, is that there is no guidance as to who can be a valid recipient of such a request. The observations offered above in relation to the second trigger event likely apply equally here.

The fifth trigger event is the landlord becoming aware of a new LDC which (a) relates to a 'lease of a dwelling in the building of which the current landlord is the landlord' and (b) contains information not included in a previous LC. There are several things to note about this new provision.

First, it again depends on an understanding of when the landlord 'becomes aware' of something (in this case a new LDC); the same considerations arise here as were discussed above.

Second, despite the apparent care surrounding the wording of the first characteristic of the triggering LDC (namely, that it must relate to 'a lease of a dwelling in the building of which the current landlord is the landlord'), another ambiguity is discernible here; does the word 'which' refer to the building or the dwelling? Grammar alone would suggest the former (the word 'building' is closer to the word 'which'). However, it is unclear why it should be necessary for the landlord to be the landlord of the whole building for this trigger event to apply. So the latter seems the better reading; if a person is landlord of leases of two dwellings in the same building, and an LDC is served on one of them, it is easier to see that a responsive LC regarding both leases should be required.

But, third, it is not entirely easy to see why information in an LDC should generate the need for a responsive LC at all. The information each type of certificate must provide is considered below, but it will be seen that there is little-to-no overlap. Yet, apparently, an LDC which contains *any* information not included in a previous LC must generate a new LC. Why this should be, or how it helps the recipient, is unclear.

10.2.5 How is an LC 'provided'?

Unlike the regime governing what is required of a landlord to obtain an LDC (see **11.4**), the 711 Regulations, reg.6 is entirely silent about modes of service. It merely states that the current landlord 'must provide' the certificate to a leaseholder. BSA 2022, s.29, which governs modes of service in relation to BSA 2022, Part 2 and Part 4, does not apply to Part 5.

In the circumstances, it seems any mode of 'provision' will suffice, but questions will doubtless emerge regarding this issue. To take one obvious example, can an LC sent by email but which goes to a spam folder properly be said to have been 'provided'? The answer to this is probably 'No' – in *Greenclose Ltd* v. *National Westminster Bank plc* [2014] 2 Lloyd's Rep 169, a document served by email was only deemed served once the recipient opened it, not when it arrived in their inbox.

It is tempting, when encountering service provisions in the property context which are silent about the mode of service, to fall back on LPA 1925, s.196(5). This, as readers may be aware, contains default provision as to the mode of serving for notices which are 'required to be served by any instrument affecting property ... coming into operation after the commencement of this Act'. However, this is unlikely to directly assist here for two reasons. First, we are concerned with certificates rather than notices as such. Second, by LPA 1925, s.205(1)(viii), a statute is expressly excluded from the definition of 'instrument' (unless it creates a settlement). A fortiori, it seems likely that secondary legislation like the 711 Regulations should be similarly excluded.

At common law, 'serving' means causing a document to be received – see *Sun Alliance and London Assurance Co. Ltd.* v. *Hayman* [1975] 1 All ER 248. It is probable that 'provided' will be given a similar meaning. An indirect method (such as giving someone a document to pass on to a third party) may be used, but there must be a sufficient causal connection between the serving party's actions, and the receipt of the notice – see *UKI Kingsway Ltd.* v. *Westminster CC*

[2019] 1 WLR 104. It was observed in that case that a notice erroneously given to a neighbour will be served if the neighbour passes it on to the correct recipient (*UKI* at [38]). By contrast, if a document were to be removed from a waste bin and passed on to the addressee, that would probably not be good service.

It is probably safe to say that, whatever mode of provision is adopted, the landlord will generally bear the risk of the LC not coming to the tenant's attention. If the tenant does not in fact receive it, that will usually mean that it was not provided. That will not invariably be so; an LC posted through a letterbox but then devoured by the tenant's dog before the tenant sees it can fairly be described as having been provided. But the situation will be different in cases of genuine non-delivery. The more reliable the mode of delivery used, the harder it will be for the tenant plausibly to assert non-receipt.

10.2.6 What must the LC contain?

The really onerous aspect of the LC regime is what the LC must contain. The form requirements are set out in the 711 Regulations, reg.6(2) and following, as (heavily) amended by the 895 Regulations. What follows is the law as set out in the 895 Regulations. If any question arises as to the validity of an LC given prior to 5 August 2023, reference must instead be made to the 711 Regulations as they stood in their unamended form.

The starting point is the 711 Regulations, reg.6(2), which remains unaffected by the 895 Regulations. It provides that the LC must comply with six basic requirements – it must:

- be in the form set out in the 711 Regulations, Sched.1;
- confirm whether or not the relevant landlord (as defined in BSA 2022, Sched.8, para.3(1)) met the contribution condition under para.3 of Sched.8;
- confirm whether or not the relevant landlord (as defined in BSA 2022, Sched.8, para.2(4)), met the condition in Sched.8, para.2(2) and was responsible for the relevant defect or was associated with a person responsible for a relevant defect;
- contain certain information referred to in the 711 Regulations, reg.6(3);
- be accompanied by the evidence set out in the 711 Regulations, reg.6(4); and
- be signed by the person who is the current landlord on the date the certificate is completed.

Consideration is given to each of these requirements in turn below.

The first requirement is that the LC should be in the form set out in the 711 Regulations, Sched.1. However, while the reference to the form is unamended, Sched.1 itself has been substituted by a new form set out in the Schedule to the 895 Regulations. This new form is referred to in the rest of this chapter as 'the Form' and can be downloaded from the Government website at **www.gov.uk/guidance/mandatory-information-required-from-leaseholders-and-building-owners**.

The Form is not unduly complicated, running to only five pages. However, it must be completed fully and precisely. It is notable that the 711 Regulations (unlike many other pieces of secondary legislation which introduce forms) give no leeway as to the Form, e.g. by stating that a document to 'substantially the same effect' as the Form will suffice. The consequences of non-completion, or erroneous completion, of the Form are considered further in **10.2.7**.

The second requirement is that the LC must confirm whether or not the relevant landlord met the contribution condition. That is, in any event, a section on the Form, appearing on the third page under the heading 'Questions as to group net worth criteria'. The 'relevant landlord' is defined here as the landlord under the lease as at 14 February 2022. Guidance as to how the landlord group's net worth is to be calculated can be found in the 711 Regulations, reg.5 and is dealt with at **9.5.2**.

The third requirement is that the LC must confirm whether or not the relevant landlord met the condition in Sched.8, para.2(2), i.e. that they were responsible for the relevant defect or associated with a person responsible for the relevant defect. Again, this is a section on the Form, appearing on the second page under the heading 'Questions as to developer criteria'. Here, confusingly, the 'relevant landlord' is defined differently: meaning not merely the landlord under the lease at 14 February 2022, but also any superior landlord at that time.

These questions present other difficulties, since they require an understanding of the concept of 'responsibility' (dealt with in BSA 2022, Sched.8, para.2(3)) and 'association' (dealt with in BSA 2022, s.121). These concepts are explained elsewhere in this book (**Chapter 9** and **Chapter 18** respectively). It is fair to say that the requirement of a tick-box, 'yes or no' answer to what are complex questions puts a heavy burden on the compiler of the certificate, particularly given that it is likely that an incorrect answer will invalidate the LC.

The fourth and fifth requirements are that the LC should 'contain the information referred to in paragraph (3)' (these being the words of reg.6(2)(d)) and 'be accompanied by the evidence set out in paragraph (4)' (reg.6(2)(e)). In one of the remarkably careless pieces of drafting which unfortunately abound in the Act and its associated legislation, paras.(3) and (4) somehow became transposed; the list of what evidence was required was originally contained in reg.6(3), with the information requirements then contained in reg.6(4). The position became more confusing still if reference was made to the Form, since the evidence requirements appeared in another tick-box list containing erroneous cross-references to the 711 Regulations. The 895 Regulations attempted to straighten out this mess by entirely replacing reg.6(3), making amendments to reg.6(4), and providing a new Form.

The information now required by reg.6(3) is as follows:

(a) the percentage of the storeys in the relevant building for which each relevant landlord was the landlord at the qualifying time;

(b) in relation to [the para.2 limitation], where a relevant landlord was part of a landlord group at the qualifying time, details of the corporate structure of the relevant landlord and any person associated with the relevant landlord and including –

- (i) the names of all the directors of each company in that group and directors of each corporate trustee, including in each case nominee and shadow directors or any person occupying the position of director by whatever name called;
- (ii) the name of any other person or persons who has the right to exercise or does exercise significant control or influence directly or indirectly over the group;
- (iii) details of the type of trust if any, the law to which it is subject and where it is tax resident; and
- (iv) in relation to trusts with an interest in the shares of any company comprised in the group, details of the economic settlor, the named beneficiaries or class of beneficiaries and protector and any other person who has the right to exercise or does exercise significant influence or control directly or indirectly over the trust;

(c) in relation to [the para.3 limitation], where the relevant landlord (defined here as just the immediate landlord under the lease in question) was part of a landlord group at the qualifying time –

- (i) details of the corporate structure of the group, setting out –
  - (aa) the companies which make up the landlord group,
  - (bb) the beneficial owner of each company in the group, and
  - (cc) if the beneficial owner of the group or any company comprised in the group is, or includes, a trust foundation or arrangement of a similar character, details of the trust and the trustees;
- (ii) the name of any other person who has the right to exercise or does exercise significant control or influence directly or indirectly over the group;
- (iii) details of the type of trust if any, the law to which it is subject and where it is tax resident; and
- (iv) in relation to trusts with an interest in the shares of any company comprised in the group –
  - (aa) details of the economic settlor;
  - (bb) the named beneficiaries or class of beneficiaries and protector, and
  - (cc) any other person who has the right to exercise or does exercise significant influence or control directly or indirectly over the trust.

The evidence which must accompany the LC is then set out in reg.6(4), which (as amended) requires the following:

(a) the set of company accounts for the relevant landlord [(which must accord with the particular requirements of the 711 Regulations, reg.5)] and, where the relevant landlord is part of a landlord group, for each company in the landlord group;

(b) a statement from a chartered accountant or finance director of the landlord company:

- (i) setting out the net worth of the relevant landlord and, where the relevant landlord is part of a landlord group, of each company in the landlord group;

   (ii) confirming the net worth is calculated in accordance with [the 711 Regulations, reg.5 and BSA 2022, Sched.8, para.3] (the 'net worth calculation');
   (iii) confirming the net worth calculations accurately represents the net worth of the relevant landlord (and, where the relevant landlord is part of a landlord group, of each of the companies in the landlord group);

(c) documents or receipts that demonstrate that the relevant building was constructed or converted before the relevant period and details of any relevant works which were carried out in the relevant period;
(d) evidence (where applicable) that –
   (i) the person who undertook works relating to the relevant defect or commissioned those works was not the relevant landlord and was not associated with the relevant landlord (as defined in [BSA 2022, Sched.8, para.2(4)]) together with confirmation of the identity of the person who did undertake such works, and
   (ii) where those works were commissioned or undertaken by a joint venture, proof the relevant landlord was not party to that joint venture, together with details of the persons who were parties to the joint venture;

(e) details of any relevant defects and any relevant measures (as defined in [BSA 2022, Sched.8, para.1]) taken in relation to those relevant defects since 28 June 2017; and
(f) details of any costs paid or due to be paid in relation to any relevant measures taken in relation to any relevant defects in the relevant building since 28 June 2017, including –
   (i) the total sum of any such costs;
   (ii) details of the number of flats between which the costs should be divided; and
   (iii) the leaseholder's maximum remaining liability.

However, in a major change made by the 895 Regulations, it is now unnecessary to set all this information out in each and every LC. The 895 Regulations seem to have recognised that some LCs would be completed in such a way as to make the provision of much of this information unnecessary – for example, if the landlord was accepting that it met the contribution condition, or was asserting that there were no relevant defects.

It is questionable however whether this attempt to streamline things has really simplified matters. The network of what information must be provided in what circumstances is now so complex that one could fairly describe it as Kafkaesque. It is further complicated by the fact that BSA 2022, Sched.8 uses the phrase 'relevant landlord' sometimes to denote the immediate landlord under the lease as at 14 February 2022 (the para.3(1) definition), and sometimes to denote the immediate landlord *and* any superior landlord at that time (the para.2(4) definition).

The effect of the 895 Regulations is set out in Table 10.2. 'RL1' means the immediate landlord as at 14 February 2022, and 'RL2' means the immediate landlord or any superior landlord at that time.

Table 10.2: Information/evidence required in landlord's certificate

Reg.	Scenario: 'LC confirms that ...'	Information/evidence required by section
2B	(a) either RL1 meets contribution condition or lease is not a qualifying lease; **and** either (b)(i) RL2 is responsible for, or associated with a person responsible for, a relevant defect or (b)(ii) RL2 did not believe at the time of completing the certificate that there was a relevant defect	[None]
2C	**Either** (a)(i) RL2 is responsible for, or associated with a person responsible for, a relevant defect; **or** (a)(ii) RL2 did not believe at the time of completing the certificate that there was a relevant defect; **and** (b) RL1 did not meet the contribution condition	3(c), 4(a), 4(b), 4(c), 4(e), 4(f)
2D	(a) neither RL2 nor associate is responsible for relevant defect; **and** (b) either RL1 met the contribution condition or lease is not a qualifying lease	3(b), 4(c), 4(d)
2E	(a) neither RL2 nor associate is responsible for relevant defect; **and** (b) RL1 exempt from contribution condition	3(a), 3(b), 4(c), 4(d), 4(e), 4(f)
2F	(a)(i) either RL2 is responsible for, or associated with a person responsible for, a relevant defect or (a)(ii) RL2 did not believe at the time of completing the certificate that there was a relevant defect; **and** (b) RL1 exempt from contribution condition	4(c), 4(e), 4(f)
2G	(a) neither RL2 nor associate is responsible for relevant defect; **and** (b) either RL1 met the contribution condition or lease is not a qualifying lease; **and** (c) value of qualifying lease on 14 February 2022 below £325,000 (if in Greater London) or £175,000 (if elsewhere)	3(a), 3(b), 3(c), 4(a), 4(b), 4(c), 4(d)

10.2.7 What is the consequence if an LC is late/wrong?

As observed above, the Regulations offer no leeway in terms of the LC's content or timing. There is no provision, for example, allowing a certificate 'to substantially the same effect' as the Form, or provided at a later time than prescribed, even if that were to be agreed.

Schedule 8, para.14(1) and (2) provide that the principal clues as to the consequences of non-compliance. As set out in **10.2.1**, they provide that the para.3 limitation is to be treated as met 'unless the landlord ... provides ... a certificate complying with any prescribed requirements ...' (or in the case of the para.2 limitation, 'that complies with any prescribed requirements').

The inference must be that if a non-compliant certificate is given, the deeming provisions in para.14(1) and (2) will apply.

A further provision to the same effect (at least regarding deemed compliance with the para.2 limitation) can be found in the 711 Regulations, reg.6(7), which as originally drafted provided that:

> If any person who is a relevant landlord under paragraph 2(4) of Schedule 8 to the Act does not provide a certificate which complies with this regulation in the form outlined in Schedule 2 to the leaseholder, the condition in paragraph 2(2) of Schedule 8 to the Act is to be treated as met in accordance with paragraph 14(2) of Schedule 8 to the Act.

In another egregiously poor piece of drafting, there was no Sched.2 to the 711 Regulations. The 895 Regulations corrected this to Sched.1. The phrase 'any person who is a relevant landlord under paragraph 2(4) of Sched.8 to the Act' has also been corrected to 'current landlord', which in turn is defined to mean 'a person who is the landlord under a lease of premises in a relevant building'. This is significant, because as originally expressed in reg.6(7) this sanction applied only to landlords under qualifying leases. Now it applies to landlords under landlords of any lease in a relevant building.

None of this quite answers the question of what exactly a certificate must do in order to 'comply with the prescribed requirements'. Attention must again be paid to reg.6(1) and (2), which set out the requirements for the time of service of an LC (see **10.2.4**) and what it must contain (see **10.2.6**).

The position regarding the time of provision is binary; a certificate will either be provided in time, or it will not. There may be room for argument about when time started to run, but once that is resolved, the consequences are clear.

In terms of the LC's content, the position is a little more nuanced. It is thought that an LC which meets the requirements of reg.6(2) is valid, even if some of the answers given are in fact wrong. So, for example, if a certificate confirms that a landlord is not responsible for a relevant defect when it actually is, or that a landlord meets the contribution condition when it does not, the certificate will nevertheless be a valid certificate in the sense that it stops the deeming provisions from having effect. By contrast, if a certificate is not in the correct form, or fails to give the confirmations, information or evidence which reg.6(2) requires, or if it is not signed, the certificate does not comply with the prescribed requirements and the deeming provisions will take effect.

Dishonest or withheld answers may then (as the notes on the Form make clear) constitute an offence under the Fraud Act 2006, ss.2 or 3. It is suggested that it will be difficult for a landlord who gives dishonest answers in an LC to argue that it was nevertheless compliant.

Finally on this topic, it is important to keep in mind that while the provision of a non-compliant LC gives rise to presumptions against the landlord, the provision of a compliant certificate does not give rise to presumptions against the tenant. In other words, an LC is not conclusive; it remains open to a tenant who disputes the LC (e.g. because the tenant believes that the landlord is wrongly denying responsibility for a relevant defect) to challenge their liability to pay a service charge in respect of that defect.

10.2.8 Can a landlord be forced to give an LC?

It would appear that the answer to this question is 'No' – at least as far as the First-tier Tribunal (FTT) is concerned. See the decision in *Will & Koterba* v. *G&O Properties* LON/00AT/HYI/2022/0003 (unreported), in which it was held that, although BSA 2022, Sched.8, para.16 contemplated that regulations might be made facilitating such an order, none had actually been made. In particular, the 711 Regulations, reg.11 (which might have been expected to deal with the point) did not do so. Regulation 11 has escaped amendment by the 895 Regulations, so this remains the position.

What reg.11 does do is enable a leaseholder to apply to the FTT if the leaseholder believes that the relevant landlord has made a false claim in the LC, or that the relevant landlord has not given the leaseholder sufficient time to provide information to prove that they have a qualifying lease.

It is not yet clear whether a tenant could obtain an injunction requiring a landlord to serve an LC. The 711 Regulations, reg.6(1) provides that 'A current landlord must provide a certificate ... to a leaseholder in each of the following circumstances ... '. It is possible that, if one of the circumstances has arisen, this obligation could be enforced by injunction in the context of an action for breach of statutory duty. On the other hand, the response might be that the Act makes clear the consequence of failing to comply with this duty, so that an injunction is not appropriate; and presumably by the time it becomes apparent that an injunction is sought, it will be too late for a valid notice to be given anyway, so to grant an injunction would be pointless.

10.3 THE FORMER LANDLORD'S CERTIFICATE

The FLC is a certificate which must be given by a previous landlord to a current landlord to enable the current landlord to provide the information required by the LC.

Provision for the FLC is made by the 711 Regulations, reg.7. This provides that a 'relevant landlord' must provide certain information to the current landlord within three weeks of a request. There is no provision as to the form in which a request must be made. This provision is made pursuant to the enabling power in BSA 2022, Sched.8, para.16(1).

A 'relevant landlord' for these purposes is a relevant landlord as defined by Sched.8, para.2(4) – that is to say, a landlord under the lease at the qualifying time (14 February 2022) or any superior landlord at that time. As stated in **10.2.3**, a 'current landlord' for the purpose of the 711 Regulations is (as a result of the 895 Regulations) 'a person who is the landlord of premises in a relevant building'.

The information which must be given is:

1. The percentage of the storeys in the relevant building for which they were the relevant landlord at the qualifying time.
2. Where the relevant landlord was part of a landlord group at the qualifying time, details of the corporate structure of that landlord's group and including:
   (a) the names of all the directors of each company in that group and directors of each corporate trustee, including in each case nominee and shadow directors or any person occupying the position of director by whatever name called;
   (b) the name of any other person or persons who has the right to exercise or does exercise significant control or influence directly or indirectly over the group;
   (c) details of the type of trust if any, the law to which it is subject and where it is tax resident; and
   (d) in relation to trusts with an interest in the shares of any company comprised in the group, details of the economic settlor, the named beneficiaries or class of beneficiaries and protector and any other person who has the right to exercise or does exercise significant influence or control directly or indirectly over the trust.

Notwithstanding the reference to a certificate in the title to reg.7, there is no provision as to any particular form in which this information must be given. A simple letter, or even oral notification, appears to suffice.

The intention behind the imposition of this duty is no doubt to enable a current landlord who is required to provide an LC, but who was not a landlord at the qualifying time, to elicit the information necessary to do so. However, it is questionable whether it is effective for that purpose. There are at least two problems.

First, the relevant landlord is given three weeks in which to provide the FLC. But, as discussed above, the period for providing an LC is usually only four weeks from the date of the trigger event. So, in theory, a current landlord would have to ascertain what information it requires, and from whom, and make the request, within days of the trigger event. Assuming the FLC is provided within the three-week period, the current landlord must then assimilate it, and incorporate it into the LC. The landlord must do this in time to provide the LC to the tenant within the four-week time frame or incur serious consequences flowing from the failure to provide a timely, correct LC. To describe this as challenging to a current landlord would be an understatement.

Second, there is no sanction for non-compliance. This is particularly unfortunate, since the enabling provision in BSA 2022, Sched.8, para.16 expressly contemplates that regulations made under it may make provision for applications to the FTT to order compliance. That said, in practical terms, and given the timetable for the provision of the FLC, it is unlikely that any order under such an enforcement power could be obtained before the deadline for providing an LC anyway. The only remedy for a current landlord in the face of a failure by a relevant landlord to provide an FLC is therefore likely to be retrospective, and could take the form of an action for breach of statutory duty. The loss recoverable would presumably be the consequences of a failure to provide a correct, complete and timely LC, and the resulting inability to recover service charges.

Finally, the FLC regime assumes that all relevant landlords still exist, when that may not be the case. The drafters of the 711 Regulations do not seem to have contemplated the possibility that a former landlord may have dissolved, leaving no one from whom the current landlord can obtain the FLC. A more sympathetic regime might have excused the current landlord from the obligation to provide information in an LC if, notwithstanding all reasonable efforts, they were unable to obtain an FLC. But that is not the legislation's current approach.

CHAPTER 11

The leaseholder deed of certificate

Andrew Butler KC

11.1 THE STATUTORY FRAMEWORK

The starting point here is BSA 2022, s.119, which sets out four requirements for a lease to be a qualifying lease. These are that:

- (a) it is a long lease of a single dwelling in a relevant building;
- (b) the tenant under the lease is liable to pay a service charge;
- (c) the lease was granted before 14 February 2022; and
- (d) at the beginning of 14 February 2022 ('the qualifying time') –
  - (i) the dwelling was a relevant tenant's only or principal home;
  - (ii) a relevant tenant did not own any other dwelling in the United Kingdom; or
  - (iii) a relevant tenant owned no more than two dwellings in the United Kingdom apart from their interest under the lease.

The concepts involved in the first of these requirements ('long lease' and 'relevant building') are explored in **Chapter 9**; to recap, a lease is a long lease if it is for a term of 21 years or more, whether or not terminable within that period, and a relevant building is one which contains at least two dwellings and is either at least 11 metres high or contains five storeys or more.

The last requirement is odd; there are three ways of fulfilling it, but the second of these adds nothing to the third. A tenant who fulfils the second will necessarily fulfil the third as well.

Whether a lease is a qualifying lease matters, because the protections against the payment of service charge set out in BSA 2022, Sched.8 apply, with only one exception, to qualifying leases only. The exception is the exclusion of defects for which the landlord or an associate is responsible, referred to in the previous chapter as 'the para.2 limitation'. This limitation applies to a lease of any premises in a relevant building.

The other point to note about the last requirement is that it is the only one which cannot be ascertained by a simple reading of the lease. Instead, its fulfilment depends on the circumstances of the relevant tenant or tenants as at 14

February 2022. The leaseholder deed of certificate (LDC) is the mode of ascertaining that information.

Schedule 8, para.13 introduces the LDC (here referred to as the 'qualifying lease certificate') in the following way:

Presumption: qualifying lease

13 (1) This paragraph applies in relation to a lease that meets the conditions in paragraphs (a) to (c) of section 119(2).

(2) The lease is to be treated for the purposes of this Schedule as a qualifying lease unless –

(a) the landlord under the lease has taken all reasonable steps (and any prescribed steps) to obtain a qualifying lease certificate from a tenant under the lease, and

(b) no such certificate has been provided to the landlord.

So, having provided in s.119 four conditions for a lease to be a qualifying lease, the Act goes on to say that only the first three need in fact be satisfied, unless certain things have happened or not happened. In particular, (i) the landlord must have taken all reasonable steps and any prescribed steps to obtain a qualifying lease certificate (which is how the Act describes the LDC), but (ii) no such certificate has been provided. It is certainly possible to imagine a more elegant way of achieving this result, in drafting terms, but the effect is clear enough.

It is important to keep in mind that the LDC's sole purpose is to prevent a qualifying lease from coming into existence by default. So only the landlord has an interest in seeking and obtaining it. A tenant does not have to take the initiative in providing an LDC and will not be prejudiced unless he or she fails to respond to requests to provide one. If that happens, a lease which might in reality satisfy the requirements of a qualifying lease will be treated as not being one. More frequently, however, it will be the landlord who fails to do what is required of it. In that case, the fiction works the other way; a lease which was not in reality a qualifying lease will be treated as being one.

It is also important to keep in mind that, while an LDC must be given by the person who is the tenant at the time it is given, it relates to the situation as at 14 February 2022 and to the personal circumstances of the tenant (whether that is the person giving the certificate, or a predecessor in title) at that date. It is thought likely that, in most cases where a lease has changed hands since 14 February 2022, the buyer will have elicited the information needed to complete an LDC as part of the process of establishing whether the lease is a qualifying lease or not. Certainly, it should now be regarded as good practice to do so.

11.2 THE 859 REGULATIONS

The secondary legislation which sets out the prescribed steps contemplated by para.13(2), and the prescribed requirements contemplated by para.13(3), is the

859 Regulations, and specifically reg.6 thereof. The 859 Regulations have been amended by the 895 Regulations.

It is the 859 Regulations which introduced the phrase 'leaseholder deed of certificate'. That phrase is synonymous with the 'qualifying lease certificate' used in the Act. As well as changing the name given to this document, the 859 Regulations announce that they will refer to the tenant as 'leaseholder', thus departing from the word used in the Act and replacing it with a much more cumbersome one. For consistency, this chapter uses the word 'tenant' throughout.

In its original unamended form, the 859 Regulations, reg.6 began by providing at para.(1) that a tenant under a lease could send the landlord an LDC. The implication was that this could be done unsolicited. The amended 895 Regulations now omit this provision. It is difficult to know what to make of this omission. It is not thought that it precludes a tenant from sending an unsolicited LDC (reg.6 still contemplates that this might happen). More likely, it was thought unnecessary to say explicitly that this could be done. That is perhaps consistent with the point made above, namely that the LDC regime is a hoop for the landlord to jump through, and which exists to stop a lease from becoming a qualifying lease by default. A tenant need not do anything unless requested – but it is thought that tenants may still take the initiative, if they so choose.

11.3 THE TRIGGER FOR THE PRESCRIBED STEPS: THE 'NOTIFICATION DATE'

As amended, therefore, the 859 Regulations, reg.6 begins at para.(2) and jumps straight into the prescribed steps which the landlord must take to obtain an LDC.

Regulation 6(2) provides as follows:

> Subject to paragraph (3), before the notification date a landlord under a lease that meets the conditions in paragraphs (a) to (c) of section 119(2) of the Act must give a notice in writing to the [tenant] which complies with paragraph (4).

So, time for compliance with the regime of prescribed steps begins with (or more accurately, before) the notification date. That phrase is defined by reg.6(11) as 'the day which is five days after the day on which the landlord becomes aware that (a) the interest in the property owned by the [tenant] is to be sold; or (b) there is a relevant defect in relation to the building in question'.

The wording here is heavily reminiscent of the trigger events for the service of the landlord's certificate (LC), discussed in **Chapter 10**. So, the problems considered there, surrounding the date a person (particularly a non-natural person) becomes aware of something, and the meaning of the phrase 'is to be sold', also arise here. The comments made in that context are equally applicable here.

The wording of second trigger event for the LDC in the 859 Regulations, namely the landlord becoming aware 'that ... there is a relevant defect in relation to the building in question', differs slightly from the wording in the 711 Regulations. The wording there is that the landlord must be aware 'of a relevant defect'. There may at first sight be little between these two differing forms of words, but the formulation 'that ... there is a relevant defect' perhaps renders it more certain that the landlord must be aware both of the defect, and that it is a relevant defect, for time to run.

The notification date is stated to be five days after the date of the landlord becoming aware of these matters. Thus, if the landlord becomes aware of them on a Monday, the notification date is the following Saturday. But, notably, the first of the prescribed steps – service of the notice required by para.(2) – must be taken *before* the notification date. So, in this example it would have to be done by Friday. There is nothing to suggest that weekends or holidays are excluded from this calculation. One can therefore imagine that, depending on when the landlord is notified, the landlord may have very limited working time within which to comply.

11.4 WHAT IS THE FIRST PRESCRIBED STEP?

As stated above, the first requirement is that the landlord must give the tenant a notice – referred to hereafter as 'the first notice' – complying with reg.6(2). However, this is expressed to be subject to reg.6(3), which provides that the first notice need not be served where, before the notification date, the landlord has received an LDC in respect of the lease. The existence of this provision makes clear that, despite the omission of reg.6(1), it is still contemplated that a tenant may submit an LDC unsolicited.

Since the whole of the regime is triggered by the first notice, it follows that if a tenant has volunteered an LDC, none of the subsequent steps need be taken.

Assuming the steps are required, the 859 Regulations, reg.7(1) provides that an LDC must be executed in relation to a lease 'by the person who is the [tenant] under that lease'. This is obviously predicated on there being a single tenant. Where there is more than one tenant, one question which might arise is whether notice must be given to all of them, or only one of them. Schedule 8, para.13(2) appears to answer this; it provides that the landlord needs to take the various prescribed and reasonable steps described in this section to obtain a qualifying lease certificate from '*a tenant* under the lease' (emphasis added). This suggests that an LDC can be obtained from any tenant, but need not be obtained from all of them.

No prescribed form for the first notice exists, but reg.6(4) states that it must:

- state that it is a notice for the purposes of BSA 2022, Sched.8, paras.13 and 15;
- include a copy of the form of the LDC;
- include a statement to the effect that failure to provide a completed LDC and the evidence required by reg.6(7):

- will result in the lease being treated, for the purposes of BSA 2022, ss.116–122 of the Act, as if it were not a qualifying lease;
- where the lease is a shared ownership lease, may result in the landlord assuming the tenant owns a 100 per cent share; and
- may result in a higher value for the qualifying lease being used under or pursuant to any provision in BSA 2022, Sched.8 to which value is relevant;

- provide the date (which must be no less than eight weeks from the date of receipt of the notice) by which a reply to the notice must be received (this is subsequently referred to as 'the reply date'); and
- provide the address of the landlord to which the reply must be sent.

Unlike the 711 Regulations, the 859 Regulations, reg.6 also provides guidance as to how the first notice must be given. In all cases, it must be left at the tenant's address or sent to that address by prepaid first class post. That address may or may not be the same as the address of the property to which the lease relates. If the tenant is a company, and the company's registered office differs from the address to which the lease relates, it is thought that notices should be sent to the registered office.

Where the tenant has provided the landlord with an email address, the first notice must also be transmitted to that email address. It is not entirely clear whether the email address must have been provided specifically for the purpose of the sending of an LDC, or whether it is sufficient if it has been provided for any purpose. It is thought that its provision for any purpose will suffice. Thus the inclusion of an email address in the lease itself, or in some unrelated communication sent before or after entry into the lease, will constitute the provision of an email address for this purpose. It should be noted that sending to an email address is not, of itself, sufficient; a hard copy must also be posted or delivered.

11.5 WHAT MUST THE TENANT DO?

The 859 Regulations, reg.6(6) provides that where a tenant receives the first notice, the tenant must by the reply date do one of two things. Either the tenant must provide the landlord with an LDC complying with the requirements of the 859 Regulations, reg.7 and the evidence referred to in reg.6(7), or the tenant must reply to the landlord in writing stating that they will not provide one.

If they elect to provide an LDC, the evidence which must accompany it is said by reg.6(7) to be:

- where the dwelling to which the lease relates was disposed of on the open market before 14 February 2022:

  - evidence of the most recent sale before that date, including an official copy of the register of title at HM Land Registry which shows the date of the sale in question; and
  - evidence of the price paid at completion (in pounds sterling to the nearest pound) in respect of that sale;
- additionally, where the dwelling was owned under a shared ownership lease at the beginning of 14 February 2022:
  - a copy of the shared ownership lease; and
  - evidence of the percentage share under the shared ownership lease held on that date.

In fact, the LDC requires some additional evidence, namely 'Evidence to show the dwelling was only or principal home at the beginning of 14th February 2022' (sic). This ungrammatical statement has gone unaltered by the 895 Regulations. As well as needing a definite article, it should be read as if the words 'of anyone who was a tenant' were interposed after the word 'home'.

No sanction is provided for a failure on the part of a tenant to fulfil the requirements of reg.6(7); the sanction is effectively that the tenant's lease may be treated as not being a qualifying lease.

Requirements as to the form and execution of the LDC are considered at **11.9**.

11.6 WHAT MUST THE LANDLORD DO IF NO REPLY IS RECEIVED?

The landlord must take certain further steps if no reply is received by the date 14 days before the reply date (assuming the minimum eight-week period was given for responding, this will obviously be six weeks after sending the first notice).

Those further steps are that the landlord must send another notice (the 'second notice') containing all the matters which were required in the first notice, except for the requirement to respond within the eight-week period. In addition, the second notice must:

- state that no reply to the first notice has been received;
- set out the reply date; and
- state that the tenant may make a request for an extension of time under reg.6(9).

The second notice must be given no later than seven days before the reply date (so effectively the landlord has a window of seven days). In contrast to the first notice, there is no provision as to how the second notice must be given, but a prudent landlord will no doubt adhere to the same service requirements as the first notice.

In addition to sending a second notice, where the landlord has a telephone number for the tenant, the landlord must telephone the tenant to draw the second notice to the tenant's attention.

By virtue of reg.6(9), if before the reply date the tenant requests from the landlord an additional four weeks to take the required steps required, the landlord must allow this. There is no requirement as to how the tenant may make this request; it seems an oral request will suffice. However, the extension requested must apparently be of four weeks. The landlord is not obliged to allow an extension of a lesser or greater time than four weeks, or allow any extension which is requested after the reply date has passed.

11.7 REASONABLE STEPS

It is not enough, however, for the landlord to simply take the prescribed steps to obtain an LDC. BSA 2022, Sched.8, para.13(2)(a) makes clear that it must take all reasonable steps to do so as well.

What constitutes reasonable steps will be a question of fact. If, for example, a landlord is in contact with a tenant during the relevant period regarding something unrelated to the LDC (say, a nuisance complaint made by or against the tenant), it may be considered unreasonable if the landlord does not refer to the issue of the outstanding LDC. It would be prudent for landlords to develop a filing system which alerts any employee dealing with a particular tenant to any unanswered request for an LDC.

11.8 THE 895 REGULATIONS: AN ADDITIONAL REQUIREMENT

The 895 Regulations impose an additional requirement on the landlord: that within one week of receiving an LDC, it must provide a copy of the same to any resident management company (RMC) or Right to Manage (RTM) company (see **12.3.2**) or named manager in relation to the building to which the certificate relates. The Regulations as amended provide that a consequence of failing to do this is that the costs of a relevant measure relating to a relevant defect in the building become prescribed costs under BSA 2022, Sched.8, para.16(4). This means they are not to be regarded as relevant costs to be taken into account when determining the amount of a service charge, and must not be met from a relevant reserve fund.

What is less clear is whether this additional requirement is intended to be one of the 'prescribed steps' which must be taken to avoid BSA 2022, s.119(2)(d) from ceasing to be relevant to the question of whether a lease is a qualifying lease. It is thought that it is intended so to be. The two consequences are capable of co-existing (Sched.8, para.16(4) applies to all leases, not just qualifying leases) and it would be odd to treat this new requirement, which is, as a matter of ordinary language, a 'prescribed step', as nevertheless not being a 'prescribed step' for the purposes of Sched.8, para.13(2).

11.9 FORM OF LEASEHOLDER DEED OF CERTIFICATE

The 859 Regulations, reg.7 provides that an LDC must be executed as a deed by the person who is the tenant under that lease, and makes provision for the form of the LDC and the information to be provided within it by reference to a Schedule to the 859 Regulations. As might be expected, the form follows the layout of BSA 2022, s.119(2)(d) and consists of a tick-box list requiring the signatory to confirm which if any of the conditions in that section applied as at 14 February 2022. The clumsily superfluous requirement of s.119(2)(d)(ii) (ownership of no other dwellings), compliance with which necessarily also entails compliance with (d)(iii) (ownership of no more than two other dwellings), is thankfully collapsed into one question, predicated on the latter.

There are also questions about the sale price of the lease on last sale (which assists in determining value for the purpose of, in particular, Sched.8, para.4) and shared ownership (which is relevant to the permitted maximum recoverable under para.5 of that Schedule).

The requirement of execution as a deed should not prove unduly problematic; the signature box on the form provides that the LDC is so executed and nothing more is required than signature alongside that statement. However, in accordance with the requirements of the Law of Property (Miscellaneous Provisions) Act 1989, s.1(3), the tenant's signature must be witnessed.

If the tenant is a company, it is possible to execute as a deed, but the requirements of the Companies Act 2006, s.44 must be complied with. The document must therefore be affixed with the common seal of the company, or signed by two authorised signatories (essentially, the directors or secretary), or by a director witnessed by a third party.

For foreign companies, reference should be made to the Overseas Companies (Execution of Documents and Registration of Charges) Regulations 2009, SI 2009/1917 which essentially apply the Companies Act 2006, s.44 with certain modifications. Questions as to who is duly authorised to act on behalf of an overseas company in executing a document are determined by the law of the company's domicile, not the governing law of the contract or document (see *Integral Petroleum SA* v. *SCU-Finanz AG* [2015] EWCA Civ 144).

11.10 SOME PROBLEM CASES

As observed in **11.1**, the LDC's purpose is not to record the situation as it is at the time of completion, but the situation as it was as at 14 February 2022.

In the vast majority of cases, this will be straightforward. The tenant completing the LDC will very probably be the same person who held the lease as at 14 February 2022, and can attest to, and evidence, their personal circumstances at that time. If the lease has changed hands, it is likely that the question of whether it was a qualifying lease will have been resolved at the time it did so. But there may, exceptionally, be problematic cases. One or two have surfaced already; it is to be expected that there may be others.

At the lower end of the scale of problem cases is the situation involving multiple tenants as at 14 February 2022. The answer to this situation is fairly straightforward; BSA 2022, s.119(4) defines a 'relevant tenant' as 'a person who, at the qualifying time, was the tenant, *or any of the tenants*, under the lease' (emphasis added). Thus, it seems that if any one tenant met any one of the requirements of s.119(2)(d) as at 14 February 2022, the lease (as long as it complies with the other requirements of s.119(2)) is a qualifying lease.

Another problem arises where the tenant as at 14 February 2022 was a corporation. It is not thought that there is any particular difficulty with the concept of a company bringing itself within s.119(2)(d). Although the definition of 'relevant tenant' quoted above refers to a 'person', it is clear from the Interpretation Act 1978, s.5 and Sched.1 that the word 'person' in a statute will also mean a company 'unless the contrary intention appears'. The contrary intention does not appear in BSA 2022. A company probably cannot satisfy the requirements of s.119(2)(b)(i), as the received wisdom is that it cannot have a home (see *Hiller* v. *United Dairies (London) Ltd.* [1934] 1 KB 57 in the context of the Rent Acts). However, there is no reason why it should not satisfy the property ownership requirements of s.119(2)(b)(ii) and/or (iii).

A third situation which has caused difficulty is where the tenant is deceased as at 14 February 2022. Whose situation is relevant for the purposes of the LDC in that situation? The answer is thought to be that it remains the position of the deceased. An executor (or administrator) only holds, in the old legal French term, 'in autre droit' (in the right of another). If – but only if – they combine that legal ownership with occupation, they will be regarded as an assignee of the lease (see *Mayor, Aldermen & Burgesses of Stratford upon Avon* v. *Parker* [1914] 2 KB 562). In that situation, the LDC should probably relate to the executor's situation, rather than that of the deceased. Assuming the executor is not in occupation, so only the deceased is relevant, then (as with a company) there can be no home, principal or otherwise. But, if the estate does not own more than the requisite number of properties, it may yet bring itself within s.119(2)(d)(ii) and/or (iii).

Finally, if the tenant is a trustee, it will nevertheless probably be the tenant, rather than the beneficial owner, who must provide the certificate. The position may however be otherwise if the tenant is a mere nominee.

11.11 THE LEASEHOLDER DEED OF CERTIFICATE – FINAL THOUGHTS

Early experience of the Act suggests that tenants, and potential purchasers of leasehold interests, are profoundly concerned about LDCs, believing them to be essential to establishing whether a lease is a qualifying lease. As has hopefully been made clear in the foregoing paragraphs, that is often – indeed perhaps usually – not the case. Unless the landlord has done all that is required of it to obtain an LDC, both by reference to the prescribed steps, and to any reasonable steps, no LDC is required. In those circumstances, a lease which complies with BSA 2022, s.119(2)(a)–(c) is, without more, a qualifying lease.

Accordingly, instead of concerning themselves with volunteering an LDC when none has been sought, tenants and purchasers (and indeed their lenders) may – particularly where the s.119(2)(d) requirements are difficult to establish – be better advised simply to ensure that the trigger for the taking of prescribed steps has been activated; this can be done by notifying the landlord that the lease is to be sold. If that is done, and the landlord does not then follow the rigorous requirements of the 859 Regulations, reg.6 to the letter (including by giving a first notice within a matter of days), the tenant and any intending purchaser of the tenant's interest can proceed on the safe assumption that the lease is a qualifying lease, without the need to provide an LDC.

CHAPTER 12

Section 112 and the new LTA 1985, section 30D

Hugh Rowan

12.1 INTRODUCTION

The building safety regime in England and Wales is a tangled web of primary and secondary legislation. One key radial of this web is the interrelation between BSA 2022 and the mechanism of LTA 1985. LTA 1985 is well established as providing the statutory framework for both landlords' and tenants' responsibilities for repair and maintenance under a lease, and the consequences of failure to comply.

The Act introduces a number of new and onerous obligations, as well as concomitant rights, for landlords and tenants in relation to LTA 1985. This chapter seeks to address the rights and obligations imposed by BSA 2022, s.112. Broadly, the purpose and effect of s.112 is an expansion of both the landlord's and the tenant's rights and remedies. This has particular relevance in terms of enforcing the parties' respective obligations under other provisions of the Act.

Section 112 incorporates various supplementary provisions into LTA 1985 with the effect of implying various additional covenants into applicable leases. These give practical powers enabling landlords to better comply with their new obligations under the Act, and also enabling tenants to force landlords to so comply. These new sections are incorporated directly after LTA 1985's provisions relating to tenants' rights with respect to insurance (LTA 1985, s.30A) and the rights of recognised tenants' associations to be consulted in relation to managing agents (LTA 1985, s.30B).

12.2 IMPLIED TERMS UNDER LTA 1985, SECTION 30C

12.2.1 Conditions for implication

Various covenants are implied into existing leases by LTA 1985; however, these new provisions will only imply terms into leases that meet two initial qualifying criteria:

- the lease must consist of or include a dwelling in a higher-risk building (HRB) (LTA 1985, s.30C(1)); and
- the lease must not be a tenancy to which LTA 1954, Part II applies (LTA 1985, s.32(1), as amended by BSA 2022, s.112(6)).

The definition of an HRB is taken from BSA 2022, s.65. This definition is addressed in detail in **Chapter 4** but can be summarised as a building that is at least 18 metres or seven stories tall, and contains at least two residential units. (More detail is provided in the 275 Regulations.) However, a different definition applies in Wales (see **Chapter 22**).

The second condition is that the lease cannot be a 'business lease' falling within the protections of LTA 1954. As a result, if the premises comprised in the tenancy are or include premises occupied for business purposes under LTA 1954, s.23(1), then that lease will not imply the covenants discussed in this chapter. This includes any mixed-use premises. It should be noted that for the purposes of this section it does not matter if the building as a whole is mixed-use, only if the lease in question is mixed-use.

It is notable that, unlike the new LTA 1985, ss.30D and 30E, there is no express definition of 'landlord' in s.30C. Sections 30D and 30E define a 'landlord' expansively to include any person who has a right under the lease to enforce payment of a service charge. However, in the more restricted context of implied covenants in the lease, it appears likely that s.30C applies to the landlord under the lease.

If both conditions discussed above are met, then a number of new covenants are automatically implied into the lease.

12.2.2 The landlord's covenant: compliance and cooperation

The landlord's implied covenant is threefold. First, where the landlord is the accountable person (AP) (as to which, see **Chapter 5**), there is implied a covenant to *comply* with their new duties under BSA 2022, Part 4 (as to which, see **Chapter 6**). Second, if they are not the AP, then the landlord covenants to *cooperate*, including taking any steps reasonably required to facilitate compliance by an AP (or special measures manager (SMM)) (see BSA 2022, s.102 and Sched.7) with their Part 4 duties. Finally, if a special measures order (SMO) (see BSA 2022, s.102 and Sched.7) exists, the landlord covenants to comply with that order.

The requirement to cooperate is given a broad definition and requires taking any steps reasonably required to facilitate the relevant persons' compliance and includes providing any information reasonably required (LTA 1985, s.30C(4); 'relevant person' is defined in s.30C(9)).

Importantly, this obligation to provide information overrides any obligation of confidence or restriction on disclosing that information (LTA 1985, s.30C(5)),[1] except if doing so would breach any data protection legislation (LTA 1985, s.30C(8)).[2]

As a result, landlords must tread a fine line between complying with their implied obligations under the lease and complying with their data protection obligations. If the landlord missteps, the landlord may either be acting in breach of the lease and liable to enforcement action under LTA 1985, s.30H (see **12.2.4**), or else be liable for a fine if they breach the General Data Protection Regulation (GDPR). These fines can be draconian (up to £17.5 million or 4 per cent of annual turnover – Data Protection Act 2018, ss.155–159) and landlords are advised to take specific legal advice if they are in doubt as to which side of the line any request for information lies.

12.2.3 The tenant's covenant: access and compliance

The tenant under a lease to which LTA 1985, s.30C applies also has a duty of compliance: just as with a landlord, a tenant must comply with their duties (under BSA 2022, ss.95 and 97: see further **Chapter 7**) and comply with any SMO.

In addition, a tenant must allow a landlord, relevant person or other party authorised in writing, access to the premises at a reasonable time if 48 hours' notice has been given. The reasons for which the tenant must allow access include inspecting premises, carrying out works to premises, or accessing parts of an HRB, in connection with a duty under BSA 2022, Part 4 (LTA 1985, s.30C(5); 'relevant person' is defined in s.30C(9)).

12.2.4 Enforcement (LTA 1985, s.30H)

The most important consequence of BSA 2022, s.112 is that is provides a means of enforcement of the parties' respective obligations under the Act. By implying these covenants into applicable leases, parties to those leases can sue on those covenants for specific performance or damages for breach of covenant.

This right to sue for specific performance of these covenants is expressly provided for (LTA 1985, s.30H), and its scope is expanded beyond the usual common law right in two key ways.

1 It is noted in passing that this disclosure carve out contains almost identical wording to a number of other recently amended statutes, including: the Trade Union and Labour Relations (Consolidation) Act 1992, s.234D; the Digital Economy Act 2017, s.40; and the Police, Crime, Sentencing and Courts Act 2022, s.30 (among others). Practitioners concerned with the meaning of this provision would be well advised to consider any parallel interpretations provided under other legislation also.

2 This is defined in the Data Protection Act 2018, s.3 and at the time of writing includes: the Data Protection Act 2018; Regulation (EU) 2016/679 (through the European Union (Withdrawal) Act 2018), s.3; and regulations made thereunder.

First, the court is entitled to award specific performance notwithstanding any equitable rule restricting the scope of the remedy. Specific reference is made in LTA 1985, s.30H(a) to a lack of mutuality not being a bar to specific performance in this sense. In other words, the historic principle that the court will only award specific performance against the defendant if it could have also – mutually – done so against the claimant[3] does not apply to the covenants implied by LTA 1985, s.30C.

Second, a tenant under a lease is entitled to sue their landlord for specific performance of their duties under the Act even if the breach does not relate to part of the building let to the tenant (LTA 1985, s.30H(b)). This expansion of the tenant's standing under the Act appears to recognise the fact that a tenant's safety is intrinsically linked to the safety of the whole building, not merely the parts demised to the tenant.

It is not possible for the parties to a lease to contract out of these provisions and protections and any attempt to do so is rendered automatically void. It is also not possible to amend the tenancy or any collateral agreement to authorise forfeiture or impose any penalty or obligation on the tenant if they enforce or rely on the landlord's obligation as set out above (LTA 1985, s.30F(1)(a)).

It is important to note that the benefit of these enforcement powers is confined to the parties to the lease. Nevertheless, it is difficult to foresee enforcement action being taken by tenants under s.30H as standard. It is unlikely that tenants will know when a landlord has, for example, failed to facilitate compliance by an AP (or SMM) with their BSA 2022, Part 4 duties. Less likely still will a tenant want to bear the potential costs and risks of taking enforcement action.

By contrast, it is foreseeable that landlords will have recourse to this provision in order to secure access to premises occupied by obstructive tenants. In this way, injunctions under LTA 1985, s.30H may take on a similar form to access injunctions for the purposes of carrying out gas safety inspections under the Gas Safety (Installation and Use) Regulations 1998, SI 1998/2451 (so-called 'Gas Injunctions').

The procedural aspects of such an application are discussed further in **Chapter 21**.

12.3 BUILDING SAFETY COSTS

12.3.1 Building safety measures and service charge machinery

BSA 2022, Part 5 and Sched.8 make detailed provision for various scenarios where landlords can and cannot recover the costs of various remediation and other works through the service charge. These are dealt with in **Chapter 9**. How-

3 *Blackett* v. *Bates* (1865) 1 Ch App 117; 71 ER 467. This reflects similar provision made in LTA 1985, s.17(1).

ever, the Act also provides for many more mundane duties of landlords and tenants. In order to ensure that these routine 'building safety measures' are recoverable through the service charge, BSA 2022, s.112 incorporates a new s.30D into LTA 1985. This provides that, for relevant leases, the costs of 'building safety measures' can always be recovered. This leaves two questions: first, what are the relevant leases; second, what are the relevant measures?

It is important to note that 'relevant leases' for the purposes of this section are not the same as 'qualifying leases' under BSA 2022, s.119. To be a relevant lease for the purposes of this section, a lease must meet five criteria:

1. First, the lease must consist of or include premises in an HRB.
2. Second, the lease must have been granted for a term of seven years or more (even if terminable sooner by a tenant's notice or re-entry/forfeiture). The lease should therefore be a registered lease (Land Registration Act 2002, ss.4(1)(c) and 27(2)(b)(i)).
3. Third, the lease must be one under which the tenant is liable to pay service charges (as defined in LTA 1985, s.18).
4. Fourth, the lease cannot be a relevant social housing tenancy (as defined in the Land Registration Act 2002, s.132).
5. Finally, the lease cannot be a business tenancy within LTA 1985, Part II (LTA 1985, s.32(1), as amended by BSA 2022, s.112(6)).

If these conditions are met, then the costs of following 'building safety measures' can be recovered through the service charge:[4]

1. Applying for registration of an HRB (BSA 2022, s.78).
2. Applying for a building assessment certificate and displaying it (BSA 2022, ss.79 and 82).
3. Assessing building safety risks (BSRs) (BSA 2022, s.83).
4. Taking reasonable steps to manage BSRs (BSA 2022, s.84(1)).
5. Preparing and revising a safety case report and notifying and providing the Regulator with the same (BSA 2022, ss.85–86).
6. Establishing and operating a mandatory occurrence reporting system, and giving information to the Regulator (BSA 2022, s.87).
7. Keeping and sharing information and documents (BSA 2022, ss.88, 89, 90 and 92).
8. Complying with duties in relation to a residents' engagement strategy (BSA 2022, s.91).
9. Establishing and operating a system for the investigation of complaints (BSA 2022, s.93).
10. Giving a contravention notice to a resident, and making an application to the county court (BSA 2022, s.96).

[4] It is possible for the Secretary of State to introduce regulations to amend this list in future under LTA 1985, s.30D(7).

11. Making a request to enter premises, or making an application to the county court (BSA 2022, s.97).

Importantly these costs do not include that carrying out of works in relation to BSRs (BSA 2022, s.84(2)). These fall to be considered separately (see **Chapter 3**). However, legal or professional fees, fees payable to the Regulator, and any management costs incurred in connection with any of the above measures, are all also recoverable costs under LTA 1985, s.30D(5).

Where LTA 1985, s.30D applies, if the taking of building safety measures is not provided for in the service charge, then the relevant lease will have effect as if the matters for which the service charge is payable under the lease included the taking of building safety measures by or on behalf of the relevant person. The 'relevant person' is the AP as defined in BSA 2022, s.115 (whether they are the immediate landlord, superior landlord or SMM).

If the lease in question contains a number of methods for apportioning costs, then any costs which the tenant is liable for only as a result of s.30D, the tenant will pay the same portion as they do for the costs incurred in connection with insuring the building (LTA 1985, s.30D(3)).

It is not possible to modify this additional service charge machinery, and any attempt to do so is rendered automatically void (LTA 1985, s.30F(2)).

It is important to note that s.30D does not exclude, modify or override the service charge regime introduced by BSA 2022, Part 5 and Sched.8 (as to which, see **Chapter 9**). The terms implied by LTA 1985, s.30D should be considered conceptually prior to any consideration of Part 5 and Sched.8. The terms implied by s.30D are concerned with what costs can be recovered under the terms of a relevant lease. Part 5 and Sched.8 are then concerned with limiting the recovery of those costs if and in so far as they are 'relevant measures' intended to remedy a 'relevant defect'.

It is foreseeable that steps taken – for example, to assess a BSR, manage a BSR, or establish a safety case report – could, in a given scenario amount to 'relevant measures' intended to remedy a 'relevant defect'. In such cases, if Part 5 and Sched.8 also operate to restrict the recoverability of service charges, then (despite the recovery of these specific costs being implied by LTA 1985, s.30D) these costs will not in fact be recoverable. In this regard, Part 5 and Sched.8 are conceptually subsequent to – and override – LTA 1985, s.30D.

12.3.2 Resident management companies and Right to Manage companies

For the purposes of this part of the Act, a Right to Manage (RTM) company is defined in accordance with the Commonhold and Leasehold Reform Act 2002. The Act also refers to a resident management company (RMC), which is given a bespoke definition in the Building Safety Act 2022 (Commencement No.4 and Transitional Provisions) Regulations, SI 2023/362, reg.3(2). For the purposes of this part of BSA 2022, an RMC is defined as a body corporate which is party to a lease of a building where either (a) the body corporate is limited by guarantee and the members of that body are tenants under leases of dwellings in the building ('leaseholders'), or (b) the majority of the shares of the body corporate are held by leaseholders.

The Act envisages that where the AP is an RMC or RTM company, those companies will appoint directors to deal specifically with the duties under BSA 2022, Part 4. To achieve this, the articles of association of any RMC that is an AP for an HRB are modified by LTA 1985, s.30E(2)(a) and BSA 2022, s.111(2) to include provision for the appointment of a director of the company. That director is appointed for the purposes of supporting the company in complying with its duties under Part 4.

Further, where an RMC appoints a paid director for a building safety purpose, then any unpaid directors of the RMC are relieved of their personal criminal liability for any breaches of duty under Part 4 (BSA 2022, s.161(4)).

In line with the other provisions discussed in this chapter, LTA 1985, s.30E now makes provision for the costs incurred in renumerating any such director (LTA 1985, s.30E(2)(b)). As with the previous section, if the lease in question contains a number of methods for apportioning costs, then the tenant will pay the same portion for any costs for which they are liable for only as a result of s.30E, as they do for the costs incurred in connection with insuring the building (LTA 1985, s.30D(3)). Just as with the statutorily implied machinery in relation to building safety measures, it is not possible to modify this service charge machinery in relation to RMCs and RTM companies, and any attempt to do so is rendered automatically void (LTA 1985, s.30F(2)).

CHAPTER 13

Service charges in respect of remediation works

Daniel Dovar

13.1 INTRODUCTION

BSA 2022, s.133 amends LTA 1985 (only in force at present for the purposes of making regulations), in order to incentivise a landlord to find some means of meeting the cost of 'remediation works' other than from the leaseholders through the service charge. To do that, the amendments operate in two ways:

- the principal amendment is through a new s.20D inserted into LTA 1985, placing an obligation on a landlord to seek out and obtain such other sources of funding; and
- the consultation requirements contained in LTA 1985, s.20 are amended and the ability to obtain dispensation under LTA 1985, s.20ZA is removed.

At present, given the lack of definition of 'remediation works' (see **13.2.2**) it is not entirely clear to what extent these limitation provisions overlap or combine with the other restrictions on service charges, such as under BSA 2022, Sched.8. These further restrictions are intended to apply in the event that the landlord has overcome the other hurdles that the Act puts in their way to recovery. Therefore consideration should first be had to the other restrictions and in particular the limitations imposed by Sched.8 before considering this chapter (see **Chapter 9**).

Further, draft Guidance has been made available online[1] ('the draft Guidance') which indicates at provisional para.13.2 that regulations will require a landlord to provide leaseholders with information about their 'pursuits for each defect' in default of which the leaseholders will have no obligation to pay towards the remediation of that defect (cf. LTA 1985, s.21B Act and the requirement to give a summary of rights and obligations with demands for service charges).

1 **https://assets.publishing.service.gov.uk/government/uploads/system/uploads/attachment_data/file/1133895/Draft_statutory_guidance.pdf**.

13.2 NEW LTA 1985, SECTION 20D

13.2.1 Introduction

The new LTA 1985, s.20D provides a limitation on the recovery of 'remediation costs' by a landlord from leaseholders by placing an obligation on the landlord to find alternative sources of funding first. In default of the landlord doing that, the leaseholder can apply for a determination that all or any of the costs of those works are not to be recovered by way of service charge.

13.2.2 Remediation costs

Remediation costs are defined as the costs of 'remediation works' on a building of a prescribed description (LTA 1985, s.20D(1)). As set out above, at the time of writing this new section was not in force, save for bringing in regulations. Those regulations, which have not yet been made, are to provide a definition of 'remediation works' as well as setting out what buildings they apply to.

The draft statutory guidance (the draft Guidance) available at the time of writing suggests that the defects which the remediation works must address are the fire and structural risks identified by BSA 2022, s.62 (see **Chapter 3**) and the building to which it applies will follow the definition of relevant building at BSA 2022, s.117 (see **Chapter 9**). However, for some reason, BSA 2022, s.133 does not directly adopt those definitions, so it may be that when the particulars are enacted, the definitions for this section are different. Given the differing definitions of building between BSA 2022, ss.65 and 117 and the 275 Regulations, reg.4, that would not be entirely surprising.

Whatever those costs are, LTA 1985, s.20D seeks to limit passing them onto the leaseholders through the service charge where a landlord has not tried first to recover them elsewhere.

13.2.3 Reasonable steps

There is no absolute requirement for a landlord to obtain alternative sources of finance, they just need to take reasonable steps: (i) to ascertain if there are any funds available; and (ii) then take reasonable steps to secure the money.

This requirement has some similarities with the requirement to mitigate losses. It is not an absolute requirement, but there is an expectation that some steps will be taken. The need to consider what the landlord would do if they were themselves otherwise to cover the costs is likely to be one consideration. In *Columbia House Properties (No.3) Ltd.* v. *Imperial Hall RTM Co. Ltd.* [2014] UKUT 30 (LC) Judge Robinson considered that when assessing what costs were recoverable in respect of a right to manage claim under the Commonhold and Leasehold Reform Act 2002, s.88, they were no more than those that the landlord would have incurred if the landlord had been personally liable for them. In the context of the obligation arising under a 'best endeavours' clause, the test set out by Geoffrey Lane LJ in *IBM United Kingdom Ltd.* v. *Rockware Glass Ltd.* [1980] FSR 335, CA seems apposite in that it obliges 'the purchaser to take all those reasonable steps which a prudent determined man, acting in his own interests and anxious to obtain planning permission, would have taken'.

The section also trails guidance by the Secretary of State about the steps to take. But it must be kept in mind that the guidance is just a draft (and part of a consultation process). When published in final form adherence to it is likely to be a factor that can be taken into account in determining whether reasonable steps have been taken (LTA 1985, s.20D(9), (10)).

LTA 1985, s.20D(8) makes it clear that the landlord should not hold up doing the works pending taking these reasonable steps. In that regard, the landlord will not be able to say that they delayed works because they wanted to pursue third parties. It is not clear how this sits with the amendments to the consultation requirements (and removal of dispensation) for recovering the cost of 'remediation costs' (see **13.3**). Statutory consultation takes time, but this amendment puts pressure on the landlord to get on with the work expeditiously.

13.2.4 Grant funding

The first alternative source of funding is grant funding. The landlord must see if there are any applicable grants and, if so, try to obtain funding.

While not expressly stating so, this seems primarily aimed at the Building Safety Fund (BSF) in its various forms and applications. The draft Guidance refers to both the BSF and the Social and Private Sector ACM Cladding Remediation Funds and 'other government funds'.

Given that the obligation is to take reasonable steps to ascertain and then obtain funding, it is likely that the landlord will have to show what attempts were made to find out whether any grant was applicable to the building. If a grant is available, the landlord will then have to show the steps it took to apply for that grant. A contemporaneous record of both of these endeavours is likely to be needed and a landlord who lost out on grant funding in whole or in part due to delay or ignorance is likely to find that it is limited in recovery of the remediation costs from the leaseholders (LTA 1985, s.20D(5)). If a leaseholder makes a s.20D application and the landlord cannot show it has taken reasonable steps, then the Tribunal may reduce or disallow all the remediation costs. New s.20ZA(5A) enables tenants to require the landlord to provide evidence to demonstrate the reasonable steps it has undertaken or will undertake (see **13.3**). It is not clear how a court or tribunal would assess the likelihood of obtaining funding or even the level of funding that would have been provided had reasonable steps been taken. The information provided under s.20ZA(5A) should provide some means of assessing the merits.

13.2.5 Third parties

After looking at the possibility of grant funding, the landlord must take reasonable steps to see if funding can be obtained from third parties. This expressly includes insurance policies, indemnities or guarantees, or making a claim against either a developer, someone involved in the design of the property or works, or someone who actually carried out works.

The draft Guidance suggests:

> Landlords should notify their insurers of a defect, and, if possible, follow any appeals procedure in the event of an unsuccessful outcome;
>
> Home warranty claims should be made where appropriate and within any warranty period or a claim made on an individual manufacturer warranty. Again, if possible, they should follow any appeals procedure in the event of an unsuccessful outcome;
>
> In the event of an insurance or warranty dispute, the landlord should consider seeking advice on whether a resolution service would provide a better option.

The potential claims against third parties have been expanded by the extensions to the limitation periods for claims in relation to building works and in particular defective cladding products (BSA 2022, ss.135, 148–150). Claims which would previously have been long statute-barred are now open. This will include those relating to the construction of the building in particular liability for defective products used in construction or a failure to build a dwelling fit for habitation (such as under the Defective Premises Act (DPA) 1972, s.1).

As a preliminary, each landlord will need to investigate who was responsible for the defects in the first place. The draft Guidance then gives some indication of the balancing act that a landlord needs to undertake in order to consider whether to make a claim against a third party. It indicates that reasonable steps will include:

- the need to seek independent legal advice as to the merits of a claim;
- following pre-action protocols to enable settlement.

The landlord will need to consider and balance the prospects of success, the time taken to pursue litigation, and the cost of litigation.

13.2.6 Impact of obtaining funding

If, as a result of the efforts of the landlord the funding comes to fruition, then LTA 1985, s.20D(4) makes the obvious point that this money should be credited to the remediation costs and the service charge reduced accordingly.

13.2.7 Application by the leaseholder

Where a leaseholder considers that a landlord has not taken reasonable steps to obtain funds from a third party, the leaseholder can apply to the prescribed court or tribunal for a determination that the remediation costs are not recoverable by way of service charge from them (LTA 1985, s.20D(5)). On such an application, the court or tribunal may make such order as it considers just and equitable (LTA 1985, s.20D(7)).

It is more than likely that a claim against third parties will not be resolved for years and will be costly. If that is the case, it is possible that at the time of a s.20D application, the requirement to continue to take reasonable steps may be continuing. The landlord will have to show, at the time of the application, that it is pursuing meritorious claims and if ultimately sums are recovered, that the landlord would credit the service charge account.

But what if a landlord dropped such a claim after recovering the sums through the service charge? There is no mechanism for repayment to the leaseholders in that scenario. Further, on an application to the court or tribunal for a determination as to whether LTA 1985, s.20D restricts recovery, what order should be made if the court or tribunal considered that the landlord is taking active steps to recover the money, but that this will take years to come to resolve and ultimately it may not be in the landlord's favour? Should the landlord be permitted to recover the sums now, with a hope that the landlord will continue to pursue the claim and then credit the service charge account? If the court or tribunal does not sanction recovery, then what if the landlord ultimately is unsuccessful in its claim against the third party? These questions are unanswered and represent formidable practical difficulties in the face of this new regime. Given that the emphasis is on taking reasonable steps, it seems that if that criteria is met, the landlord should not be penalised. If as a result of those steps, sums are then collected from third parties, this should be credited to the service charge fund, to the benefit of the leaseholders (LTA 1985, s.20D(4)).

13.3 CONSULTATION

Most readers will be familiar with the requirements of LTA 1985, s.20 and the statutory consultation required by the landlord if the landlord wishes to recover through the service charge from each leaseholder more than £250 for major works or £200 per annum for a qualifying long-term agreement. It is more than likely that remediation costs will exceed that limit, even if they are capped under BSA 2022, Sched.8, paras.5–7 (see **Chapter 9**).

If the landlord does not adhere to the prescribed consultation, then they need dispensation from the Tribunal before being able to levy more than the capped amounts. For details of the requirements and dispensation in general see Tanfield Chambers, *Service Charges and Management* (5th Edn, Sweet & Maxwell, 2021) Chapter 11.

Section 20(1), as amended, states:

> Where this section applies to any qualifying works or qualifying long term agreement, the relevant contributions of tenants are limited in accordance with subsection (6) or (7) (or both) unless the consultation requirements have been either –

(a) complied with in relation to the works or agreement, or
(b) *except in the case of works to which section 20D applies*, dispensed with in relation to the works or agreement by (or on appeal from) the appropriate tribunal. [amendment emphasised]

BSA 2022, s.133(2) amends LTA 1985, s.20 and s.20ZA, which cover consultation and dispensation. Additional consultation requirements need to be met, in particular:

- giving details to the tenants about what reasonable steps landlords have taken under LTA 1985, s.20D(2);
- giving reasons and information (yet to be prescribed); and
- having to observations made by leaseholders.

Further, it does away with the ability for a landlord to get on with the works without consultation and then seek dispensation retrospectively. The amendment carves out works to which s.20D applies from the provisions on dispensation. Unlike the general thrust of the Act which is to ensure that the landlords get on with the works and worry about funding after (i.e. see s.20D(8)), this amendment may well give landlords a reason to delay commencing so that they can follow the consultation process. Further, the costs of a dispensation application are capable of falling within BSA 2022, Sched.8, para.9 (see **Chapter 9**, and *Adriatic Land 5 Ltd.* v. *Long Leaseholders at Hippersley Point* [2023] UKUT 271 (LC) – although permission to appeal has been given in this case).

13.4 LTA 1985, SECTION 20F

Although not brought in by BSA 2022, s.133, but by BSA 2022, s.112(3), LTA 1985, s.20F places further limitations on the sums that a landlord can recover. The section sets out a number of items which are 'excluded costs' being costs that are not to be regarded as relevant costs for the purposes of determining a service charge. There are four types of excluded costs: (a) costs incurred as a result of a penalty or enforcement action by the Regulator; (b) legal costs relating to special measures proceedings; (c) costs arising out of negligence, breach of contract or unlawful activity by an accountable person (AP); and (d) costs to be prescribed by regulations, but relating to costs of an AP or special measures manager (SMM) in connection with building safety measures. At the time of writing, this provision was partially in force, but with amendments pending.

CHAPTER 14

Remediation orders and remediation contribution orders

Richard Miller

14.1 INTRODUCTION

The Government having decided to limit or, in some cases, extinguish a leaseholder's liability to pay service charges in respect of relevant measures relating to a relevant defect, the Act needed to address the situation where a relevant landlord was unable or unwilling to remediate the building. The Act's solution to this situation is to enable a specified class of interested persons to apply to the First-tier Tribunal (FTT) for an order requiring a relevant landlord to remedy defects (an RO) and a specified body corporate or partnership to make payments for the purpose of meeting the costs of remediation (an RCO).

This chapter considers these two new remedies. At the time of writing, the first RO and RCO have been made, in *Waite* v. *Kedai Ltd.* LON/00AY/HYI/2022/0005 & 0016 (unreported) and *Batish* v. *Inspired Sutton Ltd.* LON/00BF/HYI/2022/0002 (unreported), respectively. The coming months and years will no doubt see further cases and appeals which will provide valuable clarity as to the approach of the FTT to these applications. During the proof stage of this book, the FTT published another RCO decision: *Triathlon Homes LLP* v. *Stratford Village Development Partnership & Ors* [2024] UKFTT 26 (PC).

14.2 REMEDIATION ORDERS

Paragraph 997 of the Explanatory Notes to the Act explains that the policy behind ROs is to 'redress the balance of power in favour of leaseholders' where landlords are not fulfilling their obligations to ensure the building is safe.

BSA 2022, s.123 contains the provisions for ROs. The power of the FTT to make an RO is not actually contained in the Act, but in regulations made under s.123(1) (currently the 859 Regulations, reg.2, as amended by the 895 Regulations). The stated reason for enshrining the power only in secondary legislation is that the Government is expected to monitor the progress of ROs and requires the flexibility to make further or altered provisions.

Section 123(2) defines an RO as an order 'made by the FTT on the application of an interested person, requiring a relevant landlord to remedy specified relevant defects in a specified relevant building by a specified time'.

For the definitions of 'relevant defect' and 'relevant building', see **Chapter 9**.

14.2.1 Interested persons

BSA 2022, s.123(5) lists interested persons as follows:

> (a) the regulator (as defined by section 2),
> (b) a local authority (as defined by section 30) for the area in which the relevant building is situated,
> (c) a fire and rescue authority (as defined by section 30) for the area in which the relevant building is situated,
> (d) a person with a legal or equitable interest in the relevant building or any part of it, or
> (e) any other person prescribed by the regulations.

The 859 Regulations, reg.2(1) and (1A) add the Secretary of State and the Homes and Communities Agency as prescribed interested persons.

14.2.2 The relevant landlord

BSA 2022, s.123(3) defines a 'relevant landlord' for the purposes of applications for ROs as:

> a landlord under a lease of the building or any part of it who is required, under the lease or by virtue of an enactment, to repair or maintain anything relating to the relevant defect.

Section 123(4) states further that the reference to 'landlord under a lease' includes 'any person who is party to the lease otherwise than as landlord or tenant'. This is apt to include a managing agent which is party to the lease.

14.2.3 Making an application

By the 859 Regulations, reg.2(3), the application must state that it is an application under BSA 2022, s.123, identify the building, identify the defects for which the RO is sought, and identify the landlord responsible for repairing and maintaining anything relating to the relevant defects. Applications for ROs are made in Form BSA1, which satisfies these requirements.

14.2.4 The principles to be applied

The Act is not prescriptive about how the FTT should approach the issue of whether to make an RO, and, if so, in what terms. BSA 2022, s.123 and the 859 Regulations, reg.2 are drafted in very broad terms and the exercise is likely to be extremely fact-sensitive.

In *Waite* (see **14.1**), the FTT considered that the similar or analogous situations of orders for specific performance, applicable standards and tests in building regulations, the Regulatory Reform (Fire Safety) Order 2005, SI 2005/1541, and the Housing Act 2004, Chapter 1, Part 1, and the Housing Health and Safety Rating System (HHSRS) were persuasive but not prescriptive. The FTT reached this conclusion by observing that the objective of ROs has a very specific context, saying at [77] that:

> The BSA creates a freestanding regime designed to address a specific problem. Although other regimes may amount to a 'heft of good sense' they are not conclusive as to the Tribunal's jurisdiction or the extent of its powers.

Notwithstanding this, an FTT of a different constitution held in *Priory Heights* CAM/00KC/HIN/2022/0006 (unreported), which was an improvement notice appeal, that the various statutory schemes designed to address hazards in residential property do not operate in isolation. The local authority's power to act in the Housing Act 2004, s.7 in respect of a Category 2 hazard having arisen, the FTT stated at [57] that 'it is not clear why an application against the Landlord for [an RO] and/or the Landlord and/or others for [an RCO] could not be an appropriate course of action, if enforcement action is needed'. Notably in the case of the HHSRS, in November 2018 the Secretary of State for Housing, Communities, and Local Government (as it then was) produced an addendum to the Operating Guidance for the profile for the hazard of fire and in relation to cladding systems on high-rise residential buildings. Further case law will clarify the persuasiveness or otherwise of principles established in analogous regulations and relief.

As to procedure, the FTT in *Waite* considered that the interested person was under a burden to demonstrate a *prima facie* case that there were relevant defects in the relevant building, but that assigning further burdens of proof was inappropriate. Assuming there was such a *prima facie* case, the FTT envisaged the procedure involving an evidence-led enquiry primarily based on expert reports and inspections and also the panel's 'knowledge and experience'.

As a matter of practical reality, the relevant landlord is likely to have to procure any investigation reports. This is because certain interested persons, such as leaseholders, may have limited means with which to commission such reports, and also because no entity except the relevant landlord is likely to be able to access the whole of the building and have the right to undertake any invasive investigations.

14.2.5 The order

The order will require the relevant landlord to remedy specified relevant defects in a specified relevant building by a specified time.

BSA 2022, s.123 (6) defines 'specified' for the purposes of s.123 as 'specified in the order'. It is therefore prudent for leaseholders to consider drafting an RO early in the application to ensure that it complies with the requirements and provides a workable solution to remedy the relevant defects. It is likely in any event that the FTT would direct the production of draft ROs as part of early case management.

In *Waite* (see **14.1**), the FTT applied the approach taken in the High Court in *Blue Manchester Ltd.* v. *North West Ground Rents Ltd.* [2019] EWHC 142 (TCC), [2019] L&TR 13, in making a flexible order with a 'liberty to apply' provision. *Blue Manchester* was a claim for specific performance of a landlord's repairing obligations. HHJ Stephen Davies set a 'realistic' time for the landlord to comply with the order and included a liberty to apply paragraph if investigation and analysis led to the discovery that a different remedial scheme was more practicable. In *Blue Manchester Ltd.* v. *North West Ground Rents Ltd.* [2020] EWHC 2777 (TCC), the landlord did subsequently apply for, but failed to obtain, permission to carry out different works. HHJ Stephen Davies identified the comparative practicability, cost, and timeframe of the works originally ordered and the works which the landlord proposed to carry out in reaching his decision. It is expected that these factors would be persuasive should a landlord return to the FTT to propose variation of the RO.

The FTT only has jurisdiction under s.123 to make orders to remedy specified relevant defects. The leaseholders in *Waite* sought relief which exceeded that ambit, in the form of requiring a specification of works to be approved by the leaseholders, obtaining independent reports on the works following completion, and compensation for being unable to sell their flats. The FTT decided they had no power to grant this relief. To circumvent the potential difficulty regarding jurisdiction to order post-works reports, the FTT specified a desired outcome for the works, namely: 'At the very least, a post-Works Fire Risk Appraisal of External Walls (FRAEW) pursuant to PAS 9980:2022 should not prevent a satisfactory Form EWS1: External Wall Fire Review from being issued.'

The ability of leaseholders to ascertain whether a relevant landlord has complied with the terms of an RO is likely to be a problem requiring judicial guidance. Given that there will be circumstances in which the relevant landlord will not be able to recover the costs of the works from leaseholders, there will be situations in which a relevant landlord has no incentive to comply with LTA 1985, s.20 and share information and allow the leaseholders to make representations.

14.2.6 Enforcement

BSA 2022, s.123(7) provides that ROs are enforceable with the permission of the county court in the same way as an order of that court. County court enforcement is dealt with in **Chapter 21**.

14.3 REMEDIATION CONTRIBUTION ORDERS

An inevitable corollary of BSA 2022, Part 5 and Sched.8 is that freeholders, landlords, and others with repairing and maintenance obligations in respect of relevant buildings may not be able to fund remediation works. RCOs were envisaged as a way to make funding available for such works. Their main use is to enable freeholders and landlords to recover costs already paid in respect of remedying relevant defects or forward-fund projects, and in particular to allow the movement of funds from better-capitalised associated companies where the freeholders or landlords were deliberately structured to have few assets. However, the Explanatory Notes also contemplate at para.1012 a more restitutionary remedy of leaseholders recovering service charges they would not have had to pay had Part 5 and Sched.8 come into effect earlier, and that was indeed the case in *Batish* (see **14.1**).

BSA 2022, s.124(2) defines an RCO in relation to a relevant building as:

> an order requiring a specified body corporate or partnership to make payments to a specified person, for the purpose of meeting costs incurred or to be incurred in remedying relevant defects (or specified relevant defects) relating to the relevant building.

At the time of writing, *Batish* is the only known decision on an application for an RCO. It should, however, be borne in mind when considering *Batish* that the issues were not fully argued because the respondent landlord failed to submit a statement of case and was debarred from taking further part in the proceedings, and no party was represented by solicitors or counsel.

Triathlon Homes, however, was fully argued with experienced property and construction counsel on both sides, and decided by the Chamber President and Deputy Chamber President of the Upper Tribunal sitting as judges of the FTT. Its influence will be significant.

14.3.1 Interested persons

BSA 2022, s.123(5) lists interested persons as follows:

> (a) the regulator (as defined by section 2),
> (b) a local authority (as defined by section 30) for the area in which the relevant building is situated,
> (c) a fire and rescue authority (as defined by section 30) for the area in which the relevant building is situated,

(d) a person with a legal or equitable interest in the relevant building or any part of it, or
(e) any other person prescribed by regulations.

The 859 Regulations, reg.2A add the Homes and Communities Agency, the named manager, the RMC and the RTM company in relation to the relevant building as interested persons.

The Explanatory Notes provide worked examples of applications for RCOs at para.1020, which involve a freeholder applying against the parent company of the developer and the fire and rescue authority applying against a freeholder's parent company. *Batish*, the only decision at the time of writing, involved leaseholders applying against a freeholder. Whether entities without a proprietary interest in the relevant building will make use of RCOs is yet to be seen. The decision in *Priory Heights* (see **14.2.4**) suggests that local authorities should consider RCOs when deciding how to act in respect of Category 2 (if not Category 1) hazards concerning fire safety.

14.3.2 Specified body corporate or partnership

RCOs can only be made against a specified body corporate or partnership. An order cannot be made against an individual.

BSA 2022, s.124(3) provides that a body corporate or partnership will be specified only if it is:

(a) a landlord under a lease of the relevant building or any part of it,
(b) a person who was such a landlord at the qualifying time,
(c) a developer in relation to the relevant building, or
(d) a person associated with a person within any of paragraphs (a) to (c).

BSA 2022, s.124(5) defines 'developer' as 'in relation to a relevant building ... a person who undertook or commissioned the construction or conversion of the building (or part of the building) with a view to granting or disposing of interests in the building or parts of it'. 'Associated' and 'partnership' are defined in BSA 2022, s.121 and discussed in **Chapter 18**. The inclusion of associated persons is a recognition of the use of group structures with freeholders of limited capital and income and special purpose vehicles which may have been wound up after the development.

14.3.3 Relevant building

The term 'relevant building' is defined in BSA 2022, s.117, but is modified by BSA 2022, s.124(6) insofar as the Secretary of State may by regulations provide that s.124 applies, with or without modifications, in relation to a building that would, but for s.117(3), be a relevant building. Section 117(3) excludes buildings in respect of which tenants have exercised their right of first refusal or collective enfranchisement, which are leaseholder owned, or which are on commonhold land. The Explanatory Notes explain at para.1007 that the effect of s.124(6) is to allow for the possibility of interested persons in these buildings applying for RCOs in future.

The Secretary of State has exercised this power in the 711 Regulations, reg.4, subject to two modifications.

1. The following may not be specified as a body corporate or partnership for the purposes of s.124(3):
   (a) a landlord under a lease of the relevant building or any part of it where that landlord is a company owned in part or in full by a majority of residential leaseholders of the building;
   (b) person who was such a landlord at the qualifying time; or
   (c) a commonhold association, within the meaning of the Commonhold and Leasehold Reform Act 2002, s.34.
2. Section 124(5) applies as if a special measures manager (SMM) within the meaning of BSA 2022, Sched.7, para.4(2) were an interested person.

14.3.4 Making an application

Applications for RCOs are in Form BSA2.

14.3.5 The principles to be applied

The FTT can make an RCO where it is 'just and equitable to do so'. The Act does not gloss this test further and the expectation appears to be that the FTT should consider all the circumstances of the case, including the public interest in securing the safety of buildings. The same phrase is used in applications under LTA 1985, s.20C, and case law regarding that provision may prove to be of some assistance. That jurisdiction is wide and fact-sensitive, but in *Conway* v. *Jam Factory Freehold Ltd.* [2013] UKUT 592 (LC), the Deputy President held that the essential consideration is the practical and financial consequences for all those who would be affected by the order. For a more in-depth discussion, see Tanfield Chambers, *Service Charges and Management* (5th Edn, Sweet & Maxwell, 2021), 15-08ff.

In *Batish* (see **14.1**), which involved leaseholders applying for an RCO in respect of service charges paid for the purpose of meeting costs incurred or to be incurred in remedying relevant defects, the FTT said at [48] of the 'just and equitable' condition: 'We take the view that in order to satisfy the condition in this case we must be satisfied that the lessees paid for the cost of works which ought to have been met by Inspired Sutton Limited.' This logic appears, with respect, to be redundant; if the costs were not paid in respect of works to remedy relevant defects which ought to have been funded by the landlord, then the 'purpose' element of the definition of RCO would not be satisfied and the question of just and equitable would not arise.

The FTT also suggested at [50] that there could have been mitigations or other matters to be taken into account before deciding the terms of the order, but nothing had been advanced on behalf of the landlord. It is not immediately clear what the FTT had in mind when referring to mitigations, but the ability to apply to the Building Safety Fund (BSF) may be a relevant factor.

Regardless, the meaning of 'just and equitable' in the context of different interested persons and specified bodies corporate and partnerships cannot mean the same as in *Batish*, and case law will be required to elaborate the principles.

RCOs may be made for meeting costs 'to be incurred' in remedying relevant defects and the wording is clearly wide enough to cover the situation where the quantum is yet to be known with precision. Case law in the context of provisional loss may assist with ascertaining the precision with which the interested person may need to make their case: see in particular the discussion of certainty of damages in *McGregor on Damages* (21st Edn, Sweet & Maxwell, 2022), 10-001ff.

Guidance is needed from the Tribunal as to the extent to which RCOs are limited to the cost of works properly so-called or whether necessary ancillary costs, for example management fees and the costs of rehousing leaseholders if the works require vacant possession, are included. It seems that the inclusion of management fees is arguable by analogy with *London Borough of Southwark* v. *Paul* [2013] UKUT 375 (LC), in which the Upper Tribunal held in respect of service charges that overheads in the form of management fees can be reasonably incurred.

Triathlon Homes contains extensive analysis of 'just and equitable' from [236] onwards. Relevant factors include the respondent being the original developer [265], the respondent being a wealthy associated company behind which a thinly capitalised development company can hide [266], whether remediation work can be completed with or without the money [267], and shortfalls in BSF funding [268]. Irrelevant factors included the applicant's motivation [246], the fact that other parties could have been the subject of applications [248], the changing identity of ultimate beneficial owners [251], and the date when any costs to remedy relevant defects were incurred [281]. The case also gives a wide construction to 'costs incurred or to be incurred in remedying relevant defects', in that costs incurred in preventing risks from materialising or in reducing the severity of building safety incidents are included [122].

14.3.6 The order

RCOs are defined in BSA 2022, s.124(2). There is no requirement that the recipient of sums under an RCO be the applicant or be an interested person themselves, and it is evident from the list of specified persons that some applications will be made by interested persons which lack the ability to carry out works to the relevant building, such that they should not be the receiving party.

BSA 2022, s.124(4) provides:

> An order may –
>
> (a) require the making of payments of a specified amount, or payments of a reasonable amount in respect of the remediation of specified relevant defects (or in respect of specified things done or to be done for the purpose of remedying relevant defects);
>
> (b) require a payment to be made at a specified time, or to be made on demand following the occurrence of a specified event.

As with ROs, the word 'specified' means 'specified in the order'. It would therefore be prudent to consider submitting a draft RCO to the FTT at an early stage in the proceedings to ensure that the relevant defects or event which triggers the payment are included in the order with sufficient accuracy and precision.

RCOs may be subject to conditions. In *Triathlon Homes*, the FTT imposed a term that the recipient repay the contribution in the event of a successful claim against third parties. The FTT derived assistance from the principles relating to applications to dispense with consultation requirements in section 20ZA of the LTA 1985, and seemed to leave open the possibility of imposing conditions relating to the costs of the proceedings.

14.3.7 Enforcement

By the Tribunals, Courts and Enforcement Act 2007, s.27, sums payable pursuant to an RCO are recoverable as if they were payable under an order of a county court in England and Wales. Reference is again made to **Chapter 21** for more detail.

CHAPTER 15

Building liability orders and information orders

Christy Burzio

15.1 INTRODUCTION

The Act has introduced measures which aim to prevent contractors and developers from circumventing liability for development projects.

It is not unusual for special purpose vehicles, subsidiary 'shell' companies or joint ventures with very few assets to be used to develop sites. Hitherto these entities (referred to by the Act as 'the original body') have assisted in isolating risk and averting liability if the construction works are deemed defective post-completion of the project. The company that manages and owns the development is often wound up once the development is completed, and after the freehold has been sold off. A consequence of this practice is that the corporate group has no long-term liability for its developments.

Building liability orders (BLOs) introduced by the Act aim to suppress this practice by extending the liability of the original body to 'associated' body corporates and making them jointly and severally liable. The effect will be that a claimant can sue both A (the original body) and B (the associated entity) and, if the claim is successful, the assets of both A and B can be considered when damages are awarded (BSA 2022, Explanatory Note, para.1063). The solvency of the original body and associated body corporates and the degree of contribution made by each entity are factors to be taken into account when deciding whether to make a BLO.

The Act also makes provision for information orders (Ios) to prevent companies using complex and opaque structures to prevent a building owner, landlord or leaseholder from being able to prove how companies are associated, and therefore undermine the intended outcome of BLOs. They provide a tool for a party to obtain information to support their application for a BLO and thus obtain adequate recompense to correct building safety defects.

15.2 BUILDING LIABILITY ORDERS

15.2.1 The statutory framework

BSA 2022, s.130 introduces BLOs in the following terms.

Building liability orders

(1) The High Court may make a building liability order if it considers it just and equitable to do so.

(2) A 'building liability order' is an order providing that any relevant liability (or any relevant liability of a specified description) of a body corporate ('the original body') relating to a specified building is also –

(a) a liability of a specified body corporate, or
(b) a joint and several liability of two or more specified bodies corporate.

(3) In this section 'relevant liability' means a liability (whether arising before or after commencement) that is incurred –

(a) under the Defective Premises Act 1972 or section 38 of the Building Act 1984, or
(b) as a result of a building safety risk.

(4) A body corporate may be specified only if it is, or has at any time in the relevant period been, associated with the original body.

(5) A building liability order –

(a) may be made in respect of a liability of a body corporate that has been dissolved (including where dissolution occurred before commencement);
(b) continues to have effect even if the body corporate is dissolved after the making of the order.

(6) In this section –

'associate': see section 131;
'building safety risk', in relation to a building, means a risk to the safety of people in or about the building arising from the spread of fire or structural failure;
'commencement' means the time this section comes into force;
'the relevant period' means the period –

(a) beginning with the beginning of the carrying out of the works in relation to which the relevant liability was incurred, and
(b) ending with the making of the order;

'specified' means specified in the building liability order.

15.2.2 The original body and relevant liability

A BLO is an order providing that any relevant liability of the original body relating to a specified building is also a liability of another body corporate, or a joint and several liability of two or more bodies corporate, who are associated with the original body.

The Act does not define or limit the types of business that may be an 'original body', and consequently there is potentially a wide range of entities that could be caught. This could include contractors and sub-contractors, designers, architects, engineers, and other professionals (*Lessees and Management Company of Herons Court* v. *Heronslea Ltd. And others* [2019] EWCA Civ 1423).

BSA 2022, s.130(3) defines which liabilities are relevant liabilities for the purposes of BLOs:

- under DPA 1972;
- under BA 1984, s.38;
- as a result of a building safety risk.

BA 1984, s.38 creates a new cause of action which applies to any buildings for damage suffered because of a breach of building regulations. This provision was meant to be brought into force shortly after the coming into force of the Act. However, at the time of writing this has not occurred, and it remains unclear when and in what form it will become law.

BSA 2022, s.130(6) defines a BSR as a 'risk to the safety of people in or about the building arising from the spread of fire or structural failure'.

Apart from liability arising out of DPA 1972, which relates to the provision and refurbishment of 'dwellings', there is no constraint on the types of works and buildings which might incur a relevant liability under s.130(3) (see BSA 2022, Explanatory Note, para.1065). As noted above, BA 1984, s.38 allows claims in respect of any works or buildings. Likewise, the term 'building safety risk' as defined by the Act does not suggest any limitation on the categories of building to which the risk must relate. A BLO can therefore extend to commercial properties.

15.2.3 Limitation and the relevant period

BSA 2022, s.130 has both retrospective and prospective effect. BLOs can be made in respect of relevant liabilities that were incurred by the original body either before or after the Act came into force on 28 June 2022, provided that the limitation period for the relevant liability has not expired (see BSA 2022, Explanatory Note, para.1066). This suggests that where the claimant has lost the right to pursue the original body because of the passage of time it cannot pursue an associated entity using s.130.

Neither BA 1984, s.38 nor DPA 1974, s.2A were in force before 28 June 2022, therefore the only liabilities that could be incurred prior to 28 June 2022 are under DPA 1972, s.1 or in relation to BSRs.

BSA 2022, s.135 makes several changes to extend the limitation periods in respect of actions under DPA 1972, s.1, BA 1984, s.38, and DPA 1972, s.2A (see BSA 2022, s.134). These changes to limitation periods are achieved by the insertion of a new s.4B into the Limitation Act 1980.

The Limitation Act 1980, s.4B extends the limitation period under DPA 1972, s.1 to 30 years retrospectively and 15 years prospectively. This means that relevant work completed prior to the commencement of this section will be subject to a 30-year limitation period, and work completed after commencement will be subject to a 15-year limitation period.

The section also provides for a 15-year limitation period for claims under BA 1984, s.38 and DPA 1972, s.2A. These changes will apply prospectively only. BSA 2022, s.135(4) states that, in respect of DPA 1972, s.1, where a revived limitation period would last for less than one year, it will instead last for one full year (known as 'the initial period'), in order to give potential claimants the necessary time to take advice and lodge a claim.

Where a limitation period is extended retrospectively s.135 sets out two safeguards to ensure fairness in the proceedings. First, s.135(5) provides that, where an action is brought that, but for the retrospectivity provision in subsection (3), would have been barred by the Limitation Act 1980, a court hearing the action must dismiss it if it is necessary to do so to avoid a breach of a defendant's convention rights,[1] the court must dismiss the claim. Second, s.135(6) provides that, where a claim has previously been dismissed or otherwise concluded (for example, by settlement), the extended limitation period will not, of itself, be sufficient to reopen the claim.

As per BSA 2022, s.130(4), BLOs may be granted against associates of the original body if they were associated with the original body at any time within the relevant period. BSA 2022, s.130(6) defines the relevant period as (a) the beginning of the carrying out of the works in relation to which the relevant liability was incurred, and (b) ending with the making of the order.

As noted above, limitation periods have been substantially extended by the Act. The relevant period could extend over many years. Therefore, BLOs may be granted against entities that were associated with the original body and have since been disposed of or sold prior to the BLO being sought, or against entities that were incorporated or acquired after the works were carried out. These factors are likely to impact on whether a court finds it just and equitable to grant a BLO.

15.2.4 Associates

BSA 2022, s.131 expands the reach of BSA 2022, s.130 in the following terms.

Building liability orders: associates

(1) For the purposes of section 130, a body corporate (A) is associated with another body corporate (B) if –

(a) one of them controls the other, or

[1] BSA 2022, s.135(7) provides that 'Convention rights' has the same meaning as in the Human Rights Act 1998. See *URS Corporation Ltd.* v. *BDW Trading Ltd.* [2023] EWCA Civ 772 at [151]–[172].

(b) a third body corporate controls both of them.

BSA 2022, s.131(2)–(4) sets out the cases in which a body corporate is regarded as controlling another body corporate.

(2) A body corporate (X) controls a company (Y) if X possesses or is entitled to acquire –

(a) at least half of the issued share capital of Y,
(b) such rights as would entitle X to exercise at least half of the votes exercisable in general meetings of Y,
(c) such part of the issued share capital of Y as would entitle X to at least half of the amount distributed, if the whole of the income of Y were in fact distributed among the shareholders, or
(d) such rights as would, in the event of the winding up of Y or in any other circumstances, entitle it to receive at least half of the assets of Y which would then be available for distribution among the shareholders.

(3) A body corporate (X) controls a limited liability partnership (Y) if X –

(a) holds a majority of the voting rights in Y,
(b) is a member of Y and has a right to appoint or remove a majority of other members, or
(c) is a member of Y and controls alone, or pursuant to an agreement with other members, a majority of the voting rights in Y.

(4) A body corporate (X) controls another body corporate (Y) if X has the power, directly or indirectly, to secure that the affairs of Y are conducted in accordance with X's wishes.

(5) In subsection (3) a reference to 'voting rights' is to the rights conferred on members in respect of their interest in a limited liability partnership to vote on those matters which are to be decided on by a vote of the members of the limited liability partnership.

(6) In determining under any of subsections (2) to (4) whether one body corporate (X) controls another, X is treated as possessing –

(a) any rights and powers possessed by a person as nominee for it, and
(b) any rights and powers possessed by a body corporate which it controls (including rights and powers which such a body corporate would be taken to possess by virtue of this paragraph).

(7) For the purposes of section 130 as it applies in relation to a building, where a person's interest in the building is held on trust, a body corporate which is a beneficiary of the trust is to be regarded as associated with the person.

The concept of 'association' generally is the subject of **Chapter 18**; what follows is a summary relating to BLOs only.

Associated bodies corporate for the purpose of a BLO are bodies corporate where:

- one of them controls the other, or
- a third body corporate controls both of them.

The terms body corporate and limited liability partnerships are undefined in the Act. The Act does not refer to the Limited Liability Partnership Act 2000 or use terminology familiar from the Companies Act 2006 (parent company, subsidiary, undertaking or holding company). According to the Act's Explanatory Notes, the definitions are based on the Petroleum Act 1998 and the Corporation Tax Act 2010 (BSA 2022, Explanatory Note, para.1087[2]). Further, at s.130 and s.131 the Act refers only to corporate bodies, which indicates that BLOs cannot be sought against natural persons associated with the original body.

Sections 131(2)–(6) are concerned with the question of control. By focusing on control and not form, the Act effectively pierces the corporate veil to prevent developers from escaping liability in relation to the relevant liabilities.

Section 131(2) provides that a body corporate controls a company in four specified scenarios. The Act targets companies that have at least half of the associate's share capital or assets or may exercise half of the votes exercisable at the associate's general meeting. The focus is therefore on financial and/or decisive influence.

As with the broad application of the term 'original body', the provisions of the Act regarding the term 'associate' are broad enough to extend beyond group companies. Lenders of the original development company may take a large share security over the company and could be caught. However, the Building Safety (Responsible Actors Scheme and Prohibitions) Regulations 2023, SI 2023/753 expressly provide that a bank, financial institution, trust fund or other entity is not to be treated as a member of the same group by reason of the provision and terms of such debt financing and any associated security or collateral arrangements. While the cited regulation and the Act serve differing purposes, a court may be hesitant to deem a lender as an associate and would likely find that it would not be just and equitable to grant a BLO against it (see below).

Section 131(3) provides that a body corporate (X) controls a limited liability partnership if: X has a majority of the voting rights; X is a member and can appoint or remove a majority of other members; or X is a member and controls a majority of the voting rights (whether alone or by agreement with others).

Section 131(4) stands as the general catch-all provision that extends the concept of control beyond formal voting rights and focuses on the affairs of the targeted entities. While a broader test, it may be difficult for claimants to amass convincing evidence as to the internal affairs between the original body and the associate.

To be an associated body corporate, A must have been associated with B any time after the commencement of the works as a result of which the relevant liability was incurred and before the BLO is made. Consequently, the sale of projects or companies will not diminish the High Court's ability to grant a BLO against both sellers and purchasers. We are therefore likely to see greater due diligence in the purchase of companies that have been involved in the construction of projects that could incur the relevant liabilities.

2 See the Petroleum Act 1998, ss.30 and 41 and Corporation Tax Act 2010, ss.528ZA(4), 553, 617, 935, 976, 1066, 1099, 1121, 1124, 1154–1156.

A court may choose to make a BLO against an associated company based overseas, which would be enforced in the normal manner for enforcement against an overseas company.

15.2.5 Just and equitable

The court will grant a BLO order if it considers it 'just and equitable' to so do.

The Act does not provide any guidance on what will be regarded as 'just and equitable' and as such the concept will be developed on a case-by-case basis. The same phrase, used in s.124, was given extensive consideration in *Triathlon Homes*, and many of the conclusions arrived at there are likely to apply equally to its use in s.130.

During the debates in the House of Lords (Hansard, House of Lords: 29 May 2022: Lords Chambers: Building Safety Bill, Cols.1468–1469), it was suggested that the court will assess how to apportion responsibility based on the 'polluter/perpetrator pays principle' (Hansard, House of Lords: 29 May 2022: Lords Chambers: Building Safety Bill, Col.1474). It is suggested that the following non-exhaustive factors may be taken into account:

- the nature, extent and severity of the defects;
- whether the defects pose a significant and continuing risk;
- the claimant's interest in the affected property;
- the extent of the damages sought;
- whether a fair trial can take place;
- whether the claimant has an alternative method of recourse (like insurance);
- the solvency of the original body and the associate entities;
- whether the associated company (a) was incorporated or acquired after the works were carried out, (b) benefited from the original body's work, or (c) was in any way involved in the works;
- whether the original body was liable, or could be liable, to another party in respect of the defects;
- whether the claimant itself was liable, or could be liable, to another party in respect of the defects;
- the prejudice caused to the associated company if it were to be issued with a BLO;
- the extent to which the BLO will serve the purpose of the legislation (see BSA 2022, s.1(1)).

15.3 INFORMATION ORDERS

BSA 2022, s.132 enables a prescribed person to apply to the High Court for information about a company subject to a relevant liability, requiring it to provide specified information or documents relating to parties who are or have at any time in a specified period been associated with it.

15.3.1 Statutory framework

BSA 2022, s.132 introduces information orders (IOs) in the following terms.

> **Order for information in connection with building liability order**
>
> (1) A person of a prescribed description may apply to the High Court for an information order.
>
> (2) An 'information order' is an order requiring a specified body corporate to give, by a specified time, specified information or documents relating to persons who are, or have at any time in a specified period been, associated with the body corporate.
>
> (3) An information order may be made only if it appears to the court –
>
> (a) that the body corporate is subject to a relevant liability (within the meaning of section 130), and
>
> (b) that it is appropriate to require the information or documents to be provided for the purpose of enabling the applicant (or the applicant and others) to make, or consider whether to make, an application for a building liability order.
>
> (4) In this section –
>
> 'associate': section 131 applies for the purposes of this section as it applies for the purposes of section 130;
> 'building liability order': see section 130;
> 'prescribed' means prescribed by regulations made by the Secretary of State;
> 'specified' means specified in the information order.

15.3.2 The application

An IO can be applied for by a 'person of a prescribed description'. The 711 Regulations, reg 12 provides that 'any person making, or intending to make, an application for a building liability order under section 130 of the Act may apply to the High Court for an information order'.

Prior to applying, claimants should obtain readily available documentary evidence such as the articles of association, confirmation statements, persons with significant control, and the companies register of members if available through Companies House. The availability of such evidence will depend on the original body and associates' level of transparency and organisation, specifically regarding its reporting obligations.

IOs may be made if 'it appears to the court' that (a) the original body is subject to the relevant liability, and (b) it is appropriate to require the information or documents to be provided for the purpose of the claimant pursuing or intending to pursue a BLO.

The request for information should align with the necessary factors outlined in BSA 2022, ss.131(2)–(7) (see **15.2.4**).

15.3.3 Overseas companies

A court may choose to make an IO in respect of a company based overseas if it is an associated company. In practice the provisions of the Economic Crime (Transparency and Enforcement) Act 2022, which requires overseas entities to register certain details (including the identity of the beneficial owners) to Companies House, may prove helpful in this regard.[3]

15.3.4 The order

The order will require an entity to provide specified information or documents related to associates of the original body within a certain time.

Each application will turn on its facts and claimants should be able to determine precisely what information or documents ought to be provided to assist in making or deciding whether to make an application for a BLO.

15.4 A COMBINED APPROACH

The Act provides that a BLO and IO may be made by the High Court in England and Wales.

The example provided in the Explanatory Notes (paras.1074 and 1096) is where a claim under DPA 1972 is stifled as the original body is dissolved. The claimant suspects the parent company is associated and they pursue a BLO to obtain damages. However, the claimant is currently unable to show the parent company is associated to the degree necessary to be granted a BLO. The claimant in this instance applies to the High Court for an IO to be applied to the parent company. The claimant must show that they intend to seek damages under the relevant liability and that an IO could support them in applying for a BLO. In this scenario, the IO is granted, and the parent shares the necessary information. The claimant now has the information required to show the parent company directly controlled the actions of the original body. The claimant can then apply for a BLO to support them in making a claim under DPA 1972 against the parent company.

While the example foresees IOs and BLOs being utilised pre-action, there is no restriction on a claimant applying during proceedings against the original body to join the associated entity to the claim, or doing so post judgment.

[3] Examples of overseas company registers include, Canada (Corporations Canada), France (Infogreffe and INPI), Germany (Unternehmensregister), Italy (registroimprese.it), Republic of Ireland (Companies Registration Office) and Spain (Registro Mercantil de España). The European e-Justice Portal has a 'Find a Company' website, however not all member states are currently connected. In the USA, company incorporation/registration is the responsibility of state governments. The main federal repository of company information is the SEC's Electronic Data Gathering, Analysis, and Retrieval (EDGAR) database.

CHAPTER 16

Architects

Andrew Butler KC

16.1 INTRODUCTION

A little-heralded corner of the Act, from ss.157–159, makes provision for certain changes to the regulatory regime for architects. This set of provisions came into force on 28 June 2022 and consists of certain amendments to the Architects Act (AA) 1997.

16.2 DISCIPLINE AND CONTINUING PROFESSIONAL DEVELOPMENT

BSA 2022, s.157 is concerned with discipline and continuing professional development.

The first change is the insertion into AA 1997 of a new s.3(2A). This requires the Register of Architects to show disciplinary orders made in relation to a registered person. As the Explanatory Note sets out, the thinking here is to provide greater transparency to members of the public procuring architectural services. The Register is accessible through the website of the Architect Registration Board.

Disciplinary orders are to be shown 'for such period as may be prescribed'. No secondary legislation prescribing any particular periods has been made, but the Architects' Registration Board (ARB) appears to have taken the initiative here. Its Rules have been updated to provide that a reprimand will show from one year from the date of decision, a penalty order for two years from the date of decision, and a suspension order for two years from the end of the period of suspension.

Section 157 then proceeds to implement certain changes to AA 1997, s.9, which is concerned with competence to practice. Section 9(1) is amended so that a lack of recent training is added to a lack of recent practical experience as a ground for the ARB to decline to enter, or re-enter, a person's name onto the Register (or to remove a person's name from it). A new s.9(1A) is then introduced as a corollary to this, requiring the Board to consult representative bodies such as the Royal Institute of British Architects (RIBA) before prescribing what recent practical experience or training should be required.

The final change made by s.157 is to introduce a new ss.9(3) and (4) to AA 1997. The effect of these provisions is to give to an architect whose name the ARB has decided to remove from the Register a right to apply for an extension of time to attain the prescribed recent practical experience or training (as the case may be), or to satisfy the ARB in some other way of their competence to practise. Furthermore, the ARB is enjoined from removing the person's name from the Register unless either that person has not applied for an extension, or has applied but the ARB declined to grant an extension, or an extension was granted but expired without the ARB being satisfied of any the matters just described.

The phrase 'competent to practise' for the purposes of these sections is defined as having the skills, knowledge, experience and behaviours required for a person to practise as an architect (see AA 1997, s.9(4), introduced by BSA 2022, s.157(3)(c)).

16.3 ARCHITECT'S APPEALS COMMITTEE

The enhanced grounds for removal from the Register, and the preservation of an architect's disciplinary history on it, are clearly serious matters, and the Act has therefore introduced associated safeguards. One such safeguard was encountered in the previous section: the right to apply for an extension of time to convince the ARB of fitness to practise. BSA 2022, s.158 introduces another safeguard, in the form of a right to appeal decisions of the Registrar to a newly-created Appeals Committee.

The Appeals Committee is created by the insertion of a new s.1(2A) into AA 1997, and a new Part 2A into AA 1997, Sched.1. The former provision simply provides that there is to be an Appeals Committee. The latter provision empowers the ARB to make rules about the composition, membership and rules of that Committee, but provides that it must consult the Secretary of State before doing so. Such a consultation has evidently taken place, as the Rules are in force and can be found on the ARB's website (**https://arb.org.uk/wp-content/uploads/Appeals-Committee-Rules-FINAL-FOR-IMPLEMENTATION.pdf**).

The creation of the Appeals Committee required some minor consequential changes to AA 1997. For example, the Registrar, on being dissatisfied of an applicant's fitness to be registered, was previously required to refer the matter to the ARB. Now they must refuse the application (so as to engage the right of appeal – see BSA 2022, s.158(3)(a), substituting words into AA 1997, s.4(4)(b)). And, where the ARB itself decides that the name of a person who wishes their name to be retained or re-entered in the Register should not be so entitled, it must give reasons for that decision (see BSA 2022, s.158(5), adding s.9(2A) to AA 1997).

A more significant change is the introduction, by BSA 2022, s.158(6), of a new s.21A into AA 1997, which confers the statutory right of appeal to the Appeals Committee. An appeal now lies against a decision to refuse a person's application for registration, or a decision to remove (or not to re-enter) a person's name in the Register as a result of a decision by the Board that the person has not gained sufficient recent practical experience and/or training.

Section 21A(2) confers a power on the Board to make rules about certain aspects of the appeal process, including time limits, mode of proceeding, fees, procedure and interim orders – these are the same Rules as are referred to above. Section 21A(3) gives the Appeal Committee power to make any decision which could have been made by the original decision-maker (whether the Board or the Registrar). Section 21(4) provides that the Appeal Committee must communicate its decision within a prescribed time limit, which the Rules set at seven days. It is unclear what the remedy would be for a failure to comply with this requirement. However, it is at least arguable, in the writer's opinion, that it could, at the appellant's election, vitiate the process and necessitate a rehearing.

The remainder of BSA 2022, s.158 makes changes to AA 1997, s.22, essentially providing a right of appeal to the High Court (or in Scotland, the Court of Session) from a decision of the Appeals Committee. A right of appeal to those courts has always been available under AA 1997, but obviously under the previous regime this was from decisions of the ARB or Registrar, as opposed to from the Appeals Committee. A direct right of appeal to those courts (i.e. bypassing the Appeals Committee) still arises from a failure on the part of the Registrar to serve a written notice of a decision on an application for registration under AA 1997, s.6(4).

16.4 FEES

Finally, BSA 2022, s.159 makes provision for a new s.24A to be inserted into AA 1997. This allows the Secretary of State to make regulation for the charging of fees by the Board in respect of the services which it provides.

The Explanatory Note gives the following commentary on this provision, at para.1343:

> Currently, the Architects Act 1997 prescribes a small amount of services for which the Board may charge. The costs of all of the Board's functions are currently met by the annual fee for retention on the Register of Architects under section 8 of the 1997 Act, which is charged by the Board to all architects. Following the end of the EU Exit Transition Period, there will be an expansion in the services the Board provides to implement Mutual Recognition Agreements or Memoranda of Understanding relating to the regulation of architects. This section will allow the Secretary of State to lay regulations to make additional provision for separate fees for additional chargeable services, in order to keep the retention fee down for the architects that do not utilise additional services. This will be after a full impact assessment and consultation.

Little more need be said about this provision, which seems from the commentary to be related more to Brexit than to matters of building safety. No regulations under this provision have been made.

CHAPTER 17

Construction product claims

Ceri Edmonds

17.1 INTRODUCTION

This chapter considers the various remedies introduced by the Act in relation to construction products.

Buyers of new build properties have a number of options if their homes are defective, including breach of contract claims against the sellers or claims against developers under DPA 1972, s.1 for breach of the statutory duty to ensure that construction work is undertaken in a workmanlike manner so that the dwelling is fit for habitation. BSA 2022 has also inserted a new s.2A into DPA 1972, imposing a similar duty in relation to later, post-construction works. But these do not necessarily assist a property owner who discovers that their home has been built with products that are defective, for example if they pose a fire risk. The products may have been correctly installed in a workmanlike manner by contractors or developers who were not aware of the defects, and the homeowner is unlikely to have any direct contractual relationship with the supplier or manufacturer of the products.

The Act seeks to address this by creating a new cause of action, allowing a property owner to sue a manufacturer or supplier of sub-standard construction products in certain circumstances. For cladding products, there is also a separate provision imposing retrospective liability.

The Act also introduces provision for regulations, as yet unmade, which would allow the court and/or the Secretary of State to order the manufacturer or supplier to contribute towards the costs of remedial works (i.e. to make a costs contribution order (CCO)).

This is one of the few parts of the Act that also applies to Scotland (BSA 2022, ss.169(2) and (5)) and some parts extend also to Northern Ireland. This chapter deals primarily with how the Act applies in England and Wales.

17.2 NEW CAUSE OF ACTION FOR FAULTY OR UNSUITABLE CONSTRUCTION PRODUCTS

17.2.1 Overview

The new right to bring a claim is set out in BSA 2022, s.148, which came into force on 28 June 2022. Broadly speaking, it arises where a faulty product is installed during the course of building works, and it renders all or some of the dwellings unfit for habitation. Claims can be brought by lessees or by landlords/building owners against the manufacturer or, if a supplier has made a misleading statement, against the supplier.

The section is somewhat strangely worded and sets out four 'conditions' (A to D) that have to be satisfied. The conditions are set out fully below in **17.2.2**, but in summary are:

- Condition A: after 28 June 2022, a person breaches a regulatory requirement, makes a misleading statement about a construction product they are selling, or manufactures a defective construction product.
- Condition B: the construction product is then used in building works.
- Condition C: when those works are completed, the building is unfit for habitation.
- Condition D: as a result, the building is unfit for habitation.

The person who has committed the breach in Condition A (i.e. the manufacturer, marketer or supplier) is liable to pay damages to a person with a relevant interest in the building, or in any dwelling in the building. It appears from the wording of the Act that BSA 2022, s.147 imposes a strict liability (the defaulter 'is' rather than 'may be' liable). The parties cannot contract out of this liability (BSA 2022, s.148(7)).

Damages are payable in relation to personal injury, damage to property or economic loss suffered as a result of the building or dwelling being unfit for habitation (BSA 2022, s.148(6)). This would appear to include claims for loss of rent as well as the diminution in value. It is not clear that they would cover the costs of remediation works where these exceeded the cost of the diminution in value. In such cases it would appear that a CCO would be of more assistance, as described below at **17.5**.

The various definitions are discussed at **17.2.3–17.2.7**.

17.2.2 The conditions for a construction product claim

All four conditions, A to D, must be met before liability will arise.

Condition A

Condition A is set out in BSA 2022, s.148(2) as follows:

> ... at any time after [28 June 2022] –
>
> (a) a person fails to comply with a construction product requirement in relation to a construction product,
> (b) a person who markets or supplies a construction product makes a misleading statement in relation to it, or
> (c) a person manufactures a construction product that is inherently defective.

It is clear from the wording of Condition A that s.148 liability will only arise where the breach of regulations, defective manufacture or misleading statement occurs after 28 June 2022. It is not sufficient that the works were carried out after 28 June 2022.

Condition A would appear to include a breach of regulatory requirements in relation to testing products, or any requirements in relation to the labelling, storage or transport of materials. It could also include a misleading statement about the suitability of a product for a particular use, even if the product itself was not inherently defective. There is no requirement in the Act for the misleading statement to have been made knowingly and it would appear that a supplier who is simply mistaken as to the qualities of a product is still liable. It could potentially even apply to multiple parties in the supply chain, including a wholesaler who has relied on a misleading statement by a manufacturer, and a retailer who has in turn relied on the misleading information relayed by the wholesaler.

Condition B

Condition B is contained in BSA 2022, s.148(3) and is as follows:

> ... after Condition A is met, the construction product referred to in subsection (2)(a), (b) or (c) is installed in, or applied or attached to, a relevant building in the course of works carried out in the construction of, or otherwise in relation to, the building.

Condition B refers to 'works carried out in the construction of, or otherwise in relation to, the building'. This is a broad definition and would appear to include the original construction works and any subsequent works on or to a building. The term 'in the course of works' may be intended to exclude liability where a householder installs a product themselves after building works have been completed.

Condition C (where the building or dwelling is unfit for habitation)

Condition C is contained in BSA 2022, s.148(4) and is as follows:

> ... when those works are completed –
>
> (a) in a case where the relevant building consists of a dwelling, the building is unfit for habitation, or
> (b) in a case where the relevant building contains one or more dwellings, a dwelling contained in the building is unfit for habitation.

As discussed at **17.2.3** and **17.2.4**, there is an inconsistency in the description of a relevant building. Although Condition C refers to a case where the relevant building contains one or more buildings, a mixed-use building that contains only one dwelling is not a relevant building for the purposes of s.148. Condition C is not therefore satisfied where the single flat above a shop is unfit for habitation.

Condition D (causation)

Condition D is contained in BSA 2022, s.148(5) and is as follows:

> ... the facts referred to in subsection (2)(a), (b) or (c) were the cause, or one of the causes, of the building or dwelling being unfit for habitation.

Per Condition D, the supply of the defective product does not have to be the sole cause of the building being unfit for habitation. It could be that more than one defective product has been used, or that the wrong product was used (possibly due to a misleading statement) *and* it was defective, or that a defective product has been incorrectly installed, or a combination of all of these.

Similarly, it does not appear that the construction product has to be defective in order for a claim to be brought. Rather, it could simply be unsuitable for the use to which it has been put, where reliance has been placed on a statement by the supplier that the product was suitable (BSA 2022, s.148(2)(b)).

17.2.3 What is a relevant building?

A 'relevant building', for the purposes of construction product claims, is defined in BSA 2022, s.147 as '(a) a building which consists of a dwelling, or (b) a building which contains two or more dwellings'. This is different from the definition used elsewhere in the Act; understandably so, as it is for a different purpose. It would include a single house, or a block of flats, or mixed-use premises that include two or more residential units. As drafted, the definition would not include mixed-use premises that included only one dwelling, such as a shop with a single flat above.

Confusingly, however, the definition of a 'relevant interest' and the wording of 'Condition C' refer to cases where the building contains *one* or more dwellings. There is no obvious explanation for this inconsistency and it may have been a drafting error. Whatever the intention, as currently drafted, a mixed-use premises that contains only one dwelling is not a 'relevant building', even if it is possible to have a 'relevant interest' in it.

17.2.4 Who can bring a claim?

By BSA 2022, s.148(6), damages are payable to a person with a 'relevant interest' in the building. In relation to a building in England and Wales, 'relevant interest' means a legal or equitable interest in the building, where the building consists of a single dwelling, or, where the building contains one or more dwellings, a legal or equitable interest in the building or in any dwelling contained in the building. Potential claimants would therefore include the freehold or leasehold owner of a single house, any lessee of individual flats, mortgagees and freeholders or head-lessees of blocks of flats. It could also apply to developers if they had not yet sold the building. But a Right to Manage (RTM) company or a lessee-owned management company under a tripartite lease could not bring a claim unless they also held a lease of the common parts or had some other legal or equitable interest in the building.

For buildings in Scotland, 'relevant interest' means any right or interest (including a servitude or heritable security) in or over the building or any dwelling contained in the building.

As noted at **17.2.3**, the definition of a 'relevant interest' is inconsistent with the definition of a 'relevant building' and it would appear that it is possible to have a 'relevant interest' in a mixed-use premises that contains a single flat, but that this would not be a 'relevant building'. The owner of the single flat above a shop would not be entitled to damages as they would not be able to meet Conditions B and C, which refer to a 'relevant building'.

17.2.5 What is a construction product?

The Act uses the definition of a 'construction product' provided in EU Regulation No 305/2011 (regulation laying down harmonised conditions for the marketing of construction products), referred to in the Act as 'the 2011 Regulation'.[1] The regime in the 2011 Regulation was brought into UK law, as retained EU law, by the European Union (Withdrawal) Act 2018.

This is a broad definition and covers nearly all products that are incorporated into the structure of a finished building. The 2011 Regulation, Art.2 provides that:

> 'construction product' means any product or kit which is produced and placed on the market for incorporation in a permanent manner in construction works or parts thereof and the performance of which has an effect on the performance of the construction works with respect to the basic requirements for construction works.

The 2011 Regulation also includes definitions of 'kit', 'construction works' and 'performance of a construction product'. These are largely self-explanatory. 'Kit' is 'a construction product placed on the market by a single manufacturer as a set of at least two separate components that need to be put together to be incorporated in the construction works'. Construction works are in turn defined as 'buildings and civil engineering works'. The 'performance of a construction product' means 'the performance related to the relevant essential characteristics, expressed

1 Regulation (EU) No 305/2011 of the European Parliament and of the Council of 9 March 2011 laying down harmonised conditions for the marketing of construction products and repealing Council Directive 89/106/EEC (2011) OJ L 88/5.

by level or class, or in a description', and 'essential characteristics' are in turn defined as 'those characteristics of the construction product which relate to the basic requirements for construction works'.

17.2.6 What are the construction product requirements?

At present, the requirements from construction products come from multiple sources. A 'construction product requirement' is defined in BSA 2022, s.147 and includes a requirement under:

- any regulations made by the Secretary of State under BSA 2022, Sched.11, i.e. future regulatory requirements;
- existing requirements under the 2011 Regulation;
- existing requirements under the Construction Products (Amendment etc.) (EU Exit) Regulations 2019, SI 2019/465 (referred to in the Act as 'the 2019 Regulations').

The Act therefore seeks to bridge the gap between the current and future regulatory requirements, and provides for claims to be brought in relation to either or both.

A detailed consideration of the current regulatory standards covering construction products is outside the scope of this work, but it is worth noting that the system is labyrinthine. Enforcement of the 2011 Regulation is governed by the Construction Products Regulations 2013, SI 2013/1387, and both were amended by the Construction Products (Amendment etc.) (EU Exit) Regulations 2019, SI 2019/465. None of these Regulations sets out the standards, and they refer instead to standards and requirements set out elsewhere. There are over 500 standards referred to in various approved documents.

The regulatory framework for construction products, derived from the 2011 Regulation, covers some but not all of the products placed on the UK market. The framework only applies to products where a designated standard has been adopted or a UK Technical Assessment applies – some 400 product families.

The Hackitt Report (see **Chapter 1**) noted that the current system covering construction product testing, certification and marketing is complicated and makes it difficult to know whether the right products are being used. It recommended the creation of a clear, simpler, and more effective system of specification and testing of construction products, and a more effective enforcement regime with national oversight. In response, the Government has announced plans to create a National Regulator for Construction Products (NRCP), within the Office for Product Safety and Standards (OPSS), which will have overall responsibility for the national regulation of construction products.

To facilitate the creation of a new, comprehensive framework, BSA 2022, s.146 gives the Secretary of State power to make regulations in relation to the marketing and supply of construction products in the United Kingdom (including Scotland and Northern Ireland), in line with BSA 2022, Sched.11. It is hoped that this could result in the more streamlined system recommended by the Hackitt Report.

Schedule 11 gives an indication of what future regulations could contain. This includes general safety requirements, designated standards and technical assessments, and sanctions for non-compliance.

Schedule 11 introduces the concept of a 'safe product' and a 'safety-critical product'. A 'safe product' is one which, under normal or reasonably foreseeable conditions of use, presents no risk, or as low as possible a risk, to health and safety (BSA 2022, Sched.11, para.2(2)). 'Use' includes storage, transportation or packaging, and 'reasonably foreseeable conditions' include reasonably foreseeable circumstances in which the product might come under stress. Schedule 11, para.2(3) gives the example of a fire.

The intention is clearly that all construction products placed on the UK market will be safe, with government powers to ensure they are withdrawn from the market if they present a risk. It seems that it will not be sufficient merely to ensure that products would be safe for installation at the point at which they leave the factory, but they must be capable of withstanding any shocks or potential degradation caused by storage, transport or packaging, as well as being fire-safe. This again indicates the intention to have a more holistic and overarching approach to construction product regulation.

Schedule 11 also indicates an intention to impose more stringent regulatory requirements on 'safety-critical products'. Future regulations can set out a list of such products. A construction product can only be designated as a 'safety-critical product' if, in the view of the Secretary of State, any failure of the product would risk causing death or serious injury to any person. Products which are already subject to designated standards cannot be included in the list of safety-critical products, and the Secretary of State must consult as appropriate before including a construction product in the list (Sched.11, para.10(2)). The Secretary of State may by regulation set further standards – 'safety-critical standards' – for these safety-critical products.

The NRCP will not have to start from scratch in creating new regulations. Under Sched.11, para.4 the Secretary of State can designate EU harmonised standards or international standards as the standards for construction products in the UK.

The only regulations made so far under s.146 are the Construction Products (Amendment) Regulations 2022, SI 2022/712 (the 712 Regulations), which add the Secretary of State to the list of 'enforcement authorities' that can enforce existing regulations and carry out market surveillance. It is expected that further regulations will be forthcoming to set up the NRCP and to set new, and clearer, regulatory standards. As noted in the Hackitt Report (see **Chapter 1**), these standards will need to cover not only the technical characteristics of the products, but also measures to ensure they are correctly used. For example, some products may need to have a system of permanent marking making it possible to identify and trace products after they been installed.

The creation of an overarching regulatory regime in such a complex, technical area is a huge task, and it is unsurprising that the Government has not yet set out in any detail how it will work.

17.2.7 Unfit for habitation

The Act does not define 'unfit for habitation', but the Government confirmed during the passage of the bill that it intended that the 'fit for habitation' test would be equivalent to that used in DPA 1972, and not the 'fitness for human habitation test' in the Homes (Fitness for Human Habitation) Act 2018.[2] Some assistance may therefore be drawn from the case law on DPA 1972, s.1, which also refers to (but does not define) dwellings that are unfit for habitation. In *Rendlesham Estates* v. *Barr* [2014] EWHC 3968 (TCC), the court gave helpful guidance (at [68]), noting that 'fit for habitation' meant:

> capable of occupation for a reasonable time without risk to the health or safety of the occupants: where a dwelling is or is part of a newly constructed building, what is a reasonable time will be a question of fact (it may or may not be as long as the design life of the building); and ... capable of occupation for a reasonable time without undue inconvenience or discomfort to the occupants.

Defects that have been found to render a building unfit for habitation (or cited as examples of defects that could potentially render a building unfit for habitation) include defective foundations, inadequate insulation, a lift that broke down regularly, lack of emergency exits and garage doors that could not be locked (*Rendlesham* v. *Barr*; *Harrison* v. *Shepherd Homes Ltd* [2011] EWHC 1811 (TCC), (2011) 27 Con LJ 709; *Bole* v. *Huntsbuild Ltd* [2009] EWHC 483 (TCC)).

17.3 RETROSPECTIVE LIABILITY FOR DEFECTIVE CLADDING PRODUCTS

BSA 2022, s.149 makes additional provision in relation to cladding products, for past breaches of regulatory requirements. Cladding products include both a cladding system and any component of a cladding system (s.149(12)).

The provision sets out similar conditions (A to D) to those in BSA 2022, s.148, but the main difference is that liability is retrospective. A claim can be brought under s.149 where the faulty cladding has been produced/supplied or the misleading statement made before 28 June 2022. This does not affect the right to bring a claim in relation to cladding under s.148 for breaches after that date.

The wording of s.149 is similar to that of s.148. Condition A is that, at any time before 28 June 2022 (s.149(2)):

[2] Letter from Lord Greenhalgh to Lord Khan regarding issues raised during the Committee stage (third sitting) of the Bill: the levels of service charges, the costs of the appointment of a third-party professional to carry out the functions of an accountable person (10 March 2022).

(a) a person fails to comply with a cladding product requirement in relation to a cladding product,
(b) a person who markets or supplies a cladding product makes a misleading statement in relation to it, or
(c) a person manufactures a cladding product that is inherently defective.

Condition B is that, after Condition A has been met, the cladding product is attached to, or included in, the external wall of a relevant building in the course of works carried out in the construction of, or otherwise in relation to, the building (s.149(3)).

An external wall includes any part of a roof pitched at an angle of more than 70 degrees to the horizontal if that part of the roof adjoins a space within the building to which persons have access otherwise than for the purpose of carrying out repairs or maintenance (s.149(12)). This is in near identical terms to the definition of an external wall in the Building Regulations 2010 (Building Regulations 2010, SI 2010/2214, reg.2(6)(a)(iv)).

Conditions C and D are identical to those for claims under s.148.

As with claims under s.148, all four conditions must be met in order for liability to arise. The wrongdoer is liable to pay damages to a person with a relevant interest in relation to the relevant building for personal injury, damage to property or economic loss suffered by that person, and the parties cannot contract out of this provision (s.149(7)).

The terms 'relevant building' and 'relevant interest' have the same meaning as for construction product claims under s.148 and are discussed at **17.2.3** and **17.2.4**. See also **17.2.7** for a discussion of when a building is unfit for habitation.

The relevant cladding product requirements for a claim under s.149 are those in force at the time the cladding product was manufactured, supplied or marketed. These are specified in s.149(11). For products manufactured or marketed before the end of the Brexit transition period on 31 December 2020 (referred to in the Act as 'IP completion day'), the requirements are those under the Construction Products Regulations 1991, SI 1991/1620 (referred to as 'the 1991 Regulations'), or the 2011 Regulation as it had effect in EU law at that time (BSA 2022, s.149(11)(a)). For products manufactured or marketed after 31 December 2020, the requirements are as set down in the 2011 Regulation or the Construction Products (Amendment etc.) (EU Exit) Regulations 2019, SI 2019/465 (s.149(11)(b)).

17.4 LIMITATION FOR CONSTRUCTION PRODUCTS CLAIMS

17.4.1 The extended limitation periods

The Act introduces an extended limitation period for claims under BSA 2022, ss.148–149. BSA 2022, s.150 inserts a new s.10B into the Limitation Act 1980, and BSA 2022, s.151 inserts a new s.18ZD into the Prescription and Limitation (Scotland) Act 1973.

The limitation period for claims under s.148 is 15 years from the date on which the right accrued (Limitation Act 1980, ss.10B(1) and 10B(2); Prescription and Limitation (Scotland) Act 1973, ss.18ZC(1) and 18ZC(2)). For retrospective cladding claims under s.149, the limitation period is 30 years if the right of action accrued before 28 June 2022, and 15 years if the right accrued on or after 28 June 2022. There is a further extension of limitation for claims whose 30-year limitation would have expired in the 12-month period beginning with 28 June 2022 (i.e. claims where the cause of action arose between 28 June 1992 and 27 June 1993). For those claims, the limitation period expired on 27 June 2023 (Limitation Act 1980, s.10B(3); Prescription and Limitation (Scotland) Act 1973, s.18ZC(3)).

The Act has also extended the time for claims under DPA 1972 to 15 years from the date on which the right of action accrued. Where the right of action accrued before 28 June 2022, the limitation period is extended further to 30 years (Limitation Act 1980, s.4B(4)).

Although it is unlikely to matter in all but a very few cases, there is an inconsistency in the drafting of the limitation provisions which makes the exact calculation of time uncertain. Limitation is described variously as running 'from' and 'beginning with' the date on which the cause of action accrued. The courts have determined that these have different meanings, so that, where a time period is described as 'beginning with' a specified day, then that day is included in the period, but if the period is described as running 'from' or 'after' a specified day, then that day is not included in the period (*Trow* v. *Ind Coope (West Midlands) Ltd* [1967] 2 QB 899; *Zoan* v. *Rouamba* [2000] 1 WLR 1509; *Wang* v. *University of Keele* [2011] ICR 1251; *Stevenson* v. *General Optical Council* [2015] EWHC 3099 (Admin); see also *The White Book* (2023 Edn, Sweet & Maxwell), commentary at 2.8.1).

Claims under s.148 of the Act, and retrospective claims under s.149, are not to be brought more than 15 or 30 years respectively '*from* the date on which the cause of action accrued' (emphasis added). But claims under s.149, where the right of action accrued on or after 28 June 2022, are not to be brought after 15 years '*beginning with* the date on which it accrued' (emphasis added). So, where the cause of action accrues on, say, 25 February 2023, the limitation period for a claim under s.148 would expire on 25 February 2038, but for a claim under s.149 it would expire on 24 February 2038.

To add to the confusion, the terms 'from' and 'beginning with' appear to be used interchangeably for retrospective cladding claims. Although the 30-year limitation period under s.149 is described is 'from' the date on which the cause of action accrued, the further extension of time in the Limitation Act 1980, s.10B(3) refers to a case where the 'the expiration of the period of 30 years *beginning with* the date on which the right of action accrued falls in the year beginning with the commencement date' (emphasis added) (Limitation Act 1980, ss.10B(2)(a) and (3)).

This was discussed obiter in *Boxxe Ltd.* v. *Secretary of State for Justice* [2023] EWHC 533 (TCC). Mr Justice Constable noted (at [25]–[26]) that it was not immediately obvious what purpose was sought to be achieved by the different wording, and it was unclear if the drafters were using the concepts 'from' and 'beginning with' interchangeably. It would appear that the use of the phrase 'beginning with' is simply a drafting error. Other provisions in the Limitation Act 1980 refer to periods running 'from' the accrual of the cause of action.

To summarise by way of illustration, as currently drafted, it would appear that limitation works as follows:

1. For a claim under s.148 (or under DPA 1972, s.1), where the cause of action accrued on 30 June 2022, limitation would expire on 30 June 2037 (15 years from the accrual of the cause of action).
2. For a claim under s.149, where the cause of action accrued on 30 June 2022, limitation would expire on 29 June 2022 (15 years beginning with 30 June 2022).
3. For a claim under s.149 (or DPA 1972, s.1), where the cause of action accrued on 27 June 2022, limitation would expire on 27 June 2052 (30 years from the accrual of the cause of action).
4. For a claim under s.149 (or DPA 1972, s.1), where the cause of action accrued on 30 June 1992, limitation expired on 27 June 2023 (30 years, extended to the end of the year beginning with 28 June 2022).

17.4.2 When does the limitation period start?

Time starts to run for the purposes of litigation when the cause of action accrues. This is the date on which the works are completed, or, where the claim relates to a product used in the construction of the building, the date on which construction is completed (BSA 2022, ss.148(8) and 149(8)). This is similar to the wording in the extended limitation for claims under DPA 1972 (Limitation Act 1980, s.4B, introduced by BSA 2022, s.135). The limitation period does *not* start on the date on which the defective product is manufactured or the misleading statement is made. Thus it is possible to have a claim under s.149 in which time starts to run *after* the Act came into force, in circumstances where the defective product was manufactured or supplied before 28 June 2022, but the construction works were completed after that date.

As currently drafted, the provisions mean that if the cause of action accrued on, say, 27 June 2022, limitation would not expire until 27 June 2052. But if it accrued a few days later, on say 30 June 2022, then limitation would expire on 30 June 2037 (or 29 June 2037, see discussion in **17.4.1**). This could make the question of exactly when works were completed of considerable importance in certain cases in future.

In *URS Corporation Ltd.* v. *BDW Trading Ltd.* [2023] EWCA Civ 772 the Court of Appeal assumed without deciding that the completion of works for the purposes of claims under DPA 1972 meant 'practical completion'. In *Mears Ltd* v. *Costplan Services (South East) Ltd* [2019] EWCA Civ 502 the Court of Appeal (at [74]) gave the following guidance on practical completion:

1. It is easier to recognise than define, and there are no hard and fast rules.
2. The existence of latent defects cannot prevent practical completion.
3. For patent defects, there is no difference between an item of work that has yet to be completed and an item of defective work that needs to be remedied, and both will be included in snagging lists.
4. Practical completion is a state of affairs in which the works have been completed free from patent defects, other than ones to be ignored as trifling.
5. Whether or not an item is trifling is a matter of fact and degree, to be measured against 'the purpose of allowing the employers to take possession of the works and to use them as intended'.
6. There is no rule of law that the mere fact that the defect is irremediable means that the works are not practically complete.

17.4.3 Exceptions to the extended limitation

For retrospective claims under BSA 2022, s.149, the extended limitation periods will not apply (and the court must dismiss a claim that, but for Limitation Act 1980, s.10B(2) (or the Prescription and Limitation (Scotland) Act 1973, s.18ZD (2)), would be statute-barred), if it is satisfied that it is necessary to do so to avoid a breach of the defendant's rights under the Human Rights Act 1998/European Convention on Human Rights (BSA 2022, s.149(9)). A similar provision applies for claims taking advantage of the retrospective extension of liability under DPA 1972 (BSA 2022, s.135(5)).

The most obvious reading is that the exception to extended liability is intended to apply where the right to a fair trial may be at risk due to the poor quality of evidence available. At the time of writing there is no case law on s.149, but the equivalent carve out in s.135 was discussed, obiter, in *URS Corporation Ltd.* v. *BDW Trading Ltd.* [2023] EWCA Civ 772. The Court of Appeal noted that a party who had destroyed critical documents which might have provided a defence to a claim under DPA 1972, because they had assumed that under existing law any relevant claims would be statute-barred, may be able to deploy this fact at trial.

In addition to the general case law on what constitutes a fair trial, there may be some assistance in the case law on the application of the Prescription and Limitation (Scotland) Act 1973, s.17D. Section 17A of that Act, introduced by the Limitation (Childhood Abuse) (Scotland) Act 2017, disapplies the time limit for a claim for damages for personal injury in cases brought by victims of childhood abuse. Section 17D creates an exception to this extended liability in cases where the defender satisfies the court that it is not possible for a fair hearing to take place. Factors such as the death of material witnesses and the loss of documentation, particularly before any claim had been intimated could, in appropriate circumstances and depending upon all other relevant factors, lead the court to a conclusion that a fair trial was not possible. But the burden is on the defendant to show that a fair trial cannot take place (*GD* v. *Sisters of Nazareth* [2023] SC Edin 27).

17.5 COSTS CONTRIBUTION ORDERS

17.5.1 Overview

BSA 2022, ss.152–155 introduce powers for the Secretary of State to make regulations in relation to CCOs, which are orders requiring the defaulter to pay compensation. These provisions apply to the whole of the UK, including Northern Ireland. So far, the Secretary of State has not exercised his powers to make regulations, and the only regulations made under BSA 2022, Sched.11 are the 712 Regulations (see **17.2.6**). It is therefore unclear exactly how CCOs will work in practice, including who the potential beneficiary of any costs order would be.

However, there is some indication in the wording of the various provisions. The Act anticipates that these orders could be made either by the courts, on the application of the Secretary of State (BSA 2022, s.153), or by the Secretary of State himself (BSA 2022, s.154). In either case, the Act provides that CCOs will only be made where specified conditions, A to D, are met. These are similar to the conditions for a construction product claim, described at **17.2.2**, save that the defaulter must have been convicted of an offence.

There is an obvious overlap with construction product claims under BSA 2022, ss.148–149. But there are some clear differences, in particular the fact that CCOs are to be made by, or on the application of, the Secretary of State, and with reference to the costs of the remedial works needed to make the building or dwelling fit for habitation. It would appear that CCOs would be of most benefit to homeowners in situations where the costs of remedial works would exceed the diminution in value caused by the defects.

More fundamentally, it is unclear whether a homeowner or building owner will be able to apply for a CCO or whether this will be entirely at the instigation of the Secretary of State (or the assessor, see **17.5.5**).

It is unclear how regulations under s.153 and s.154 – for orders to be made by the court and the Secretary of State respectively – are intended to interrelate. It may be that the Secretary of State has effectively a choice between making regulations that allow him to apply to the courts for an order, or regulations that set up a government-managed system. But if the Secretary of State issues regulations bringing both types of orders into force, it is unclear in which circumstances either form of order would apply. It is possible that CCOs in relation to an individual building will be made by the Secretary of State, but where the problem is nationwide – because a particular product has been found to be defective – the Secretary of State will apply to the court for an order covering the total costs of remediation works on all buildings where the product has been used.

17.5.2 The conditions to be satisfied for a CCO

As noted in **17.5.1**, the Act provides that CCOs will only be made where conditions A to D have been met, which are similar to those for construction product claims. These are in addition to any other conditions that may be prescribed by regulations.

Accordingly, Condition A is that a person has been convicted of an offence consisting of a failure to comply with a construction product requirement in relation to a construction product (BSA 2022, s.153(3) and s.154(3)). The Act does not itself create any offences in relation to construction products but there are a number of existing offences. For example, under the Construction Product Regulations 2013, SI 2013/1387, regs.3 and 6 non-compliance with certain requirements in the 2011 Regulation is an offence. As set out above (see **17.2.6**), the Government has made clear its intention to overhaul the current regulatory regime, and this may set out further offences.

The terms 'construction product requirement' and 'construction product' are defined in BSA 2022, s.152 and are identical to those used for construction product claims, save for Northern Ireland. In Northern Ireland a construction product requirement also includes a requirement under the Construction Products (Amendment etc.) (EU Exit) Regulations 2020, SI 2020/1359, for which the definition of a construction product in reg.2 of those regulations will apply.

In contrast to Condition A in BSA 2022, ss.148 and 149, there is no mention as to when the conviction has to have occurred for the purposes of liability for a CCO. This may be clarified in any future regulations, but as drafted it seems that a CCO could be made any time after a conviction, including one made before the Act came into force.

Condition B is that, *after* the failure to comply with a construction product requirement (but not necessarily after the conviction), the construction product has been installed in, or applied or attached to, a relevant building in the course of works carried out in the construction of, or otherwise in relation to, the building (BSA 2022, s.153(4), s.154(4)). As with construction product claims, this would appear to apply to pretty much all construction works. Again, there is an inconsistency in the terminology. A 'relevant building' is defined in s.152 as a building which consists of a dwelling, or which contains *two* or more dwellings (emphasis added). So, despite the reference in Condition C to cases where 'the relevant building contains one or more dwellings', it would appear that a mixed-use premises containing only one residential unit would not be a relevant building and no CCO could be made in relation to such a building.

Condition C is that when the works are completed, a dwelling contained in the building (or where the building consists of a dwelling, the building itself) is unfit for habitation (BSA 2022, s.153(5), s.154(5)). Again, fitness for habitation is not defined, but the test would appear to be the same as that used for the purposes of DPA 1972 (see discussion at **17.2.7**).

Condition D is that the failure to comply with the construction product requirement was *a* cause (but not necessarily the sole cause) of the building or dwelling being unfit for habitation (BSA 2022, s.153(6), s.154(6)).

17.5.3 The payer and payee of a costs contribution order

The Act does not specify clearly who is to benefit from a CCO, and who is to pay. Rather, BSA 2022, ss.153(9) and 154(9) state that future regulations may set out the factors to be taken into account by a court or, as the case may be, by the Secretary of State, in determining 'against whom, and in favour of whom' to make a CCO.

That said, the Act provides that a 'defaulter' is to pay. This is the person who has been convicted of the offence in relation to the construction product. The most obvious target of a CCO is therefore the manufacturer of a defective product. But it may be that, when the Regulations are overhauled as planned, a supplier who knowingly misleads a buyer as to the suitability of a product will also commit an offence. There may be situations where there is more than one party at fault, for example, if more than one defective product has been used, or if a supplier has made a misleading statement and the product itself turns out to be defective.

Similarly, the beneficiary is to be a person with a 'prescribed interest' in the building or dwelling (ss.153(7) and 153(8)). So, it may be that even though it is the Secretary of State who brings a claim, the money is to be paid to a homeowner. It remains to be seen whether the beneficiary will include a freeholder of a block of flats or a third party with a lease of the common parts, such as a management company named in a tripartite lease. But if the defects are in the common parts, so that the freeholder or management company has a responsibility for remedying the defects, it would seem logical that they should be included as a potential beneficiary in any future regulations. This is especially so if the costs of the works are liable to be passed on to the flat owners through the service charge.

It is less clear if the regulations would include an RTM company or other lessee-owned management company who does not hold any estate in any of the common parts. It would be sensible to include such a party, as they may be responsible for remedial works where the defect lies in the common parts. But it is not clear that a 'prescribed interest' could include a party who does not hold any legal estate or interest in any part of the building. It is also unclear whether a former homeowner who sold their property at a reduced value due to a defect could be a potential beneficiary.

It seems that a CCO could provide for each flat owner within a block to receive a share of the total costs of remedial works. This may also help to address any difficulties with an RTM company being a beneficiary, especially if the Secretary of State has standing to bring applications under BSA 2022, s.153 on behalf of all lessees.

17.5.4 Quantum of CCOs

The relevant factors for determining the amount to be paid under a CCO are a matter for regulations (BSA 2022, ss.153(9)(b) and 154(9)(b)). But it is clear that the amount is to be determined with reference to the cost of any remedial works. Under BSA 2022, ss.153(8) and 154(8), a CCO will require the defaulter to pay an amount that the court (or Secretary of State) considers 'just and equitable' in respect of the costs of remedial works required to make the building or dwelling fit for habitation. This includes either the costs actually incurred, or that are likely to be incurred. It would appear therefore that there is no scope for the inclusion of an amount to compensate homeowners for distress and inconvenience, rather that the amount of costs will be capped at the total cost of the remedial works. But it would also appear to allow homeowners to recover potentially all of the remediation costs, even where these exceed the diminution in value that has been caused by the defects.

The Act recognises the risk of double-recovery by a homeowner who makes a construction product claim and is also a beneficiary of a CCO. Under ss.153(11) and 154(11), future regulations can make provision to ensure that a person does not incur liability, or is not entitled to be reimbursed, more than once for the same costs. Future regulations can also prevent a beneficiary of a CCO from pursuing other legal remedies to recover the same sum. This may prove to be complicated, as the heads of loss under ss.148 or s.149 construction product claim differ from those under ss.153 and 154. There is no good reason why a homeowner who has suffered personal injury caused by a defect in their home should not be able to recover damages for personal injury as well as a contribution towards the costs of remedying the defect. But it may be difficult to disentangle the economic loss recoverable under s.148 from the costs of remedying the defect. It is logical that a landlord who has suffered a loss of rent as a result of the defect should be able to recover that loss as well as the cost of remedial works, in order to restore the landlord to the position the landlord would have been in but for the breach of regulations. But it is less obvious that a flat owner who has bought property at a discount due to the defect should be able to recover the full cost of works.

It is clear that a CCO can be made both before or after any remediation works. It is less clear whether it is a condition of any CCO that the remediation works are in fact carried out. The provision for regulations to appoint a person to assess the cost of remedial works indicates that there would need to be at least a settled intention to do the works.

There is scope for an award of costs, in addition to a CCO, but it appears that this only applies to costs incurred by the Secretary of State. Under s.153(10), regulations may provide for the court also to award costs, including the costs of making the application and the costs incurred by the Secretary of State in relation to the assessment, as per the regulations under s.155. Similarly, under s.154(13), regulations may provide for the defaulter to pay any costs incurred by the Secretary of State. However, there is no provision for costs to be awarded to a homeowner who has taken steps to procure an order under s.154.

17.5.5 The assessor

The Act provides for the Secretary of State to make regulations covering the appointment of persons to assess quantum, referred to as 'assessors'. More specifically, under BSA 2022, s.155(1) the assessor will assess:

- whether the conditions for a CCO are met (including whether a building is unfit for habitation);
- the works required to make a building or dwelling fit for habitation;
- the interest a person has in a building or dwelling;
- the costs that a person has reasonably incurred or is likely to reasonably incur in undertaking the remedial works;
- the amount that a person should be required to pay under a CCO.

Again, at the date of writing no regulations have been enacted under this provision, and it is unclear exactly how this will work in practice. But the assessor can assess costs both under BSA 2022, s.153 and s.154, i.e. for applications to be determined by the Secretary of State, or applications to be determined by the courts per s.155. Either way, the assessment will be provided to the Secretary of State, either as applicant, under s.153, or as adjudicator, under s.154. The criteria for appointment as an assessor is a matter for regulations.

The Explanatory Notes that accompany the Act explain that, following a successful prosecution for failure to comply with construction product regulations, the Secretary of State would be able to appoint an assessor to undertake an assessment of buildings where the defective product has been used. It appears therefore that the intention is that there will be a single, systemic investigation in such cases.

Regulations may provide for the assessor to require 'persons' to provide any information it reasonably requires (BSA 2022, s.1, s.155(3)). It remains to be seen to which persons, and to what information, this will apply. It may be that manufacturers of defective products could be compelled to provide details of the costs of replacement materials. But it may be that regulations go further, so that manufacturers or suppliers could be compelled to investigate the costs of remedial works. It is unclear what information, if any, could be required from third parties who are not the potential subject of a CCO, but it appears nonetheless that there is power to require information from such third parties.

The Act does not directly create an offence of failing to provide required information, or providing misleading information for the purposes of an assessment, but it authorises the Secretary of State to make regulations that include provision for such an offence (s.155(4)).

It is unclear whether a court will be bound by the assessor's assessment of the costs, but it would appear that the court would ordinarily not be asked to determine the total costs of remediation works. This may help to reduce the complexity of court proceedings for CCOs, as the court will be focusing primarily on the share of costs to be paid.

17.5.6 Further provisions where CCOs are to be made by the Secretary of State

BSA 2022, s.154 authorises regulations to cover a number of further provisions in relation to CCOs, where such orders are to be made by the Secretary of State. These include:

- a system of warning notices before any CCO is made by the Secretary of State;
- a prescribed form for a CCO made by the Secretary of State;
- prescribed information that such an order should contain;
- the method of service of a CCO made by the Secretary of State;
- the person on whom it is to be served;
- a right to apply to the Secretary of State for a review of a s.154 CCO;
- appeals to a court or tribunal.

There is no express mention of how the Secretary of State will delegate any powers under s.154. It is unclear whether the intention is to have a national office or agency who will have responsibility for making CCOs, or whether it is to be delegated to local authorities.

CHAPTER 18

Liability of associated persons and personal criminal liability

Charles Joseph

18.1 INTRODUCTION

The Act contains provisions in Part 5 which can lead to liability in the form of a remediation order (RO) (see **Chapter 14**), a remediation contribution order (RCO) (see **Chapter 14**) or a building liability order (BLO) (see **Chapter 15**). An RO can only made against a relevant landlord (as defined) and so is not considered further in this chapter. An RCO or a BLO can be made against a wide range of persons or entities (called 'associated persons') linked to a landlord or to a developer of a building. A building is a relevant building for the purposes of an RCO if it is at least 11 metres high or has at least five storeys, and it contains at least two dwellings. However there is no similar restriction on the type of building as regards a BLO. These associated persons may not otherwise be directly liable for the relevant defects or the sums in question. The primary purpose of BSA 2022, Part 5 and Sched.8 is to relieve tenants, in a variety of ways, of much of the liability to pay service charges which would otherwise cover all or part of the costs of works required to cure a relevant defect, or to relieve tenants from the liability to pay for the costs of remediation under the Act. The Act is designed to ensure that there is someone available upon whom the burden of paying for the works will fall, rather than that burden falling on the tenant.

This chapter seeks to address the issues around what the Act calls 'associated persons', but it is not possible to do this in isolation and so the context in which the provisions arise is necessarily referred to from time to time. The relevance of 'associated persons' is that, as pointed out above, an associated person can be made subject to various court orders requiring payment even if that person would otherwise have no liability for the relevant defect or defects in the building. It should be noted that, while the term 'body corporate' used in the Act is for simplicity frequently referred to in this chapter as a 'company', a limited liability partnership is also a body corporate pursuant to the Limited Liability Partnerships Act 2000, s.1(2).

Additionally and for convenience this chapter also deals with the personal criminal liability of individuals connected with a body corporate or a partnership in circumstances where the body corporate or a partnership has committed an offence under BSA 2022, Part 2 or Part 4, although it is right to observe that such individuals are not expressly described as associated persons in the legislation.

18.2 BSA 2022, SECTION 121 AND WHO IS ASSOCIATED

18.2.1 Section 121

BSA 2022, s.121(1) provides that a partnership or a body corporate is associated with another person in the circumstances set out later in the section. For the purposes of the Act that other person is usually a landlord. It is important to note here that the concept of association in the Act appears to apply only to a partnership or a corporate body and does not appear to include an individual for the reasons given at **18.2.3**. Accordingly it seems that an individual is not an associated person for the purposes of BSA 2022, ss.122–125 or indeed Sched.8. It is not beyond the bounds of possibility that, for example, a developer or a builder (and thus 'a person responsible for a relevant defect' within Sched.8, para.2(2)(b)) might be an individual, but nevertheless the developer/builder would not be an associated person for the purposes of the Act.

18.2.2 Trusts

Trusts are addressed at BSA 2022, s.121(2), which provides that where 'a person's' interest in a relevant building is held on trust at the qualifying time (which is defined at BSA 2022, s.119(2)(d) as 14 February 2022) then 'any partnership or body corporate' which was a beneficiary of the trust at that time will be associated with that person. This does not appear to deal with the position which might obtain if a person's interest is held on trust but there is no partnership or body corporate which is a beneficiary. So, for example, if a relevant property was held on trust only for an individual then, as noted above in respect of s.121(1), it does not seem that the individual, or indeed the trust, is caught by this provision.

18.2.3 Partnerships and directors

'Partnership' as a term is defined at BSA 2022, s.121(11) for the purposes of s.121 as meaning a partnership within the meaning of the Partnership Act 1890 or a limited partnership under the Limited Partnerships Act 1907. The position of individuals who are co-owners of property is not expressly addressed, but the draftsman will no doubt have had in mind the definition of partnership in the Partnership Act 1890, namely 'the relation which subsists between persons carrying on a business in common with a view of profit' (s.1(1) of the Partnership Act 1890). It seems unlikely that co-owners would be the proprietors of the sort of buildings envisaged by this part of the Act unless they held the property for the purpose of making some sort of profit; if they are, they will be partners within the Partnership Act definition and thus within the scope of these parts of BSA 2022, s.121 and Sched.8. It should be noted that although the definition here does not expressly include a limited liability partnership under the Limited Liability Partnerships Act 2000, as pointed out at **18.1** such entities are bodies corporate (pursuant to the Limited Liability Partnerships Act 2000, s.1(2)) and so fall within s.121(1) by that route.

Relatively uncontentious provisions are made at s.121(3) and (4), which provide that a partnership is 'associated' for the purposes of the Act with anyone who was a partner in the five years prior to 14 February 2022 (although it should be noted that there is an express exclusion for partners who are limited partners and who are accordingly not caught by this provision); and a body corporate is 'associated' with any person who was a director of that entity in the five years prior to 14 February 2022.

However it seems likely that the references to partners or directors in the five years prior to 14 February 2022 do not refer to natural persons, but rather to corporate bodies or partners which were themselves directors or partners. This is because it is clear from the provisions of BSA 2022, s.124(2) and 124(3) (see **18.2.7**) and from BSA 2022, ss.130(2) and 131 (see **18.4.4**) that an RCO and a BLO can only be made against a body corporate (or, in the case of an RCO, a partnership). Accordingly, and since there is no scope for an individual natural person to be liable, it seems likely that the associated persons referred to in ss.121(3) and (4) must be corporate bodies or partnerships. This is because there would have been no point in creating a category of associated persons (namely individual natural persons) against whom no remedy is available.

18.2.4 Control

As noted at **18.1**, a body corporate includes a limited liability partnership, but for simplicity is referred to in the following paragraphs simply as a company. BSA 2022, 121(5)–(8) deals with how and when one company is to be regarded as associated with another company. This includes the important concept of 'control'.

Section 121(5)(a) stipulates that one company is associated with another if they each had a common director at any time in the period of five years ending on 14 February 2022. There is no apparent reason why such a director could not be a natural person for this purpose. The 'association' is between companies, not between a company and the director. Second, s.121(5)(b) stipulates that one company is associated with another if on 14 February 2022 one of the companies controlled the other, or a third company controlled both of them.

Section 121(6)–(8) sets out the circumstances in which one company is to be regarded as controlling another, and thus associated with it for the purposes of this section of the Act. It should be noted that there are some similarities with the definition of 'subsidiary' in the Companies Act 2006, s.1159 as further explained at Sched.6 of that Act. Although this is not the place for an analysis of company law, it should be borne in mind that by the Companies Act 2006, s.136 the general rule is that a subsidiary company cannot be a member of its holding company.

Section 121(6) states that one company controls another company if the first company possesses or is entitled to acquire (a) at least half of the issued share capital of the second company; or (b) such rights as would entitle the first company to exercise at least half of the votes in the second company in general meeting; or (c) such part of the issued share capital in the second company as would entitle the first company to receive at least half the amount distributed out of income; or (d) such rights as would entitle the first company to receive at least half of the assets of the second company on a winding up or otherwise. In all of these cases the first company is to be taken to control the second company. Existing shareholdings can be traced through filings at Companies House, but of course it is likely to be much more difficult to find out the true position if there is some arrangement which is either undocumented or where the documentation is not required to be registered on any public register. It may be possible, however, for anyone making or intending to make an application for a BLO (but not an RCO) to obtain relevant information by way of an application for an information order about associated persons by way of an application to the High Court pursuant to BSA 2022, s.132 and the 711 Regulations, reg.12.

Section 121(7) makes provision for when a company controls a limited liability partnership. A company controls a limited liability partnership where it holds a majority of the voting rights in the partnership; or where it is a member of the partnership and has the right to appoint or remove a majority of other members; or where it is a member of the partnership and it controls, either by itself or by way of an agreement with other members, a majority of the voting rights in the partnership. It should be noted that although there is no express provision for the reverse position (i.e. where a limited liability partnership controls a company), a limited liability partnership is itself a body corporate (see **18.1**) and so that position would fall within s.121(5)(b) and (6).

There are two further provisions in s.121 which should be mentioned. By s.121(8) the Act provides that one company controls another company (and is thus associated with it) if the first company:

> has the power, directly or indirectly, to secure that the affairs of [the second company] are conducted in accordance with [the first company's] wishes.

It is not clear from the statute what is intended to be covered by the idea of indirect power to control a company. It is possible that what was envisaged is, or at least includes, some form of controlling influence, perhaps in a family context, in circumstances where the formal shareholdings are less than 50 per cent per shareholder and there is no formal voting agreement between shareholders, but nevertheless a corporate shareholder in practice controls what some or all of the other shareholders do and thus by extension controls the second company.

There is a possible similarity with the concept of a shadow director, defined at the Companies Act 2006, s.251 as 'a person in accordance with whose instructions the directors of the company are accustomed to act'. In *Ultraframe (UK) Ltd.* v. *Fielding* [2005] EWHC 1638 (Ch) the court interpreted this to mean that at least a consistent majority of the directors must be accustomed to act in that way. It should also be noted that in the same case it was decided that if the directors of the company had to act in a certain way pursuant to the requirements of a major lender or a customer for the protection of that person's interests, then that person would not be a shadow director. However the drafter of s.121(8) appears to have made a conscious decision not to use the familiar phrase 'shadow director' and so it might be inferred that something somewhat different was intended. Ultimately, the full meaning and extent of s.121(8) will have to be determined by the courts on a case-by-case basis.

18.2.5 Nominees

By BSA 2022, s.121(10) it is made clear that where a company acts through a nominee then for the purposes of the section the company is to be taken as possessing all the rights and powers otherwise vested in the nominee; and a company which controls another company is to be taken to possess any rights and powers vested in that other company.

None of these provisions is intended to be exclusive of any of the others. The Explanatory Notes to the Act give by way of example a situation involving a complex corporate structure where five separate entities are all to be taken to be associated with one another, so that if one of them has an interest in a relevant building with a relevant defect then all or any one of the other entities could be the subject of an RCO.

18.2.6 Summary

By way of summary, for the purposes of BSA 2022, Part 5 and Sched.8, a partnership or a body corporate can be an associated person if relevantly linked to another person. This can apply in some cases where there is a trust involved, and it will also cover the position where the partnership or body corporate formerly had common partners or common directors as the case may be. The Act also provides that a partnership which was itself a partner in another partnership in the period of five years before 14 February 2022 can be associated with that partnership; and a body corporate which was a director of another body corporate in the period of five years before 14 February 2022 can be associated with that body corporate. It should be noted that there is no requirement that the partner or director should in either case have been in office for the whole of that period, nor that they should have ceased to be in office after that period.

18.2.7 Application

The practical application of this is to be found in the main body of BSA 2022 at s.124 and in Sched.8. By BSA 2022, s.124 the First-tier Tribunal (FTT) can make an RCO against a person associated with a landlord or former landlord, or a developer. But as pointed out above, in general terms an associated person cannot be an individual. This is reinforced here by s.124(2) and by the opening words of s.124(3) which in each case refer only to a body corporate or a partnership. Accordingly an RCO cannot be made against an individual under s.124(3)(d) because the associated person must be a body corporate or a partnership. Schedule 8 is addressed below at **18.3**.

18.2.8 Insolvency

By BSA 2022, s.125 the court can make an order that a body corporate or a partnership which is associated with a company which is being wound up should make contribution to the company's assets or even to make a payment directly to another person. Despite the marginal note in the Act ('Meeting remedial costs of insolvent landlord') the wording of the section refers only to a company being wound up and to the appointment of an insolvency practitioner. Acting as an 'insolvency practitioner' is defined at s.125(4) by reference to the Insolvency Act 1986, s.388. That section of the Insolvency Act provides that (so far as a company is concerned) an insolvency practitioner may be appointed as a liquidator, provisional liquidator, administrator, administrative receiver or monitor or as nominee or supervisor under a voluntary arrangement. Accordingly the company being wound up need not necessarily be, or have been adjudged to be, insolvent. For example, in some cases a charge-holder can appoint an administrator even if there may be no question of an insolvency. And as advisers will be aware, any solvent company can be wound up if the members choose to cause it to be wound up.

18.3 BSA 2022, SCHEDULE 8 AND REMEDIATION COSTS

BSA 2022, Sched.8 is brought into effect by s.122. The Schedule relates to service charges, and who may be liable to pay since the tenant is largely excluded from liability. By para.1 of Sched.8 'associated' is defined for the purposes of the Schedule by reference back to BSA 2022, s.121 (as to which, see **18.2**).

18.3.1 Who may be liable

By BSA 2022, Sched.8, para.2(2) no service charge is payable in respect of a relevant measure relating to a relevant defect if a relevant landlord is either responsible for the defect or is associated with a person responsible for the defect (e.g. a builder or a developer). Accordingly, it can be seen that the question who is associated with the landlord may have significant consequences, particularly if the landlord is, for example, impecunious. But, as pointed out at **18.2.3**, this appears to be applicable only to a partnership or a body corporate. Individuals generally do not appear to be 'associated' as defined because neither an RCO nor a BLO can be made against an individual. The consequence of this may be that (i) if a relevant landlord is not responsible for the defect, and (ii) if the builder or developer who is responsible for the defect is an individual and not a body corporate or a partnership, then the protection conferred on tenants by para.2(2) will not apply.

18.3.2 Contribution condition

Moreover by Sched.8, para.3 no service charge is payable under a qualifying lease in respect of a relevant defect where the landlord meets the contribution condition. The contribution condition is defined by reference to the net worth of the 'landlord group'. By para.3(4)(a) the landlord group is defined as the relevant landlord and any person 'associated' with the relevant landlord. Since for the reasons above (see e.g. **18.2.1**, and note again that for the purposes of Sched.8 'associated' is defined by reference to BSA 2022, s.121) it appears that a natural person cannot generally be a person associated with the landlord, it follows that a natural person cannot be part of a landlord group (unless of course that natural person is the landlord).

18.3.3 Net worth of individuals; spouses and civil partners

There is special provision for the purposes of calculating the net worth of a relevant landlord where the landlord is an individual. The 711 Regulations, reg.5 (as amended) deals with how the net worth of a landlord group is to be calculated at the qualifying date, namely 14 February 2022. However where the landlord is an individual, reg.5(6) provides that the assets and liabilities of the landlord include those of their spouse or civil partner at the same date, namely 14 February 2022. It is to be observed that the spouse or civil partner is not here described as being 'associated' with the landlord, but that their net wealth is nevertheless liable to be part of the calculation of the landlord's own net wealth.

It seems likely that this investigation of the wealth of an individual landlord and their spouse/civil partner will be regarded as somewhat invasive, and perhaps therefore contentious. Moreover, as time passes it may in future be quite difficult to carry out the intended valuation exercise since it may take place some years after the qualifying date. It may cause a certain amount of friction, or even embarrassment or resentment. For example, it is possible that spouses or civil partners may keep, or wish to continue to keep, some or all of their respective financial affairs separate from one another, and perhaps confidential. Disclosure might be very difficult to achieve. It is possible that these provisions (which arise from secondary legislation rather than primary legislation) may be subject to challenge based on the privacy rights arising from Art.8 of the European Convention on Human Rights (incorporated into English law by the Human Rights Act 1998). It is also possible that when the time comes for the relevant calculations to be carried out, the parties to a marriage or civil partnership may have separated or may have been divorced. In the course of that separation or divorce the parties may have made certain financial arrangements or such arrangements may have been imposed by a court, perhaps rendering the back calculation required by reg.5(6) highly artificial. And lastly, it is possible that there may be significant data protection issues here. All these matters will need to be worked out by the courts on a case-by-case basis, but until this happens it is inevitable that there will be some uncertainty about how and to what extent reg.5(6) actually works.

18.3.4 Modification of who is associated for purposes of landlord group

It should also be noted that where what is under consideration is whether a person is to be treated as associated with the landlord for the purposes of the landlord group provisions, for the purpose of BSA 2022, Sched.8, para.3 the definition of who is associated has been modified by the 711 Regulations, reg.3 (as amended) so as to exclude as an associate a person who would otherwise have been considered to be associated by reason of BSA 2022, ss.121(4) or (5)(a). It will be recalled that s.121(4) provides that a body corporate is associated with anyone who was one of its directors in the relevant period and that s.121(5)(a) provides that a body corporate is associated with another body corporate if at any time in the relevant period a person was a director of both of them. These are excluded from consideration in the context of para.3, so that the director or body corporate, as the case might be, is not to be regarded as an associated person for the purpose of the definition of a landlord group. What this means is that, for the purposes of working out who is in a landlord group, neither a person who was a director in the relevant period nor another company which had a common director will be associated, and so neither will be part of the landlord group. The current form of this exclusion made by reg.3 is the result of amendments made to the 711 Regulations by the Building Safety (Leaseholder Protections) (England) (Amendment) Regulations 2023, SI 2023/126. It is understood that this was considered to be necessary because in their initial form the 711 Regulations had mistakenly excluded parent companies and sister companies.

18.4 BSA 2022, SECTION 130: BUILDING LIABILITY ORDERS AND WHO IS ASSOCIATED

BSA 2022, ss.130–132, which deal with BLOs, also rely in part on the potential liability of associated persons. By s.130 the High Court may make a BLO against a company, providing that at least one other body corporate is already subject to a relevant liability. As noted at **18.1**, a body corporate includes a limited liability partnership (see the Limited Liability Partnerships Act 2000, s.1(2)) but for simplicity such entities are referred to here simply as companies. In order for the court to have the power to make a BLO against another company then the company or companies which are to be made liable must be, or must have been in the relevant period, 'associated' with the first company.

18.4.1 Who is to be regarded as associated for BLOs

Association is defined for these purposes at BSA 2022, s.131. As with s.121, the key issue for determining whether one company is associated with another is the question of control. The provisions of s.131 are in many respects similar to those appearing in some of the subsections of s.121. However unlike s.121, partnerships (other than limited liability partnerships), and partners and directors in post in the five years preceding 14 February 2022 are not included in s.131.

18.4.2 Control

By BSA 2022, s.131(1) a company is associated with another company if one of them controls the other or if a third company controls both of them.

By s.131(2) it is provided that one company controls another company if the first company possesses or is entitled to acquire (a) at least half of the issued share capital of the second company; or (b) such rights as would entitle the first company to exercise at least half of the votes in the second company in general meeting; or (c) such part of the issued share capital in the second company as would entitle the first company to receive at least half the amount distributed out of income; or (d) such rights as would entitle the first company to receive at least half of the assets of the second company on a winding up or otherwise. In all of these cases the first company is to be taken to control the second company.

Section 131(3) makes provision for when a company controls a limited liability partnership. A company controls a limited liability partnership where it holds a majority of the voting rights in the partnership, or where it is a member of the partnership and has the right to appoint or remove a majority of other members, or where it is a member of the partnership and it controls, either by itself or by way of an agreement with other members, a majority of the voting rights in the partnership.

Section 131(4) stipulates that a company controls another company if the first company has the power, directly or indirectly, to secure that the affairs of the second company are conducted in accordance with the wishes of the first company. There is no indication as to what is meant by indirect power, but as with BSA 2022, s.121(8) (see **18.2.4**) it may be that some form of corporate control by, for example, a dominant family member may fall within this provision.

For the purpose of applying these subsections, by s.131(6) the first company is to be treated as possessing all the rights and powers of any nominee for it together with any rights and powers possessed by any other company which it controls.

In all these cases a company (meaning a body corporate and thus including a limited liability partnership) will be associated with another company and so fall within the scope of a BLO.

18.4.3 Trusts

So far as the provisions of BSA 2022, s.131 are concerned, by BSA 2022, s.131(7) where a person's interest in a building is held on trust, a company which is a beneficiary of the trust is to be regarded as associated with that person.

18.4.4 Summary: partnerships excluded from liability for a BLO

Under BSA 2022, s.131 the High Court can make a BLO against an associated body corporate, but partnerships (other than LLPs, which are bodies corporate) are not included in s.131 as capable of being associated persons. It is not immediately obvious why partnerships should be excluded from liability for a BLO given that by BSA 2022, ss.121 and 124 they are to be regarded as associated persons for the purpose of an RCO in the same part of the Act. The Explanatory Notes to s.131 do not appear to address this.

18.5 BSA 2022, SECTION 161 AND PERSONAL CRIMINAL LIABILITY

BSA 2022 at s.161 deals with the personal criminal liability of the individuals described below in respect of certain offences created by BSA 2022, Part 2 and Part 4.

18.5.1 The relevant offences

The offences in BSA 2022, Part 2 are those of intentionally obstructing an authorised officer or impersonating an authorised officer (BSA 2022, s.23(1) and (2)), and the knowing of or reckless provision of false or misleading information to the Regulator in the circumstances set out at BSA 2022, s.24(1).

The offences in BSA 2022, Part 4 are more numerous. They include the relevant AP's liability for the occupation of a residential unit in an HRB without a completion certificate (s.76); the failure of the PAP to apply for a building assessment certificate (s.79); provisions relating to the display of a building assessment certificate (s.82); the failure of an AP to give prescribed information to the Regulator (s.87); the failure of an outgoing AP to give prescribed information to an incoming AP or to the Regulator (s.90); the failure of an AP to comply with a compliance notice (s.99); and the contravention of a relevant requirement by an AP which puts a person in or about the building at significant risk of death or serious injury (s.101).

18.5.2 Who may be liable

By BSA 2022, s.161(1), where any of these offences is committed by a body corporate (which includes a limited liability partnership – see the Limited Liability Partnerships Act 2000, s.1(2)) and that offence is committed with the consent 'or connivance' of any director, manager, secretary 'or other similar officer' of the body corporate, or 'any person who was purporting to act' in any such capacity, then that person also commits the same offence. Moreover, where the offence of the corporate body is 'attributable to any neglect' on the part of any such person, then that person will likewise be guilty of the same offence as the body corporate.

It should be noted that by BSA 2022, s.40 a new s.112A is inserted into BA 1984. This makes similar provision for personal liability as regards criminal offences committed under that Act.

It can be seen that these are wide-ranging provisions aimed at piercing the corporate veil, so that the specified individuals are not permitted to hide behind corporate status. This applies to managers as well as to those who are truly officers of the company such as directors and company secretaries, and it applies to those who act as such even if they have no formal status in that capacity.

Furthermore, it applies to individuals who have neglected to do something, and this neglect has resulted in the commission of the offence. So, for example, if a company failed to apply for a building assessment certificate then the individual person or persons at a managerial level responsible for the company's failure will be guilty of the criminal offence created by the Act just as much as the company itself. The Act does not limit the number of people who may fall into this category and so it is entirely conceivable that there may multiple persons at different rungs of managerial and/or director levels, each of whom is liable for failing to ensure that the company has complied with its obligations.

18.5.3 Possible application of previous authority

Previous authority may, however, provide some degree of amelioration of the regime described in **18.5.2**. The Explanatory Notes to BSA 2022, s.161 expressly state that s.161 has been modelled on the Health and Safety at Work Act 1974, s.37. In respect of that similarly worded legislation, the House of Lords held in *R. v. Chargot Ltd. (t/a Contract Services)* [2009] 1 WLR 1 that in order to prove the offence the prosecution had to establish the relevant state of mind of the defendant, and that circumstances would vary from case to case. It was said by Lord Hope of Craighead, giving the leading judgment and building on previous authority, that the question will always be whether the company's officer should have been put on inquiry so as to take steps to determine whether or not there had been compliance with the relevant statutory provisions. He said that it would be a relatively short step to infer connivance or neglect if the circumstances under which the risk arose were under the direction or control of the defendant, but that the more remote the defendant's area of responsibility was from those circumstances the more difficult it would be to draw that inference. Connivance can, however, be simply shutting one's eyes to the obvious, i.e. 'Nelsonian' or 'blind eye' knowledge.

In *Re City Equitable Fire Insurance Co. Ltd.* [1925] Ch 407 Romer J made it clear (at 429 and 430) that where a director, acting honestly, properly left certain duties to others who were apparently competent and qualified to carry them out (including a fellow director) then the director was not liable in negligence for the fraud which was, unknown to the director, being carried on. The judge said that there has to be a degree of trust in business: 'Men in responsible positions must be trusted by those above them, as well as by those below them, until there is reason to distrust them.' This principle was more recently applied in *Huckerby* v. *Elliott* [1970] 1 All ER 189. In that case a director of a company which had operated a gaming business without the necessary licence would have been criminally liable, together with the company, if she had neglected to ensure that the company had the necessary gaming licence. She had in fact left the task of obtaining the licence to a co-defendant who was both the company secretary and also a director of the company. Since she had properly left it to him, and had no reason to distrust him or his abilities, she was not guilty of neglect. The Chief Justice pointed out that one director did not have to supervise his co-directors.

18.5.4 When some directors can escape liability

It should be noted that there are certain specific requirement as to who is, or who is not, a director for the purposes of this section of BSA 2022 at s.161(2) and (4). By s.161(2), if the body corporate is managed by its members, then any member is to be regarded as a director. But by s.161(4), where the AP is a company which is a resident management company (RMC) as defined, or an RTM company, or a commonhold association, then if a director has been appointed for building safety purposes and is entitled to remuneration from the company, s.161 is disapplied so far as concerns the directors who are not entitled to remuneration. Accordingly in such circumstances the unpaid directors will not be criminally liable for offences committed by the company. This is likely to be seen as a substantial incentive for such companies to appoint someone as a director expressly for building safety purposes.

18.5.5 Summary

By way of summary of the provisions of the Act as to the criminal liability of individuals for the offences created by Parts 2 and 4, the Act creates multiple criminal offences potentially affecting multiple individuals with management responsibilities, regardless of whether they operate at director level or as company secretary, and regardless of whether they have job titles which reflect that responsibility. The Act aims to look at the substance of what the individuals do. As and when prosecutions take place, and if the facts permit, defendants are likely to seek to rely on the body of law which has built up in respect of similarly worded provisions in the Health and Safety at Work Act 1974. Also, if an RMC or RTM company or a commonhold association has appointed a paid director expressly for the purpose of dealing with building safety, then the unpaid directors of those bodies will escape liability.

CHAPTER 19

Transactional issues for residential conveyancers: acting for the seller

Ian Quayle

19.1 INTRODUCTION

The Act creates several problems for those acting for sellers in a residential conveyancing transaction. In particular, conveyancers should be aware of the following:

1. The need to provide information, explanations, and advice concerning the application of the Act to the transaction and ensuring the seller client is aware of the significance of the Act to the transaction.
2. The need for the conveyancer and to an extent the client seller to understand the additional documentation required where the Act applies.
3. The need to appreciate the problems and issues with the Act itself.

The risk of a claim concerning Act-related advice being made against the conveyancer acting for the seller may not be obvious. Claims could however arise in relation to explanation and advice or lack thereof concerning the preparation and completion of the leaseholder deed of certificate (LDC) or the TA7 leasehold information forms. Claims could also arise as a result of failing to clarify whether the Act applies or does not apply to a particular transaction.

In addition to a risk of a claim, a failure to appreciate the application of the Act to a transaction could lead to client complaints arising from a failure to ensure documentation is provided to the buyer's conveyancer in a timely manner or at all.

19.2 DOCUMENTATION WHICH THE SELLER MAY BE REQUIRED TO PRODUCE

19.2.1 The TA7 form

The TA7 form is now in its third edition and contains additional questions concerning the Act. In order to be Conveyancing Protocol compliant, a TA7 will have to be produced in every transaction to which the Protocol relates.

As with all the TA forms, the seller is expected to answer the questions without assistance or guidance from their conveyancer. The forms themselves contain a warning to that effect for the seller, but the conveyancer should reinforce that warning in the retainer.

Several of the questions in the TA7 form have implications relevant to the Act. For example:

Question 1.1 – 'Who owns the freehold?'

The answer to this question could also be useful in determining who is the accountable person (AP) or principal accountable person (PAP) for higher-risk buildings (HRBs). It may also assist in discovering who owned the building on 14 February 2022 and therefore whether the provisions of Sched.8 apply.

It will be necessary if acting for the seller to check that the information the seller provides is correct.

Question 1.3 – 'Who is responsible for managing the building?'

The answer to this question is important for the same reasons as are set out in relation to Question 1.1 above.

Question 2.2 – 'Please supply a copy of any correspondence from the landlord, any management company and any managing agent'

The correspondence could be significant as it could include a request from the landlord for the production by the seller of an LDC, a response from the landlord to a notification of sale, or a request by the seller for the provision of a landlord's certificate (LC) due to remediation work being required for a relevant defect. More generally, correspondence might be available relating to remediation costs for relevant or non-relevant defects, or the landlord's obligation to consult on proposed service charge costs under LTA 1985, as well as information concerning building safety and building safety costs under both BSA 2022 and LTA 1985.

Question 2.3 – 'Please supply a copy of any invoices or demands and any statements and receipts for the payment of (a) maintenance or service charges for the last three years, (b) ground rent for the last three years'

As with correspondence provided in response to Question 2.2, where documentation is provided in connection with Question 2.3 it needs to be considered in order to ascertain whether the landlord has incurred or could incur service charges costs relating to remediation work for relevant defects as defined by BSA 2022. Where the conveyancer is aware of any relevant information which the seller has not disclosed, the position should be corrected and the relevant information included.

Question 4.5 – 'Does the seller know of any expense (e.g. the cost of redecoration of outside or communal areas not usually incurred annually) likely to be shown in the service charge accounts within the next three years? If yes, please give details'

The seller may need some guidance as to what information the seller should provide relating to expenses not usually incurred. Any knowledge is likely to stem from information provided by the landlord. Again the safest approach is to ensure that the seller discloses any information and reveals any knowledge of relevant expenses.

Question 4.8 – 'Does the seller know of the existence or suspected existence in the building of cladding or any defects that may create a building safety risk? If yes, please give details'

To answer this question a seller will need to be assisted with an explanation of what cladding and defects that may create building safety risks (BSRs) are. The seller should be told to answer this question only where the seller has received information from the landlord or a third party that mentions cladding or BSRs.

This question is problematic, as the seller may not know of the existence or suspected existence of cladding or BSRs other than from information provided by the landlord, AP or PAP. The client could usefully be directed to check documentation received from the landlord. Further, it may be worthwhile asking the seller if they have had any surveys or valuations undertaken that might provide insight.

Question 5.2 – 'Has the seller received any other notice about the building, its use, its condition or its repair and maintenance? If yes, please supply a copy'

The safe course of action here is to advise the client to volunteer any documentation from the landlord or PAP concerning the condition of the building or repair or maintenance.

A conveyancer for the seller would be unwise to be selective, and should instead ensure any potentially relevant information is included.

A new section 11 has been introduced into the TA7 in the following terms:

Question 10.1 – 'Have any remediation works on the building been proposed or carried out?'

The problem with this question is that a seller is unlikely to know what remediation works are. The question is not limited to remediation works as defined by BSA 2022, but remediation work generally. As stated previously, the client will be likely to need guidance in answering this question.

Question 10.2 – 'Is the lease of the property a qualifying lease?'

The same problem arises. The seller is only likely to be able to answer this question if their conveyancer has explained to them what a qualifying lease is, or has confirmed to them that the lease is or is not a qualifying lease. Assuming the seller was not the owner of the property at 14 February 2022 it may not be possible to confirm with certainty that the dwelling was the relevant tenant's only or principal home on that date as required by BSA 2022, s.119(2)(d). Although supporting evidence on that point may be available with the LDC, caution should be exercised with the response to the question. The seller should be warned that the tenant on 14 February 2022 is in the best position to answer this question. Where the seller or the producer of the LDC was not the owner on that date, the seller should be warned of the consequences of providing incorrect information which may lead to a buyer concluding the lease is a qualifying lease when this is not the case or vice versa. As a result, the client should be warned about the need to undertake reasonable investigation before confirming that the lease is a qualifying lease. It may be appropriate to state that the seller does not know or cannot confirm the status of the leaseholder as at 14 February 2022, and the buyer should rely on their own enquiries.

Question 10.3 – 'Is there a Leaseholder Deed of Certificate for the property? If yes: (a) Did the seller (the current leaseholder) complete the deed of certificate or was it completed by a previous leaseholder? (b) Please supply a copy of the Leaseholder Deed of Certificate and the accompanying evidence'

The seller should be able to confirm whether there is an LDC, but this question does highlight two issues:

1. The importance of ensuring the LDC is kept safely, as it is now an important document in the conveyancing process. Where the LDC has to be prepared, the conveyancer needs to ensure that the client is guided as to how it is to be completed and what is to be done with it.
2. Whether the landlord has asked for or has been provided with an LDC is a crucial question for a buyer. This is significant when considering BSA 2022, Sched.8, para.13, which creates a presumption that a lease is a qualifying lease, unless the landlord has taken all reasonable steps (and any prescribed steps) to obtain an LDC and no such document has been provided.

See **11.1**.

Question 10.4 – 'Has the freeholder/landlord been notified of the intention to sell?'

This is an important question, as notification triggers the need for a landlord to produce an LC within four weeks. It also triggers the timetable for the performance of the prescribed steps which the landlord needs to take to obtain an LDC. For detailed examination of these issues, see **Chapters 10** and **11**.

It is important to ensure that the seller is able to confirm the date and the method of notification, as the buyer could ask for more information from the seller where the landlord has not produced an LC or an issue arises as to whether an LC was provided out of time. The Act does not make clear what notification is required, and as a result it would be sensible for formal notification by post or email to be made and a record kept of the date of that notification. The issue of whether the landlord has been notified of an intended sale and the date of notification could become significant where the LC is not provided or when the four-week window for the provision of the LC is in dispute.

Question 10.5 – 'Has the seller received a Landlord's Certificate and the accompanying evidence? If yes, please supply a copy of the Landlord's Certificate and the accompanying evidence'

This is another important question, as where a seller has not received an LC within four weeks of the landlord being notified by the seller of a sale, or receiving a request from the seller for an LC, then (assuming the lease is a qualifying lease) the landlord cannot claim certain historical remediation costs for relevant defects. This protection would benefit the seller, the buyer and subsequent owners.

When acting for a seller, a conveyancer should ask the client whether the landlord was notified of the intended sale and whether the seller has asked for an LC, and if so when and how the request or requests were made and what the response of the landlord was.

In summary, the client should be reminded that the information provided by them as seller needs to be carefully considered, and a warning should be given that if the seller gives inaccurate information, the seller could be liable to the buyer and subsequent owners of the property for misrepresentation, and may possibly even commit a criminal offence under the Fraud Act 2006, s.2.

Given the complexities of the Act and the risks associated with the seller providing incorrect information, the conveyancer should check the information provided by the seller against the information on file, and should check for accuracy generally and of course check that the document has been properly executed as a deed.

Finally, the seller should be warned of the need to update any of the replies if relevant additional information or documentation comes to light during the conveyancing process.

19.2.2 The LPE1 form

The LPE1 form is now in its fourth version and includes a number of additional questions, such as:

- whether an LDC has been served on the landlord in relation to the sale of the property, or remedial works required for the property;
- whether an LC has been served; and
- whether there is any outstanding enforcement action against the landlord, AP or PAP, such as outstanding enforcement notices.

The form also includes new requests for documents including the LDC and the LC, as well as information relating to any known enforcement action being taken.

The amended document includes new definitions for the LDC and the LC, plus an amendment to the definition of a Right to Manage (RTM) company.

Where the LPE1 form includes a disclaimer as to the accuracy of the information within it or the accuracy of the information of documents accompanying it, the seller client should be told, as should the buyer.

A conveyancer for the seller should check the information within the LPE1 form to ensure it has been properly and fully completed, and that the information it contains is consistent with any answers provided by the seller in the TA7. At the time of writing, the proposed new guidance for landlords produced by the Association of Residential Managing Agents is still awaited.

19.2.3 Commercial enquiries before contract

Where a transaction is a mixed-use or commercial sale, Commercial Property Standard Enquiries (CPSEs) should be insisted upon rather than the TA7 and LPE1 forms. These should capture everything that the seller is aware of in respect of the property which the buyer is unable to determine from public information or an inspection.

Care must be taken when acting for the seller to determine who has completed the CPSE form and the extent of their knowledge. Where knowledge or information is limited, consideration should be given to explaining that limitation or including a disclaimer in the CPSEs.

Both the conveyancer for the seller and for the buyer should ensure that the answers given to the CPSEs are as full and complete as possible.

It should be remembered, if acting for a seller in commercial property transactions, that it is possible to limit or exclude liability for information generated in CPSEs, as the attitude of the courts is that commercial parties can distribute risk between them.

CPSEs can be pre-populated by the lawyer acting for the seller. If this is done, the client needs to understand that the information in the CPSEs is information that could lead to the client being liable to the buyer for misrepresentation.

The current version of CPSE.6 (version 1.6) 'Supplemental pre-contract enquiries for property subject to residential tenancies' includes questions relating to the Act which must be completed where relevant.

This form includes additional questions concerning the Act including at page 22:

- Question 21.1 – 'Is the Building a "relevant building" ...?'
- Question 21.2 – 'Please provide all information necessary to complete the landlord's certificate and provide all required supporting evidence ... '
- Question 21.3 – 'Is the seller aware of any breach of any of the following:
  - Regulation 6(1) of the BS(LP) Regulations[1] (the duty to provide a landlord certificate to a leaseholder);
  - Regulation 6(9) of the BS(LP) Regulations (the duty to provide copy landlord certificate to other landlords and AP or PAP);
  - Regulation 6(10A) of the BS(LP)(I) Regulations[2] (the duty to provide copy leaseholder deed of certificate to certain third parties)'
- Question 21.4 – 'If any of the regulations 3, 4, or 5 of the BS(LP)(I) Regulations applies to the seller, please confirm the seller has served the relevant notices and provide copies (unless already supplied).'
- Question 21.5 – 'Unless already supplied, please provide copies of all notices sent to any leaseholder in the building under Regulation 6(2) and 6(8) of the BS(LP)(I) Regulations together with any written request received from any leaseholders pursuant to Regulation 6(9) of the BS(LP) (i) Regulations where a leaseholder deed of certificate has not yet been received by the seller.'
- Question 21.6 – 'Unless already supplied, please provide copies of all leaseholder deed of certificate (including all the supporting information as referred to in Regulation 6(7) of the Regulations which have been received from leaseholders in relation to the building and confirm that the originals will be handed over on completion.'
- Question 21.7 – 'If Section 20D of the Landlord and Tenant Act 1985 (as inserted by section 133 of the BSA) applies to any works that have been or are to be carried out at the property:
  - (a) what steps have you taken come to comply with section 20D?
  - (b) what was the outcome of those steps?'

When acting on a sale of a relevant commercial property it is important for the conveyancer to ensure the seller client completes this form and, just as with the TA7 form, is aware of the dangers of doing so incorrectly.

1 Building Safety (Leaseholder Protections) (England) Regulations 2022, SI 2022/711 (the 711 Regulations).

2 Building Safety (Leaseholder Protections) (Information etc.) (England) Regulations 2022, SI 2022/859 (the 859 Regulations).

In a residential transaction, if acting in circumstances where the building has recently been sold, it would be helpful to extract a copy of the form from the landlord to check or cross check information provided by the landlord in any landlord certificate produced as part of the conveyancing process although a landlord would not be obliged to provide it.

19.2.4 The LDC

It is important for the conveyancer to appreciate that where an LDC is produced by the seller it performs three functions:

1. It sets out information which a landlord or AP will require to establish if a leaseholder holds a qualifying lease.
2. It will allow a landlord to calculate the remediation cap.
3. It provides the buyer and the buyers' conveyancer with information which confirms that the building in which the flat or apartment is situated is a relevant building, which (combined with a lease is that is a qualifying lease) means the seller and subsequent owners are afforded the protection provided by BSA 2022, s.122 and Sched.8.

There are some other important practical points to appreciate:

1. A leaseholder can produce an LDC at any point, to affirm an entitlement to the protection for qualifying leaseholders (or to reveal that there is no such protection).
2. It is not necessary for the leaseholder to serve an LDC on a landlord, and a failure to do so would not on its own prevent or exclude qualifying lease status. As mentioned earlier, and importantly, where a landlord does not hold an LDC and has not asked for one from a seller leaseholder, this can benefit a subsequent buyer due to the presumption contained in BSA 2022, Sched.8, para.13 (see **11.11**).
3. A leaseholder selling a qualifying lease in a relevant building will usually be required to provide a valid and completed LDC as part of the conveyancing process, because a buyer properly advised would not be willing to proceed without one, and a lender is likely to require one. While the Act does not impose a sanction for the failure to provide an LDC, such a failure is likely to prevent or delay a sale.

As examined in **11.1**, a leaseholder does not have to volunteer an LDC and is not prejudiced by failing to do so. The position is different when a building owner requests an LDC.

Reference should be made to **11.3** and **11.4** in order to be aware of what the landlord must do by way of prescribed steps and reasonable steps to obtain an LDC, and required timings. Put simply, where a request is made by the landlord, the leaseholder must provide an LDC within eight weeks of the request, but can ask for an extension of time of a further four weeks.

It should be remembered that a leaseholder does not have to provide an LDC to the landlord voluntarily and there is no time limit for providing an LDC if providing it voluntarily; and that there are potential benefits for a buyer where the landlord has not been provided with, and has not asked for, the LDC.

Although there is no need for a landlord to formally accept an LDC, it would make sense when the deed is sent that the conveyancer for the seller makes a request for a receipt or acknowledgement, or for there to be some evidence of it being sent in case a dispute arises in the future.

Where a lease qualifies and the leaseholder has completed and sent the LDC, then the building owner can either treat the lease as qualifying for relevant protections or, where there is evidence that information within the LDC is incorrect or the LDC is defective (for example, it has not been properly executed) it could be challenged. Conversely where a landlord has taken all prescribed steps and any reasonable steps to obtain an LDC, and the leaseholder fails to provide it within time, the lease is not a qualifying lease.

The conveyancer for the seller should exercise caution in assisting the seller to complete the LDC. Put simply, the seller should be warned about the need to ensure the information in the deed, and the supporting evidence or documentation, is accurate. The seller must also be warned that if the information is not correct or the deed defective, then the seller could be liable to the buyer and or future owners of the property for misrepresentation. The same approach taken in advising the seller to complete the TA forms should be adopted.

19.3 POTENTIAL PROBLEMS WHEN ACTING FOR THE SELLER

19.3.1 How can a conveyancer for the seller ascertain if the building is a relevant building for the purposes of BSA 2022, Sched.8?

A conveyancer is dependent on either the landlord, the seller, or a third party such as a surveyor to confirm that the height or number of storeys of the building in which the property being sold is situated is such that the building is a relevant building. The position is much easier when acting on a sale of a property in an HRB, as the height issue is clarified where the building has been registered. Where that has not occurred, a conveyancer may not be able to confirm the height or status of a building. The seller should be warned that this is the case. There is a problem here in that, at the time of writing, although the register of HRBs is required to be an open register, this is not currently the case, meaning that the only way to check if a building has been registered as an HRB is for the building owner, AP or PAP to provide proof of registration.

It is now possible to search the register of HRBs using the website **www.register-high-rise-building.service.gov.uk/public-register/search**. A search can be undertaken by typing in a postcode and the register, which is free to access, will reveal the following, assuming the building has been registered:

- the address of the property;
- the number of floors above the ground;
- the height measured from ground level to the top floor not the roof;
- the number of residential units;
- when the building was completed;
- who is responsible for the building's safety (usually the AP) and what they are responsible for; for example, the routes that residents can walk through, like corridors, staircases and fire doors, and maintenance of plant and equipment such as lifts, firefighting equipment and any other machinery in the building.

The register will also reveal who is the PAP responsible for registering the building and making sure the information held by the BSR is updated, and for telling residents how to contact them, make complaints or ask questions (part of their residents' engagement strategy).

19.3.2 Can the conveyancer insist that the landlord produces an LC?

The only case law on this point so far suggests that the answer is 'No' – see *Will & Koterba* v. *G & Properties* Lon/00AT/HYI/2022/0003 (unreported), referred to at **10.2.8**. Whether it would be possible to secure an injunction based on the wording of the 711 Regulations, reg.6(1) is as yet undecided. However, lenders for the buyer often insist on the production of an LC as a condition of the mortgage. A practical problem then arises.

Subject to the possibility of obtaining an injunction, the Act does not provide a solution to the problem. Limited comfort can be taken from Sched.8, paras.14(1) and (2) (see **10.2.7**) which explains that the lack of the LC provides some protection to the buyer. As far as any lender is concerned, the only course of action is to advise the buyer's conveyancer to contact the Department of Levelling Up, Housing and Communities to put pressure on the lender to change and relax their requirements for the production of an LC or to maintain pressure on the landlord in the hope that an LC is forthcoming, remembering that if it is provided out of time the buyer retains the comfort mentioned previously.

19.3.3 Can a conveyancer for the seller verify the content of the LDC or LC?

Obviously, the answer is that it would not be sensible for the conveyancer for the seller to verify or provide any form of warranty as to the accuracy of some information provided by the client or the landlord in any document.

Taking each document in turn:

1. The LDC – while a conveyancer for the seller should be able to confirm the information contained in the first three requirements of BSA 2022, s.119(2)(a)–(c), the requirement in subsection (d) (regarding the ownership occupation issue as of 14 February 2022) will be problematical. The produ-

cer of the certificate might not provide the correct information, may be mistaken or may deliberately lie. However the seller's conveyancer should highlight to the buyer's conveyancer the potential use of BSA 2022, Sched.8, para.13 to circumvent the problem (see **Chapter 11**).
2. The LC – the information in an LC is likely to be complex accountancy information or information concerning the history of construction and/or remediation work undertaken in connection with the building. It would be difficult if not impossible for a conveyancer to be able to confirm or verify the accuracy of any information provided.

19.3.4 Conclusions

When acting for a seller of a residential property to which the Act might apply, caution should be exercised:

1. While a conveyancer might want to avoid any of the problems associated with the Act by limiting the scope of the retainer, it must be appreciated that it will be implied into the retainer that it is for the conveyancer to clarify if any matters are excluded: *Hurlingham Estates Ltd.* v. *Wilde & Partners* [1997] 1 Lloyd's Rep 525. There needs to be fully informed consent of the client, so in the context of acting for a seller the client needs to be aware of the potential problems of providing the buyer with incorrect information.
2. It is implied into a conveyancer's retainer that they will proffer advice which is reasonably incidental to the work that they are carrying out. In determining what advice is reasonably incidental, it is necessary to have regard to all the circumstances of the case, including the character and experience of the client: *Minkin* v. *Landsberg* [2015] EWCA Civ 1152, [2016] 1 WLR 1489 at [38].
3. The care and skill of a reasonably competent practitioner is assessed to the standards usually applied to the profession: see *Midland Bank Trust Co Ltd* v. *Hett Stubbs & Kemp* [1979] Ch 384 at 402–403.
4. There is an obligation on the conveyancer to protect the interests of their client and to advise on all matters relevant to the retainer: *Tiffin Holdings Ltd.* v *Millican* 49 DLR (2d) 216, approved by the Supreme Court of Canada [1967] SCR 183, (1967) 60 DLR (2d) 469.
5. It is unreasonable and artificial to define that scope by reference only to the express instructions of the client: matters which fairly and reasonably arise in the course of carrying out those instructions must be regarded as coming within the scope of the retainer: *Gilbert* v. *Shanahan* [1998] 3 NZLR 528.
6. In respect of matters which come to the solicitor's notice in the ordinary course of business, to identify any matters which are or may be important to the client and to bring them to the client's notice, for example anything which might be materially adverse to the client's interests.

7. If the role of the conveyancer acting for the seller is considered in the light of the above, there is a duty to ensure that the seller provides the buyer with all the documentation necessary to enable the buyer's conveyancer to undertake appropriate due diligence. Care needs to be exercised where that document is produced by the seller, such as the TA7, but that care would not normally extend to other documentation. For example, it would not normally be necessary for the seller or a conveyancer acting for a seller to check service charge accounts or the LPE1 provided by the landlord for accuracy, but if the seller or conveyancer was aware of a glaring error in those accounts it would be necessary for the matter to be disclosed. Putting this into the context of the examination of the Act in this book, it would not be for the seller or conveyancer to audit and verify the accuracy of an LC or LDC provided by a third party before it was provided to the buyer, unless either was aware of a glaring defect. Where the seller is producing an LDC the position would be different, and the seller should be warned of the dangers of providing inaccurate or defective information in an LDC and the risk of a claim being brought by the buyer or subsequent owners of the relevant property where this is the case.

CHAPTER 20

Transactional issues for residential conveyancers: acting for the buyer

Ian Quayle

20.1 INTRODUCTION

Where a conveyancer is asked to act for a buyer in the acquisition of a residential leasehold property, the conveyancer must be particularly careful to ensure that explanation is provided to the buyer of the following:

1. What has been described in the amended Conveyancing Quality Scheme Guidance 2022 as the 'bigger picture' of leasehold ownership; the radical difference between leasehold and freehold ownership; and the duties and obligations created by the lease and the landlord relationship.
2. The peculiar nature of leasehold ownership and in particular the obligation of the buyer to pay a service charge. That explanation should contain general advice about the statutory protection afforded to leaseholders concerning service charge.

Where the leasehold property may be affected by the Act (because it is in a relevant building, or higher-risk building (HRB), or both), the conveyancer should additionally explain:

1. The problems presented by the Act, notably the difficulties in being able to conclude whether Sched.8 protection applies to the property being acquired, and also the likelihood, particularly where the target property is within an HRB, that service charge costs are likely to increase due to the additional duties and responsibilities being imposed on the landlord.
2. The fact that, where previous years' service charge accounts are disclosed by the seller or where, on a new build, estimated service charge accounts are provided, neither is a safe or reliable indicator of likely service charges in the future.
3. Consideration should also be given as to whether any client buying a property that is currently not within a relevant building or an HRB could

encounter some of the protection afforded by Sched.8 or some of the additional costs associated with the duties on the building owner, landlord, accountable person (AP) or principal accountable person (PAP) on a building which is an HRB if the building is developed and additional storeys are added or the height of the building is increased.

This chapter considers how to manage the process, starting with the retainer and the pre-contract enquiries, and moving on to the report on title.

20.2 SCOPING THE RETAINER

20.2.1 Appreciating the difficulties

It is important that clients appreciate the difficulties which the Act and associated regulations pose to conveyancers.

Rather than relying on the provision of relevant information to the buyer client when reporting on title at a later stage in the process, a conveyancer should, when bringing a client on board in connection with a transaction to which the Act could apply, scope the retainer at the earliest opportunity to explain the difficulties with the following:

1. Ascertaining if or to what extent the Act applies to the building in which the property is located and/or the property.
2. The issue of whether BSA 2022, Part 5 and Sched.8 apply to provide protection to the seller and/or to the buyer, and or future owners.
3. Where Sched.8 could potentially apply, explaining – in terms that the client can understand – the limited protection afforded in connection with some remediation costs for some relevant defects and the protection that applies to all residential leases whether held under qualifying leases or not.
4. Establishing whether the building in which the property is situated is an HRB.
5. If the property is in an HRB, the increased duties and obligations imposed both on landlord and leaseholder and the potential for involvement of APs and a PAP.
6. Whether other aspects of the Act apply to the transaction, for example where the property is a new build, and if so, what the implications of this will be.

20.2.2 Essential objectives

As problematic as the Act potentially is for the conveyancer acting for the seller (as explored in **Chapter 19**), it has the potential to generate even more problems for buyers and conveyancers acting for them.

When scoping the retainer, a conveyancer should keep in mind the following essential objectives, namely:

1. Reducing or limiting liability to the client for loss sustained as a result of breach of contract or negligence.
2. Identifying precisely the work the conveyancer will be doing on behalf of the client and any limitations on that work.
3. Highlighting work that a client might presume a conveyancer will do but which will not be undertaken.
4. Emphasising where the conveyancer will be reliant on third parties during the conveyancing process, including where documentation must be provided by the landlord, AP, PAP, managing agent, surveyor or valuer, and of course the seller.
5. Providing information, explanation and advice to the buyer client as to the conveyancing process; the duties and obligations owed by the seller and buyer; and the risks associated with the conveyancing process and how those risks can be identified and assessed. This can be done directly in the retainer, or alternatively the retainer could refer to documentation which contains that information or explanation.

20.2.3 The desirability of a written retainer

The problems with the Act warrant a review of conveyancers' standard retainers which should explicitly deal with the issues mentioned earlier but, before that, some basic points are worth remembering:

1. Although there is no formal requirement for the retainer to be in writing, it is good practice that it should be.
2. The client should be asked to sign a copy of the conveyancer's retainer, the conveyancer's engagement letter, and/or the conveyancer's standard terms of business. Of course, the contract can be implied by the client acknowledging receipt of the retainer letter or standard terms of business and then instructing the conveyancer to proceed, but good practice advocates that the retainer is in writing incorporating all the contractual terms of the conveyancer/client relationship and that is signed to that effect by the buyer client(s).

20.2.4 Effect of not having a written retainer

A failure to put in place a written retainer will disadvantage the conveyancer. The case of *Griffiths* v. *Evans* [1953] 2 All ER 1364 is a reminder of the problems which arise when parties dispute the terms on which the solicitor has been engaged, and in particular as to the scope of the duty undertaken by the solicitor as regards advising the client. In that case, the Court of Appeal held that where there is a dispute between a solicitor and the client about the existence or the terms of an oral retainer, the court may prefer the client's evidence. Denning LJ stated:

> On this question of retainer, I would observe that where there is a difference between a solicitor and his client upon it, the courts have said, for the last 100 years or more, that the word of the client is to be preferred to the word of the solicitor, or, at any rate, more weight is to be given to it. The reason is plain. It is because the client is ignorant, and the solicitor is or should be learned. If the solicitor does not take the precaution of getting a written retainer, he has only himself to thank for being at variance with his client over it and must take the consequences.

The Court of Appeal made the point that the lack of clarity around what the professional was instructed to do, and whether in acting for their client there had been a breach of their duty of care, is difficult to determine without a clear and precise retainer. Where a clear written letter of engagement or retainer setting out the scope of the services is provided to the client and is agreed upon with the client, the task of identifying what duty of care is owed is more straightforward.

20.2.5 Limitations on work

As stated previously, the retainer or engagement letter should also explain where appropriate what is *not* to be done. It is prudent for a conveyancer to state clearly that advice will not be provided on certain matters, and that the conveyancing process does not protect a buyer client from all risks associated with that process. This chapter will explore this in the context of BSA 2022 in detail.

It follows that if engagement letters or retainer documentation are vague as to the scope of services to be performed, or (even worse) there is no engagement letter at all, the conveyancer is more vulnerable to claims of negligence or for breach of contract.

Where a written retainer has not been provided, or is vague or ambiguous, it is open to the courts to infer the existence or extent of a retainer from the conduct of the parties. *Midland Bank Trust Co Ltd* v. *Hett, Stubbs and Kemp* [1978] 3 WLR 167 is useful by way of example. In that case, a solicitor failed to register an option over a property as a land charge. The court considered what steps should have been taken by the solicitor in the conduct of the transaction. The claimant alleged that the solicitor defendant was acting under some sort of general retainer, imposing a duty to consider his interests generally whenever he was consulted. The court held that there is no such thing as a general retainer in that sense. The concept of a client having a solicitor was meaningless in seeking to establish any duty broader than that arising out of the particular matter in which the solicitor's services are retained. The court found the extent of the duties owed to a client by a solicitor depended upon the terms and limits of the retainer and any duty of care must relate to what the solicitor is instructed to do.

20.2.6 The extent of the duty of care

As for the extent of the duty of care owed to the client, the test adopted by the courts is what the reasonably competent practitioner would do having regard to the standards normally adopted in the relevant profession. Subject to certain overriding principles which will be examined below, the duty is limited to the confines of the written retainer.

When a retainer is agreed, the scope of the work being undertaken should be regularly monitored, and if it becomes clear that the scope has changed, then this should be addressed either by sending an update to the engagement letter, or at the very least it should be discussed with the client and recorded in an attendance note. This is an issue which concerns professional indemnity insurers in connection with the Act, and which requires addressing by conveyancers undertaking this type of work.

Where a conveyancer provides a retainer that is clear on what they are being instructed to do, it may be difficult to establish negligence in respect of something falling outside that retainer. The Canadian case of *Spence* v. *Bell* [1982] 6 WWR 458 provides an example. In that case, a solicitor was retained to prepare a lease for a mobile home park. The lease drafted by the solicitor did not meet the requirements of financial institutions. However, the retainer had not required the solicitor to satisfy those requirements. The solicitor had undertaken what he was required to do with reasonable skill and care, and the claim was accordingly dismissed, the decision being upheld on appeal.

20.2.7 Additional work

Care should be taken where additional work becomes necessary in the performance of a conveyancing transaction. Whether the work involves the provision of information, explanation or advice, consideration should be given to whether the work falls within an existing retainer, or whether that retainer requires explicit extension or amplification. Not only should an extension or modification of the retainer be considered, but also whether the client should be charged for the additional work about to be undertaken. Any transactional work involving the Act should be regarded as specialist work enabling higher fees to be charged, and where additional work beyond the retainer is required the client can fairly be charged for it, provided the position is explained to the client and the increased fee agreed upon with the client before the work is undertaken.

20.2.8 'Reasonably incidental'

It is implicit that the conveyancer's retainer includes the need for advice to be proffered which is reasonably incidental to the work being carried out within the retainer. To determine what advice is reasonably incidental, it is necessary to have regard to 'all the circumstances of the case, including the character and experience of the client': see *Minkin* v. *Landsberg* [2016] 1 WLR 1489 at [38].

This issue came before the courts in *Spire Property Development LLP* v. *Withers LLP* [2022] PNLR 27. This case involved a commercial property transaction where, after the completion of the purchase, questions were asked by the client about problems that had arisen. The court had to consider whether the solicitors only owed a duty simply to answer those questions, or to go further and suggest what legal remedies the former client might have.

The claimant having succeeded at first instance, the Court of Appeal allowed the appeal, clarifying that the requirement that the solicitor carry out work 'reasonably incidental' to the retainer did not stretch so far as to require them to carry out investigative tasks in areas that they had not been asked to deal with, however beneficial to the client that might in fact have turned out to be.

Another recent example can be found in the case of *Lennon* v. *Englefield* [2022] PNLR 3, where the court held that if a client instructs their solicitor to send the proceeds of a conveyancing transaction to an intermediary, it is usually no part of the solicitor's duty to proffer advice about the commercial wisdom of that step.

Additional words of caution are required concerning over-reliance on the written retainer. There may be matters that fairly and reasonably arise in the course of carrying out instructions which must be regarded as coming within the scope of the retainer, even if not explicitly spelt out.

Absent the express exclusion from a retainer of advice about the effect of the Act, it could well be that such advice would be held to be reasonably incidental to a conveyancing transaction in connection with a residential leasehold purchase.

20.2.9 Duty to warn

Another point of note is that there is a duty to warn the client about particular risks by pointing out hazards of a kind which should be obvious to the conveyancer but which the client, as a layman, may not appreciate. In the case of *County Personnel (Employment Agency) Ltd* v. *Alan R Pulver & Co.* [1987] 1 WLR 916 at 922D, it was held:

> If in the exercise of a reasonable professional judgment a solicitor is or should be alerted to risks which might elude even an intelligent layman, then plainly it is his duty to advise the client of these risks or explore the matter further.

The important point to extract from the case law would appear to be that it is not possible when acting for a buyer to scope the retainer to avoid any liability arising from the application of the Act to the transaction, but that it is possible to limit the retainer to avoid liability for work which a conveyancer could otherwise reasonably be expected to undertake. This might include:

- the verification of the height of a building or the number of storeys contained within it;
- the accuracy or validity of the content of a landlord's certificate (LC);
- the accuracy or validity of information within a leaseholder deed of certificate (LDC) provided by the seller.

It is suggested that it is not part of a conveyancer's function to advise on the accuracy of service charge accounts provided by the seller or landlord (unless holding out that such advice can and will be given), but a conveyancer may reasonably be expected to draw this limitation to the attention of the client, with the recommendation that specialist advice should be obtained if the client requires it.

Put simply, a buyer client must be made aware of the potential impact of the Act on service charge, but it is not thought that a conveyancer can fairly be criticised for failing to explain its precise impact on the property with which the client is concerned.

20.2.10 Final thoughts on scoping

In summary, therefore, the conveyancer should ensure:

1. The client is made aware that it may not be possible for the conveyancer to confirm definitively whether the Act applies to the lease.
2. The client understands that there is a risk that the Act may operate to reduce or enlarge the service charge payable under the lease, but that the conveyancer will not be undertaking a full investigation or assessment of that risk.
3. The client understands that additional work could be undertaken (for an additional fee, and if the conveyancer is willing to offer this service) to ascertain the impact of the Act on the service charge, and that additional specialist advice might be required from third parties (again, at a cost).

Where appropriate, and depending on the status of the building in which the property is situated, some of the information below could also helpfully be explained to the client:

1. Where contractors or third parties have done work to the building where the property is located and that work requires remediation, the landlord will be obliged to pursue these contractors or third parties for the cost incurred before compelling the leaseholder to pay for it by way of a service charge.
2. The landlord will be required to attempt to recover costs incurred for remediation work from government schemes and funds established to meet remediation costs before compelling the leaseholder to pay for those costs by way of service charge.

3. Part of BSA 2022 could apply to the lease where the building in which a flat or apartment is situated is within a building that is at least 11 metres or five storeys in height, and which contains two or more residential units.
4. The landlord will be unable to add to the service charge costs incurred resulting from remediation work undertaken by the landlord for defective works which had been performed by the landlord or a party associated to the landlord, assuming the building is a relevant building and it does not matter whether a lease is a qualifying lease.
5. The landlord will be unable to add to the service charge costs it incurs resulting from remediation work undertaken by the landlord in connection with cladding.
6. The landlord will not be able to include remediation costs for relevant defects in the service charge where the landlord under the lease at 14 February 2022 had a net worth more than £2,000,000 multiplied by the number of relevant buildings owned by the relevant landlord.
7. The landlord will not be able to include remediation costs for relevant defects within the service charge where, as at 14 February 2022, the property was worth less than £325,000 (if located in Greater London) or £175,000 in all other cases.
8. There will be a cap on service charge costs incurred relating to remediation for relevant defects where the Act applies:
   (a) if the premises are in Greater London Greater London the cap is £15,000; otherwise, £10,000;
   (b) where the value of the flat or apartment as at 14 February 2023 exceeded £1,000,000 but did not exceed £2,000,000, the cap is set at £50,000;
   (c) where the value of a flat or apartment as at 14 February 2023 exceeded £2,000,000, the cap is set at £100,000.

Rather than simply providing the client with all this information when reporting on title or reporting on the lease, and thus risking overload, it might be useful to provide the information above early on in the transaction to heighten awareness and to enable the conveyancer more effectively to highlight any issues which actually apply when reporting on title later. This information could be provided independently of the retainer.

20.3 ADDITIONAL ENQUIRIES BEFORE CONTRACT

Chapter 19 looked at the issue of the information generated by a seller in the TA forms generally, and in the new section 11 of the revised TA7 in particular.

A conveyancer acting for a buyer needs to appreciate that it is important to identify when either a leaseholder or landlord has requested information or asked for documentation, as this may affect the qualifying status of the lease or the recoverability of service charges. Where a request has been made by a landlord for an LDC, it is important to establish if and when it was provided (see **11.5**). Similarly it is important to know whether the leaseholder has requested the landlord to provide an LC (and if so whether one was provided), or has notified the landlord of an intended sale (see **10.2.4**). For the most part enquiries of this kind are covered by the amendments to the forms identified in that chapter, but a conveyancer should not be slow to augment those standard questions with additional enquires should the situation render that helpful.

20.4 REPORTING ON TITLE

20.4.1 Introduction

Even though the buyer client should, in the retainer or elsewhere at the start of the conveyancing process, have been warned about the disadvantages and limitations of leasehold ownership, it would be prudent to repeat those warnings in the report on title. Both Solicitors Regulation Authority (SRA) and Conveyancing Quality Scheme (CQS) guidance requires a conveyancer to explain these matters, as well as the protection provided by statute, and the Act has unfortunately made this task more onerous.

Given the complexities of the Act and the broad scope of its application, it is important to highlight that a report on title:

- may need to be wider in scope than before the Act existed;
- should treat clients as inexperienced in matters relating to the Act, regardless of whether they have bought leasehold properties in the past.

20.4.2 Case law

Before exploring what the report on title should deal with in the post-Act world, it might be useful to look at case law to revisit some general principles. For example, *Clark Boyce* v. *Mouat* [1994] 1 AC 428, per Lord Jauncey:

> When a client in full command of his faculties and apparently aware of what he is doing seeks the assistance of a solicitor in the carrying out of a particular transaction, that solicitor is under no duty whether before or after accepting instructions to go beyond those instructions by proffering unsought advice on the wisdom of the transaction.

The point to be made here is that, given the complexity of the law created by the Act and the problems with the property market generally as a consequence, there is a case for spelling out the problems which might be encountered to a greater extent than contemplated by Lord Jauncey in this passage.

In *Yager* v. *Fishman & Co.* [1944] 1 All ER 552, per Lord Goddard:

> The nature and amount of advice which, in a matter of this sort, a solicitor would be expected to give to a person wholly unacquainted with business may differ very materially from what he would offer to an experienced businessman, who would naturally decide for himself the course he thought it in his interest to take.

The novelty of the Act and accompanying Regulations, and the extensive impact of both on leasehold ownership, would suggest that the buyer client be treated (at least as regards matters involving the Act) more as 'a person wholly unacquainted with business' than 'an experienced businessman'.

And finally, *Credit Lyonnais SA* v. *Russell Jones & Walker* [2002] EWHC 1310 (Ch), [2002] PNLR 2, per Laddie J:

> if, in the course of doing that for which he is retained, [the solicitor] becomes aware of a risk or a potential risk to the client, it is his duty to inform the client. In doing that he is neither going beyond the scope of his instructions nor is he doing 'extra' work for which he is not to be paid. He is simply reporting back to the client on issues of concern which he learns of as a result of, and in the course of, carrying out his express instructions.

It is certainly possible to imagine these dicta having resonance in, for example, the acquisition of an HRB where there is potential for service charge liability to increase to a significant extent.

20.4.3 What should be explained to the client in the report on title?

This chapter focuses specifically on what the report on title should say about service charge, both generally, and in the context of the Act.

First, and obviously, simply reciting the terms of a lease or a contract or indeed parts of the Act 2022 or regulations will not be adequate. Explanation and, where appropriate, advice is required. Given the amount of information which can potentially be provided to a client in a report on title, it might be wise to produce a separate report on the content of the lease, including ancillary matters of which the application of the Act would be part. Alternatively, if that is impractical, separate reports on the lease and ancillary matters such as service charge should be considered.

So far as service charge generally is concerned, the following should be explained:

1. The conveyancer has not inspected the property, and is unable to advise on the physical condition of the property. This could be particularly important as there could be defects in the flat or apartment or the building itself which are relevant defects requiring remediation to which BSA 2022, Sched.8 applies, or there could be defects which are not relevant defects but which require addressing either by the leaseholder or the landlord. In the case of the latter, the defects might require remediation due to the obligations imposed on either landlord or leaseholder by the Act. Advice should be given that the buyer should arrange for a survey of the property to be car-

ried out if this has not already been arranged. Where a survey has been obtained it should be considered by the conveyancer and any general issues concerning any physical defects in the property identified, the significance of any potential relevant defects highlighted and where appropriate or necessary the client told to seek clarification or further information from the surveyor or valuer.

2. No steps have been taken steps to verify independently any information supplied by the seller in an LDC, or the TA forms including the TA7. While the buyer should be advised that it may be possible to sue the seller for misrepresentation if information provided is incorrect, proceedings for misrepresentation are expensive and uncertain of outcome. It is better for the buyer to verify the information for themselves.
3. No steps have been taken to verify the accuracy of any statements made or documents provided by the landlord, management company or managing agent including the LPE1, any replies to landlord enquiries or replies to additional enquiries or the LC.
4. It is not possible to provide an opinion on the commerciality of the transaction, including by giving advice on the value of the property.
5. Ownership of the property will require the buyer to pay an annual service charge as the lease prescribes, including an obligation to pay the service charge and a contractual commitment for a future unascertained and unascertainable future ongoing expense.
6. There are statutory controls on service charge (as to which, see **20.4.4**).
7. It is impossible to confirm what the service charge will be going forward.
8. A failure to pay the service charge demanded by the landlord will be a breach of covenant and the consequences (including the possible risk of forfeiture) should be explained to the client.
9. The lease will enable the landlord to potentially transfer remediation costs as well as other costs and expenses into service charge liability. Those costs could include the cost for remediation of relevant defects and could, in the context of HRBs, involve additional management costs incurred in case of building safety management.
10. Care is needed where the lease permits the landlord to borrow money to pay for unusual or one-off items of expenditure. While the aim of the provision is to permit the landlord to borrow money and spread the cost of the expenditure into more than one year's service charge, it is important to appreciate that BSA 2022, Sched.8, para.18 probably prevents the use of such a clause to exclude or limit the protection afforded by it.
11. The lease may compel the landlord to create a reserve or sinking fund for unusual or one-off items of expenditure. If this is the case it should be explained to the client that payments will need to be made by the leaseholder and that funds held by the landlord in the reserve or sinking fund can be used by the landlord. The buyer needs to be aware that a conveyancer cannot advise whether, if there is a reserve or sinking fund, it will be

adequate or sufficient to meet unusual or one-off items that could be incurred in the future. The buyer must also be advised that the landlord cannot use this fund as a means to exclude or limit the scope of the protection afforded by Sched.8 (see para.10).

12. It may be useful to make the buyer aware that there are sources of help available to a leaseholder (such as Citizens' Advice, or the Leasehold Advisory Service) and how to engage those. It could also be suggested that if there are problems with the landlord generally or service charge in particular, further instruction could be given to the conveyancer's firm with a view to resolving that.

So far as the impact of the Act on the service charge is concerned:

13. Consistently with (4) above, it is not possible to advise a client whether the Act increases or reduces the value of the property.
14. Just as it is impossible to predict what future service charges will be in the future, it will also usually be impossible to confirm with certainty whether the potential protection provided by BSA 2022, s.122 and Sched.8 applies.
15. The Act provides protection against certain types of service charge costs. As a result, the Act could limit the amount of service charge a leaseholder is required to pay in connection with some remediation work for relevant defects assuming the building in which the property is situated is a relevant building and the lease is a qualifying lease.
16. The Act only affects service charges relating to defects of a certain type and will not eradicate or limit all service charges.
17. Unless the position is clear, it will be difficult to confirm whether a building in which a flat or apartment is situated is a relevant building or HRB for the purposes of the Act. It is of course possible that the building has been registered as an HRB; the register is currently under the control of the HSE, and although an enquiry can be made of the HSE asking if a building is registered, it is envisaged that the Building Safety Regulator will publish the register. When the register will be available online is, at the time of writing, unknown. Current practice involves a request being made to the party who registered the HRB to access the register and for that entity to provide evidence of registration.
18. Where the building is an HRB, the service charge will be made up of expenses which the landlord/management company/managing agent incurs in fulfilling the duties and obligations imposed on it by the lease or by the Act.
19. Given the additional duties and responsibilities imposed on the landlord, either as a landlord or as an AP or PAP, the landlord is likely to face increasing costs and so is likely to charge more by way of service charge than before.

20.4.4 Summary of the statutory controls on service charge outside the Act

The buyer should be made aware of the statutory protection available to leaseholders apart from the Act. As to this, Tanfield Chambers' book on service charges and management (now in its 5th edition) is a useful point of reference.[1] Whether the buyer is made aware of this protection in general terms (perhaps by referring to the Leasehold Advisory Service website and in particular the leaflet 'Do you Know Your Lease'), or by going into the law in more detail, is for the conveyancer to decide. Where detail is to be provided, the explanation and advice should include the following points:

1. The landlord can only provide services and charge for those services if the lease contains provisions to enable this.
2. LTA 1985, s.19 states that a service charge is only recoverable by a landlord in so far as the costs have been reasonably incurred. The section also states that the service charge is only recoverable if works carried out for the charge are of a reasonable standard. The First-tier Tribunal (Property Chamber) or the Leasehold Valuation Tribunal in Wales has jurisdiction to determine whether the reasonableness test is met and whether a service charge is recoverable. In addition those tribunals are empowered to find whether a service charge is payable at all or how much must be paid.
3. LTA 1985, s.20 (as amended by the Commonhold and Leasehold Reform Act 2002) imposes an obligation on the landlord to consult with leaseholders where the cost of an individual item of service charge is more than £250 per item, or more than £100 per item where the item of service charge lasts for more than one year. If the landlord has failed to go through the consultation process properly or at all, the liability of each leaseholder is capped at £250 or £100. A landlord can apply in certain circumstances to the First-tier Tribunal (FTT) to dispense with the need to consult, but must obtain permission before the expenditure is incurred except in exceptional circumstances. An important point to note is that it is not possible to dispense with the need to consult in connection with remediation costs for relevant defects. The Act also prevents a landlord from applying to the FTT to waive the obligation to consult for costs relating to Sched.8 expenditure. This is due to the amended LTA 1985, s.20(1) which now reads:

   > Where this section applies to any qualifying works or qualifying long term agreement, the relevant contributions of tenants are limited in accordance with subsection (6) or (7) (or both) unless the consultation requirements have been either –
   >
   > (a) complied with in relation to the works or agreement, or
   > (b) except in the case of works to which section 20D applies, dispensed with in relation to the works or agreement by (or on appeal from) the appropriate tribunal.

[1] Tanfield Chambers, *Service Charges and Management* (5th Edn, Sweet & Maxwell, 2021).

LTA 1985, s.20D refers to remediation works and the need for the landlord to seek funding from third parties.

4. LTA 1985, s.20B requires a landlord to notify a leaseholder within 18 months of service charge costs being incurred or to demand payment from the leaseholder. Where a landlord fails to comply with this timescale, the landlord will not be able to recover the charges.
5. The landlord will only be entitled to recover any service charge if the demand for payment includes the landlord's name and address, and must also include a 'summary of leaseholders' rights and obligations', which will include details of the leaseholder's right to apply to the FTT to assess the reasonableness of the service charge being claimed. Where the demand does not comply, the leaseholder has a legal right not to pay unless and until the service charge is demanded in the proper manner. The relevant law is contained in the Service Charges (Summary of Rights and Obligations, and Transitional Provision) (England) Regulations 2007, SI 2007/1257.

Particularly where the building is an HRB, a landlord might be required to undertake additional works in order to comply with the Act and the requirements of the Building Safety Regulator. These requirements are likely to increase costs incurred by the landlord relating to the management of the building which the lease is likely to permit to be passed on in the service charge.

20.5 THE RISK OF A BREACH OF CONTRACT OR NEGLIGENCE CLAIM

When acting on the purchase of a leasehold property, a conveyancer should be aware of the potential for claims issues for breach of contract and or negligence arising from the Act. Claims could involve:

1. Failing to advise a buyer that the information from the seller contained within the TA7 or LDC may not be correct, and the consequences of that.
2. Failing to advise a buyer that the protection under BSA 2022, s.122 and Sched.8 applies with regard to a service charge for remediation relating to relevant defects.
3. Failing to advise a buyer that the protection under BSA 2022, s.122 and Sched.8 does not apply with regard to service charges for remediation relating to relevant defects.
4. Failing to advise a buyer of a flat or apartment in an HRB of the existence of implied terms in the lease of the property due to the introduction, by BSA 2022, s.112, of a new s.30C into LTA 1985.
5. Failing to advise a buyer of the potential for increased service charges as a consequence of buying a flat or apartment in an HRB.

20.6 ACTING FOR LENDERS

Finally, it is hopefully helpful to say a few words about the position of a conveyancer who is acting for a lender. The important point to make here is the lender's instructions are critical.

If the lender is asking for confirmation or verification as to the information contained in an LC or LDC, then it would be dangerous to act, and the same would apply in connection with a lender asking a conveyancer to verify the height of a building, or whether the lease is a qualifying lease, or whether Sched.8 protection applies.

The UK Finance Mortgage Lenders' Handbook has been updated with a new clause 5.14.17 which reads:

> 5.14.17 This section applies only to leasehold property purchases in England situated in a 'relevant building' as defined in the Building Safety Act 2022 ... See Part 2s for our requirements on purchases and remortgages. Where the security will comprise such a leasehold flat you must request the following information from the seller's conveyancer about the safety of the building in which the flat is situated:
>
> - Confirmation as to whether the building has been or will be remediated under the Building Safety Act 2022.
> - Copies of any Landlord's Certificates, signed by the Landlord in the form set out in the Building Safety (Leaseholder Protections) (England) Regulations 2022.
> - Copies of any executed Leaseholder Deed of Certificate (in the form set out in the Building Safety (Leaseholder Protections) (England) Regulations 2022) and confirmation that they have been submitted by the relevant leaseholder to the landlord.
>
> You may want to consider any guidance from your professional body and/or regulator about the information and advice you should provide to the home-buyer relating to building safety. You should also consider any implications for section 4.4 of the Handbook.

The above requirements, in particular the confirmation as to whether the building has been or will be remediated, will be impossible to provide in most cases.

Lenders' Part 2 instructions of course vary.

Where a lender is asking for copies of the LC or LDC that should not warrant any concern, provided, of course, the documents are to hand. Where a lender is asking for the conveyancer to verify the content of the document, that becomes impossible. A conveyancer is unlikely to be sufficiently qualified or able to verify the content of an LC, never mind determine whether it generates any form of risk to the lender. So far as the LDC is concerned, again a conveyancer cannot verify statements made by the seller or previous owner of a property as to the requirements of BSA 2022, s.119(2)(d).

At the time of writing, lenders seem reluctant to rely on the BSA 2022, Sched.8, para.13 presumption of a qualifying lease as a way of circumventing that problem.

Also at the time of writing, some lenders seem to be frequently amending their Part 2 instructions and so extreme caution is required. Conveyancers should check lenders' instructions on receipt, and check again before exchanging contracts in order to see if the lenders' instructions have changed.

20.7 CONCLUSION

At the time of writing, paralysis in the residential leasehold conveyancing market remains. Conveyancers are reluctant to act in purchase transactions due to:

- concerns relating to professional indemnity insurance cover in relation to defective advice concerning the application of the Act;
- the additional documentation being generated as a consequence of the Act;
- concerns about the reliability of information being provided within the LDC or LC;
- the failure of sellers or landlords to produce LDCs or LCs;
- concerns about information being provided concerning the height of buildings;
- the requirements of lenders;
- the inability to charge appropriate fees for the work and additional documentation, and the additional risk it creates.

Subject to the relaxing of lender instructions, it is suggested that it should be possible to act on a purchase of a property to which the Act potentially applies, provided:

1. The retainer must be drafted in a such a way that the client is aware of the risks the Act creates, the difficulties a conveyancer faces when advising on the application of the Act, and the vulnerability of the buyer arising from documentation needed being created by third parties, for example the LDC and LC.
2. Any retainer creep should be monitored.
3. The report on title must reinforce the message that it is difficult to provide definitive advice concerning the application or otherwise of the protection afforded by BSA 2022, Sched.8.
4. Risk assessments must be undertaken on onboarding the client and throughout the transaction.

CHAPTER 21

Courts and tribunals

Mattie Green and Daniel Dovar

21.1 INTRODUCTION

The Act is replete with references to procedural applications and appeals to the courts and tribunals. In the vast majority of cases, such applications and appeals are made to the Tribunal, which means the First-tier Tribunal (FTT), and allocated to the Residential Property part of the Property Chamber (FTT). This chapter considers those applications, as well as the more modest number which the Act provides must be made to the county court. Reference has already been made to many of these types of application in earlier chapters of this work, dealing specifically with the various parts of the Act which make provision for them. This chapter draws the applications together, and also deals with some of the practical and procedural questions which might arise.

At present the direction for some applications is unclear; the Act specifies only that regulations will provide for whether applications should be to the FTT or the county court (i.e. see proposed LTA 1985, s.20D, as amended by BSA 2022, s.133: see **Chapter 13** and, in relation to appeals against compliance and stop notices, new BA 1984, s.39A).

21.2 THE FIRST-TIER TRIBUNAL

21.2.1 Remediation orders

As considered in detail in **Chapter 14**, BSA 2022, s.123(2) provides that:

> A 'remediation order' is an order, made by the First-tier Tribunal on the application of an interested person, requiring a relevant landlord to remedy specified relevant defects in a specified relevant building by a specified time.

The terms used in s.123(2) are all closely defined in the Act and are fundamental to the FTT's jurisdiction. For example, an application for an order under s.123(3) can only be made by an 'interested person' such as the Regulator, local authority, fire and rescue authority or any person with a legal or equitable interest in the building (BSA 2022, s.123(5)). Note that under the 859 Regulations, reg.2, the Secretary of State and the Homes and Communities Agency are also an 'interested person'.

Procedurally, the 859 Regulations, reg.2 provides that:

> (3) An application for a remediation order must –
>
> (a) state it is an application under section 123 of the Act;
> (b) identify the building to which the application relates;
> (c) identify the defects to the building for which a remediation order is sought;
> (d) identify the landlord (as defined in section 123(3) and (4) of the Act) which the applicant considers is responsible for repairing or maintaining anything relating to the relevant defects.
>
> (4) Where the First-tier Tribunal makes a remediation order it must as soon as is reasonably practicable send a copy of the order to –
>
> (a) the person who made the application; and
> (b) the relevant landlord.

At present, there are no specific FTT rules or practice directions applicable to applications under the Act. They are therefore covered by the general procedural rules for FTT proceedings, in particular the Tribunal Procedure (First-tier Tribunal) (Property Chamber) Rules 2013, SI 2013/1169 (the 2013 Rules), rule 26(2). An important point to note is that the provisions as to costs in the 2013 Rules, rule 13(1) apply. The effect of this is that a successful party will not be entitled to their costs unless limited exceptions apply, such as unreasonable conduct.

The FTT has published an application form (Form BSA1) which covers s.123 applications and meets all the above procedural requirements. The relevant application forms are available online (**www.gov.uk/government/collections/residential-property-first-tier-tribunal-forms**). Note that under the 2013 Rules, rule 26(5), an application must be accompanied by the appropriate fee.

As far as defects with applications are concerned, there is a distinction between a failure to comply with s.123 or the regulations on the one hand, and a failure to comply with an FTT direction or rule. Failure to comply with s.123(2) itself and/or the regulations may go to the FTT's jurisdiction. If the FTT lacks jurisdiction, it must strike out an application in whole or in part (2013 Rules, rule 9(2)(a)). However, the FTT has a separate power to add or remove a party under the 2013 Rules, rule 10 which should be kept in mind when issues of jurisdiction arise. A mere failure to comply with the 2013 Rules does not invalidate the application, although it may provide grounds for a respondent to apply to strike out (see the 2013 Rules, rule 8(1)).

21.2.2 Remediation contribution orders

Remediation contribution orders (RCOs) have also been discussed in **Chapter 14**. BSA 2022, s.124(2) provides that:

> 'Remediation contribution order', in relation to a relevant building, means an order requiring a specified body corporate or partnership to make payments to a specified person, for the purpose of meeting costs incurred or to be incurred in remedying relevant defects (or specified relevant defects) relating to the relevant building.

Once again, each requirement is a defined term in the Act itself and will be relevant to the FTT's jurisdiction to deal with the application.

As set out above in relation to remediation orders (ROs), there are no specific FTT rules or practice directions, and such applications are again covered by the general procedural rules for FTT applications set out in the 2013 Rules.

The Tribunal's application form, Form BSA2, covers s.124 applications and meets all the above procedural requirements.

21.2.3 Appeals against notices requiring recovery of remediation costs from other landlords

The 859 Regulations, regs.3–5 contain detailed provisions which allow a landlord who has paid or is liable to pay the cost of a relevant measure relating to a relevant defect which, but for BSA 2022, Sched.8, would have been payable as a service charge by a tenant under a lease, to recover a prescribed amount from other landlords.

In each case, regs.3(5), 4(4) and 5(8) provide the other landlords with a right to appeal within 30 days of the relevant notice.

The grounds of appeal are specified in regs.3(6), 4(5) and 5(9). The grounds of appeal are broadly limited to a challenge on the basis that the landlord concerned is not a 'responsible landlord' (reg.3(8), 'contributing landlord' (reg.4(7)) or 'relevant landlord' (BSA 2022, Sched.8, para.12(2)) or that the amount specified in the notice does not represent the cost of the relevant measure. Under reg.5(9), it is an additional ground that the remediation amount determined for the landlord is incorrect.

Again, there are no specific FTT rules or practice directions applicable to BSA applications. These appeals are therefore again covered by the 2013 Rules, rules 26(2) and (4).

The FTT Form BSA4 covers appeals by a landlord against a notice relating to liability to pay, or pay a share of, a remediation amount and meets the requirements of rule 26.

21.2.4 Landlord's certificates

Landlord's certificates (LCs) have been considered in **Chapter 10** and reference should be made to that chapter for a detailed discussion on that topic.

For the purposes of this chapter, it is important to note that the 711 Regulations, reg.11 allows a lessee to apply to the FTT in the following circumstances:

1. Where the lessee believes that a relevant landlord has made a false claim in the LC provided under the 711 Regulations, reg.6, including but not limited to:
   (a) stating that the relevant landlord is not the developer (see BSA 2022, Sched.8, para.2(4) for the definition of 'developer') or is not associated with the developer; or
   (b) stating that the relevant landlord does not meet the contribution condition; or
2. The relevant landlord or current landlord has not given the leaseholder sufficient time to provide information to prove they have a qualifying lease (BSA 2022, s.119 defines a 'qualifying lease').

Applications are again covered by the 2013 Rules, rule 26(2). The FTT Form BSA3 covers such applications and meets the requirements of rule 26.

The decision in *Flat 16 Grove House, 76 Sidmouth Avenue, Isleworth, Middlesex, TW7 4FQ* LON/00AT/HYI/2022/0003 (unreported) related to an application under reg.11. In that case, the landlord completely failed to provide an LC, and the leaseholder applied to the FTT for an order requiring it to do so. The Chamber President found that regs.11(2)(a) and (b) made no provision for leaseholders to seek orders requiring freeholders to provide LCs. The FTT struck out the application on jurisdictional grounds, noting that this appeared to be a lacuna in the regulations.

21.2.5 Appeals against decisions of the Regulator under BSA 2022, Part 4

BSA 2022, s.104 provides that affected persons have the right to appeal decisions of the Regulator where the Regulator:

- declines to register a higher-risk building (HRB) on an application under BSA 2022, s.78(1) (s.104(1)(a));
- removes an HRB from the register under BSA 2022, s.78(3) (s.104(1)(b));
- where an application for certification is refused under BSA 2022, s.81(3) (s.104(1)(c)); or
- where the Regulator gives a direction to the accountable person (AP) under BSA 2022, s.83(2) (s.104(1)(d)).

The grounds for appeal are that the decision was based on an error of fact; the decision was wrong in law; and/or the decision was unreasonable (s.104(3)).

In s.104(1), 'affected person' means:

- in relation to a decision mentioned in s.104(1)(a) or (b), an AP or a person who would be an AP for the building if the building were an HRB (s.104(4)(a));
- in relation to a decision mentioned in s.104(1)(c), an AP for the HRB (s.104(4)(b)); and

- in relation to a decision mentioned in s.104(1)(d), the AP subject to direction (s.104(4)(c)).

BSA 2022, s.106 provides that in relation to an appeal under BSA 2022, s.103, s.104, and s.105 (see **21.2.6**), the FTT must consider the decision appealed against afresh and may take into account evidence that was not available to the Regulator. The FTT may confirm, vary or quash the decision of the Regulator.

21.2.6 Appeals against decisions of the Regulator made under regulations

BSA 2022, s.105 provides that a prescribed person may appeal to the FTT against a prescribed decision of the Regulator made under regulations under BSA 2022, Part 4. Such an appeal may be made only on prescribed grounds.

At the time of writing, the 907 Regulations, reg.15 provides:

> (1) A decision to refuse a request under regulation 7(1) of the Building Safety (Registration of Higher-Risk Buildings and Review of Decisions) (England) Regulations 2023 (request to regulator to remove building from register) is prescribed for the purposes of section 105(1) of the 2022 Act.
> (2) The person prescribed for the purposes of section 105(2) of the 2022 Act is an AP for the building or any person who would be an AP for the building if the building were a higher-risk building.
> (3) The grounds of appeal prescribed for the purposes of section 105(3) of the 2022 Act are –
>
> (a) that the decision was based on an error of fact;
> (b) that the decision was wrong in law;
> (c) that the decision was unreasonable.

21.2.7 Determination as to the identify of the AP/PAP (BSA 2022, s.75)

As discussed in **Chapter 5**, for the purposes of BSA 2022, Part 4, an 'accountable person' (AP) is defined by BSA 2022, s.72. However, BSA 2022, s.75 provides that an 'interested person' may apply to the FTT for a determination as to who is an AP or principal accountable person (PAP) for an HRB, or to determine the parts of the HRB for which any AP is responsible.

'Interested person' is defined by s.75(3) as either:

- the Regulator;
- a person who holds a legal estate in any part of the common parts of the building; or
- a person who is under a relevant repairing obligation in relation to any part of the common parts.

An application could be made when it is not clear who the AP or PAP is in relation to relevant parts of the structure or exterior, or when an AP refuses to acknowledge being the PAP.

If, upon an application to the FTT for a determination as to who is the PAP, it appears to the Tribunal that there is more than one AP that satisfies the definition in s.75, the Tribunal can decide as to who the PAP is, as it considers appropriate. This could be where an AP holds a legal estate in possession of the structure and exterior and has a relevant repairing obligation in relation to the relevant parts of the structure and exterior of the building. The consideration of who is appropriate gives the FTT a wide discretion as to the factors it takes into account in coming to that determination. No doubt it will take into account factors such as: the extent of the area over which an entity has relevant obligations; past performance; ability to coordinate with the other APs; and expertise (whether the AP's own ability or the AP's ability to obtain expertise from professional third parties).

One of the objectives of the Act is that there should be a clearly defined dutyholder during occupation who is under a statutory obligation to maintain the fire and structural safety of the building. This provision ensures there is certainty as to who has the obligations of the AP or PAP and in respect of the latter ensures that the entity with the ultimate reporting and monitoring obligations, the PAP, is clearly identified.

The FTT's decision will bind the person it determines as the AP or PAP, and that person will be liable for the relevant obligations under the Act considered in **Chapter 6**.

21.2.8 Appeals against compliance notices (BSA 2022, s.103)

Under BSA 2022, s.99, the Regulator may give a compliance notice to an accountable person (AP) for an HRB who appears to the Regulator to have contravened, be contravening or be likely to contravene a relevant requirement. Compliance notices have been considered in detail in **Chapter 8**.

BSA 2022, s.103(1) provides that a person who has been given a compliance notice may appeal to the Tribunal.

An appeal may be on the following grounds:

- the person has not contravened, is not contravening, or is not likely to contravene, a relevant requirement (s.103(2)(a)); or
- that it is unreasonable to require the person to do anything specified to be done in the notice (s.103(2)(b)).

The effect of an appeal differs depending on whether or not the compliance notice is an urgent notice (for which see BSA 2022, s.99(4) and the discussion in **Chapter 8**). An appeal against a compliance notice that is not an urgent notice will suspend the effect of the notice pending the resolution of the appeal (s.103(3)). Whereas an appeal against an urgent action notice will not suspend its effect unless and until the Tribunal determines that it should (s.103(4)(a) and(b)).

An application can also be made to the FTT by a person to whom a compliance notice has been given under s.103(5) to extend the time for the doing of anything specified to be done in the notice.

21.2.9 Enforcement of decisions of the First-tier Tribunal and Upper Tribunal

BSA 2022, s.107 provides that a decision of the FTT or Upper Tribunal made under or in connection with Part 4 is enforceable with the permission of the county court in the same way as an order of that court (s.107(1)), save for decisions ordering the payment of a sum (s.107(2)).

The FTT does not have enforcement powers of its own, other than powers to enforce payment of a sum of money (Tribunals, Courts and Enforcement Act 2007, s.27(1)). This provision ensures that the FTT's decisions are enforceable. Within the framework of the Civil Procedure Rules (CPR), Part 70.5 deals with the enforcement of orders made by tribunals other than the High Court and county court.

21.3 THE COUNTY COURT

21.3.1 Introduction

The following paragraphs assume that the reader has at least a working knowledge of the court system and process and is familiar with the CPR. It concentrates on the new jurisdictions and scenarios where matters will be dealt with by the county court by reason of the Act.

21.3.2 Access to premises (BSA 2022, s.97)

Where an AP requires entry to a flat to carry out their duties, but that is refused, the AP can apply to the county court for an order for access. New LTA 1985, s.30C implies a covenant into each residential lease that access will be given to enable an AP to carry out their duties.

The duties that this relates to are:

- those contained in BSA 2022, ss.83 and 84 and relating to the assessment of BSR (**Chapter 6**); or
- those contained in BSA 2022, s.95 and concerned with whether a resident or owner has contravened their own duties (**Chapter 7**).

Before an application is made, the AP must make a request in writing, setting out the reason for access. They must give at least 48 hours' notice and access must be requested at a reasonable time. In *Dorrington Residential Ltd.* v. *56 Clifton Gardens Ltd.* [2022] UKUT 266 (LC) the Upper Tribunal considered the requirements of access in a lease on 24 hours' notice at a reasonable time. At [25], the Deputy President stated:

> In this case no right of entry exists unless and until the landlord has given 24 hours' notice. It must also request access at a reasonable time. What amounts to a reasonable time includes the day itself and the time of day, but I would not interpret the restriction too narrowly so as to exclude other relevant considerations. It might well not be reasonable to expect the tenant always to be available at such short notice. If, for example, the landlord sought access on a day when the tenant was not at home and could not reasonably be expected either to change their plans (for example because they were abroad on holiday) or make alternative arrangements for access to be permitted, it would be possible to say that the time at which access had been requested was not a reasonable time. The period of notice specified in the definition of Requisite Notice is a minimum period and the landlord is not prevented from offering longer notice, as happened in this case when a month's notice was given. The longer the period of notice given the more difficult it may be for the tenant to argue that consideration of its own convenience made the suggested time an unreasonable one.

If refused, then an application can be made to the county court, presumably on form N244, for an access order.

The county court has a discretion as to whether to make an order; BSA 2022, s.97(4)(a) says it 'may' make an order. However, before the discretion arises, the court must be satisfied that 'it is necessary to do so for the purpose mentioned in the request'. So it is important that the AP sets out clearly the purpose in the written request to the resident or owner, and that that is the same basis upon which they apply for an order. If an order is made, it must specify either a date or a period within which access is required.

As well as an order requiring access to an AP, it can also specify (at the request of the AP) an authorised person to have access; i.e. a surveyor or builder. In the event that an AP seeks an order of this kind, the AP should set out in the application who should be given access, and why.

In addition to access, s.97(3)(b) provides that an application to be made by the AP can include a request for authorisation to take measurements, photographs, recordings or samples. The terms of the order that can be made by s.97(4)(a) can include, where necessary, authorising such steps to be taken.

21.3.3 Other implied covenants

LTA 1985, ss.30C–30E imply various terms into residential leases imposing obligations on both landlord and tenant. The new s.30C has been referred to above in relation implied terms for access, but it also implies various obligations and duties on a landlord who is an AP in relation to their building safety duties. It extends to a term that the landlord will cooperate with any other person complying with their building safety duties. So in the latter case, it may be that an order may be made against a landlord to allow access or provide documents or provide information to further that end (see the definition of 'cooperate' at s.30C(4)).

The new LTA 2022, s.30G provides that the county court has jurisdiction to deal with any claim or other proceedings arising under these sections, and also provides there is no limit – financial or otherwise – on the jurisdiction of the court for this purpose.

21.3.4 Contravention notices

Enforcement of contravention notices under BSA 2022, s.96 is allotted to the county court. These notices can be given by an AP to a 'relevant person' where it appears that they have contravened or are contravening a duty under BSA 2022, s.95. The duties have been dealt with in **Chapter 7**.

The notice must be given by the AP, being the person who is responsible for the part of a building in question. The 'relevant person' is the person with a duty under s.95, being either the resident of a flat or the owner. Their duties include not to create a risk of a BSR; not to interfere with safety items; and to comply with requests for information.

If they breach any of those duties, the AP can serve them with a contravention notice, which specifies the alleged contraventions, the remedial action required, and anything that should not be done, and sets out the steps for enforcing the notice. It may also seek a sum of money, being an amount to repair or replace a safety item, which has been caused by the contravention.

An AP can make an application to the county court for an order for one or more of the following: (a) the provision of information; (b) to do something within a specified time; (c) to stop doing something; or (d) to pay a sum. The requirement that 'it is necessary to make the order' sets the bar relatively high.

21.3.5 RCOs: insolvent landlord (BSA 2022, s.125)

While most applications for RCOs (see **14.3**) will be made to the FTT (see **21.2.2**), where the landlord is undergoing insolvency, an insolvency practitioner can make an application to court for an RCO out of the landlord's assets. This should be on similar lines to an application in relation to a solvent landlord, save that (a) it can only be made by an insolvency practitioner, and (b) as the order is in such sum as is just and equitable, other considerations on insolvent distributions may impact on the sum awarded, such as the available assets and funds for distribution and the demands of creditors, and possibly any arrangements that are in place to deal with the insolvency.

CHAPTER 22

The Building Safety Act in Wales

Hugh Rowan

22.1 INTRODUCTION[1]

In so far as it is in force, the new statutory and regulatory regime implemented by the Act applies in its entirety to England. However, it has a far more restricted scope in Wales. Nevertheless, Wales is poised for equally thorough legislative and regulatory changes. As part of the drafting process of the Act, the Welsh Government requested the UK Government to make and implement various changes to BA 1984 on its behalf, and has provided its consent to the various provisions as required.

The intention in Wales is that these changes, detailed below, will give the Welsh Government sufficient power to bring forward primary legislation in the Senedd Cymru to implement a system appropriate to the practical and political landscape of Wales. The proposed system and application of the Act in Wales is set out in the Welsh Government's White Paper, 'Safer buildings in Wales' (December 2021) (the Welsh White Paper).

22.2 THE REGULATOR AND ITS FUNCTIONS

In England, the Act creates a new Building Safety Regulator – a division of the UK Health & Safety Executive (HSE) – and acts as an independent body with various responsibilities and powers in respect of the Act and in particular higher-risk buildings (HRBs). This body is discussed further in **Chapters 1, 2** and **6**.

BSA 2022, Part 2, which creates this new body, has no effect in Wales. Indeed, there is no proposal for such a new independent body in Wales. Rather, it is intended that the regulation and oversight of the design, construction and refurbishment of HRBs and the building control system in Wales will be addressed through the extension of local authorities' and Welsh Ministers' functions.

1 The author and editors express their gratitude to Daniel Beynon of Hydrock for allowing his work to be used in this chapter.

In relation to HRBs in particular, the Welsh White Paper proposes extending the current role of local authority building control to cover any additional regulatory regimes. In addition, the Welsh White Paper proposes a Joint Inspection Team (JIT): a body with no legal authority but with practical expertise that can assist in advising local authorities. A similar body already exists in England.

22.3 HIGHER-RISK BUILDINGS

The new definition of HRB (inserted at BA 1984, s.120D, and also at BSA 2022, s.65) does not apply in Wales. Instead, under BSA 2022, s.31 and BA 1984, s.120I, an HRB in Wales falls to be defined by Welsh Ministers in appropriate regulations. At present, the intention appears to be to adopt a similar – but not identical – definition to that employed in England. As with the definition in England, there is a difference between an HRB during the design and construction phase (covered by BA 1984), and then during the occupation stage (covered by BSA 2022, Part 4).

During the design and construction phase, the Welsh Government proposes to adopt a very similar definition to that for England with one key difference. While an HRB must contain at least two residential units in England (BA 1984, s.120D and the 275 Regulations, reg.2; see further **Chapter 4**), in Wales it is proposed that it only need contain at least one residential unit (Welsh Government, Consultation – 'Summary of Responses and the Government Response for the consultation on the Building Safety proposed definition of a Higher Risk Building', September 2023). It is also proposed that certain buildings be excluded from the definition of HRBs, including: secure residential institutions (e.g. prisons); temporary leisure establishments (e.g. hotels); and military premises (e.g. military barracks). This reflects similar provision in the 275 Regulations, reg.7 as applies to England.

The Welsh reform of the building safety regime during the occupation phase – which is addressed by BSA 2022, Part 4 – is being considered by the Government separately. The definition of HRB and the categories of buildings coming within that regime may be different, although it is unclear at this stage to what extent it will be or not. As a result, none of the provisions of BSA 2022, Part 4 yet has any application in Wales.

22.4 AMENDMENTS TO BA 1984

Since 31 December 2011 – following the Welsh Ministers (Transfer of Functions) (No.2) Order 2009, SI 2009/3019 – building regulation powers under BA 1984 have been devolved to Wales. As a result, the UK Government has worked with the Welsh Government to secure the necessary consents to amend BA 1984. Notwithstanding, as a result of this devolution there are a number of small, but important, differences in how the amendments to BA 1984 (set out in BSA 2022, Part 3) take effect in England and in Wales. The first of these differences is the definition of HRBs discussed above.

The second key difference, also touched on above, is that while the 'regulatory authority' in England is the new Building Safety Regulator, in Wales the authority is defined as the Welsh Ministers. This includes the authority to whom information should be given, where required in the regulations (BA 1984, Sched.1, paras.1D–1E). As described above, the Welsh White Paper indicates that these powers and responsibilities are then likely to be devolved onto local authorities.

This has the potential to create a conflict, where a local authority may be both the relevant regulator and the developer in relation to an HRB. In such cases Welsh Ministers are empowered under BA 1984, s.91ZD to make regulations that would enable them to designate a different local authority as the building control authority for those works.

Third, BSA 2022, ss.42–52 – concerning the regulation of the building control profession – apply equally in England and Wales save in so far as the regulatory authority is different. It should be noted that there is a specific summary offence in Wales of a registered building control approver failing to comply with a notice requiring information relating to the exercise of their building control functions. This may reflect the fact that there is no requirement in Wales to establish a facility to enable specified persons to give specified relevant information, and no requirement for the regulator in Wales to keep a register of that information. In England these requirements are imposed by BSA 2022, s.53.

22.5 OTHER PROVISIONS ABOUT SAFETY, STANDARDS, ETC.

Importantly, BSA 2022, ss.116–125 and Sched.8, for the remediation of certain defects (including remediation orders (ROs) and remediation contribution orders (RCOs)) do not apply in Wales. This means that the service charge regime in the Act, and the restrictions imposed, do not apply in Wales. In addition, the new limitation on service charges inserted into BA 1984 by BSA 2022, s.133 only applies in England.

In March 2023, First Minister Mark Drayford indicated that it was the Welsh Government's view that 'whereas [BSA 2022, ss.116–125] expose leaseholders to bills up to £10,000', in Wales the intention was 'that leaseholders should not be required to pay for the remedial action that is required to their buildings'. Moreover, during the same session Mark Drayford stated that 'whereas sections 116 to 125 require leaseholders to instigate legal action against a developer who they consider is not remediating fire safety defects, in Wales it will be the Welsh Government who will take that action on behalf of the leaseholders so that they don't end up having to foot the bill for doing so'. At this stage however, it is not clear how this will be managed practically (Senedd Cymru [Welsh Parliament], Y Cyfarfod Llawn [Plenary], 7 March 2023).

In addition, the provisions in relation to building industry schemes (BSA 2022, ss.126 and 127); prohibitions on development and building control (BSA 2022, ss.128 and 129); and new build home warranties (BSA 2022, ss.144 and 145) have no application in Wales.

Beyond these limitations, BSA 2022, Part 5 does otherwise extend its application into Wales. This includes building liability orders (BLOs) (BSA 2022, ss.130 and 132); the New Homes Ombudsman Scheme (BSA 2022, ss.136–143); liability in relation to construction products (BSA 2022, ss.146–155); and various amendments to the Regulatory Reform (Fire Safety) Order 2005, SI 2005/1541 (BSA 2022, s.156).

Index